# CHINA, MAN

# China, Man

## A YEAR OF MISADVENTURE TEACHING ENGLISH IN SHANGHAI

### EDUARDO MESTRE

CHINA, MAN

*A Year of Misadventure Teaching English in Shanghai*

ISBN   978-1-5445-0099-7  *Paperback*

978-1-5445-0098-0  *Ebook*

*For everyone who ever encouraged me to step off the beaten path*

# CONTENTS

## JIASHI, WANDERING FISH

*Out of a discarded pumpkin wire*
*Folk, customs, Chrysanthemum cold,*
*Corn, pine, nut speculation,*
*Synchronous emblem of incense fish.*
*Huangshan pair of winter,*
*The vast operation*
*Calming and ingredients of*
*The Taiping Sun.*
*The red side tang of the wild*
*Folk customs, simplicity,*
*Hospitality, altar artillery*
*Food science and modern philosophy.*

—OLD CHINESE PROVERB, MING DYNASTY

# PREFACE

The Jiashi proverb was an incantation popular among agrarian families in China during the height of the Ming Dynasty. With each repetition of the third stanza, the youngest son would yell his own name backwards, ceremoniously decapitate a chicken using only his teeth, and then deposit the carcass into a sack of rice, as a sacrifice to Zhonghua, the Rice God, in hopes of a good harvest.

Actually, I'm just messing with you. All twelve lines of the above proverb, plus the title, are actually food items from a single English translation of the menu at a restaurant that I visited in China. It's restaurants like these where you inadvertently receive a side order of deep fried Golden Retriever. Good luck ordering food. Welcome to China.

# Part One

*Wowsers, there's a lot of Chinese people here.* Shanghai. Shanghai is in China. China has a lot of...yeah. I wasn't crazy. Or was I?

移民

Hmm. I stared up at the little symbols. The first looked like a bear hugging an electricity pole. The second was an "R" with a crowbar jammed through it. I couldn't jimmy any meaning.

"Customs and Immigration," the sign read underneath. Merciful English.

I peered down at my new Tag Heuer watch, a college graduation present from my parents for limping across the finish line. My final GPA was at least a full point away from a Rolex. I strolled briskly toward "Customs and Immigration." I came upon an unmanned kiosk, with several stacks of forms spread across a marble countertop. In big letters on top, it said "QUARANTINE." I stopped.

Chinese men in business suits whizzed by, grabbed a piece of paper from the kiosk, filled it out in two seconds, dropped it into a slot, and sped toward "移民" without breaking stride. They all had very serious expressions on their faces. So many faces. One of them could have been a celebrity. Maybe they thought I was a celebrity. My Argentine cousins always told me I looked like Ricky Martin. I don't.

First things first. I grabbed a "QUARANTINE" form and started reading.

QUARANTINE
名字 / NAME: _____
护照 / DOCUMENT NUMBER: _____
日子 / DATE: _____
飞机 / FLIGHT: _____
请确认，如果您有任何下列疾病

☐  HIV/AIDS
☐  Avian Flu
☐  Tuberculosis
☐  Hepatitis C
☐  Ebola
☐  Venereal Disease
☐  Yellow Fever
☐  Bubonic Plague
☐  Pregnant

I paused on the checkboxes and bit my bottom lip. No tidy English instructions. Was I supposed to check the boxes if I didn't have the assorted illnesses, or was I supposed to check the boxes if I *did*?

The immigration queue was going to get long if I didn't make a move, so I checked the box next to every single disease, deposited my form in the same slot as everyone else, and proceeded forward to Customs and Immigration.

The "Foreigners" line was still mostly empty. The agent stamped my passport and smiled at me from behind the plexiglass with a wicked flash of the teeth, like someone who had just decapitated a chicken. With his teeth.

I emerged with my head attached, plucked my two duffels from the baggage claim conveyor belt, and sought out the director of Fudan International School, whom I knew only from a grainy online photo.

My baggage cart rolled smooth and true, with wheels like a fresh pair of rollerblades. Then I saw her. The Fudan International School director, Linda, was a welcome white-woman-at-a-Chinese-airport sight. She wore a giant smile and held her two arms outstretched, trying to hug me from forty feet away. Her shoulder length gray hair had some bounce to it. I waved and drove my baggage trolley toward her with an effortless push. Our eyes met, and she clapped her hands together excitedly, retracting her earlier hug offer.

"Hi there!"

"Linda, we meet at last." We did an awkward handshake-hug-pat-on-the-back trifecta.

"You made it."

"I made it."

"Welcome to China."

China. It suddenly felt real. We exited the airline terminal and met our Chinese van driver curbside by the international arrivals area. With mutually awkward smiles and nods, the driver assisted me in loading my pair of duffel bags into the back of the giant blue van. It had five rows of seats, but I was the lone pickup.

"*Xie xie ni*," I tiptoed, attempting to say "thank you" to the driver. This was one of about four phrases that I had learned during my ten hours of lessons. His smiled. It worked! Holy smokes. Away we accelerated, into the concrete abyss.

"How was your trip from New York?"

"Mostly stress free, though that Quarantine form was a little intimidating."

"They list a lot of scary diseases! I have to fill that thing out every time I arrive back in China after a trip from the States. God help anyone that checks off any of the boxes."

I coughed, "Excuse me, don't you mean you worry for anyone who leaves the boxes blank?"

"No, the form asks if you are carrying any of those diseases."

*Fuck. I'm patient zero.*

"Right, right. That's what I meant," I played it off cool, as my heart shrank a little bit knowing that I had been in China for fifteen minutes and already there was a piece of paper with my name and passport number indicating that I simultaneously had Ebola, AIDS, and VD. Plus I was pregnant.

"But anyway." Linda quickly changed the subject.

She continued, "Remember your passport when you haggle for a cell phone. Cash only. Elbows up as you exit an elevator. Our school is located north of city center. Mr. Wu has deep pockets. Unfrosted massage parlor front window glass is good. Beware high taxi license numbers.

Bamboo is a sturdy construction material. Wine's cheap, cigarettes are counterfeit, and I hope you don't take milk in your coffee. School starts in a four days."

"Welcome to Fudan International School orientation."

Linda's voice projected confidently to the new faculty as we musical chair'ed into our...chairs. There were about twenty of us in a large room in our school building. Tall, empty bookcases lined the bare walls, and a ceiling fan hummed rhythmically overhead, clicking purposefully with each revolution, as if to remind us that we were in *China. China. China. China.* It smelled like fresh paint—a bit toxic, almost. The high-achieving graduates from Duke were probably settling into investment banking orientation right about now. I was sandwiched among a bunch of Chinese people breathing in paint fumes.

The walls were straightjacket white, the electric outlets along the baseboard boasted a cryptographic Da Vinci Code pattern that could only be solved by Robert Langdon, and the noon daylight eked through three windows on the far wall, its radiance muted by dense cloud cover and smog overhead.

About half of my peers appeared to be Chinese, the rest white or foreign born. *Fudan International School.*

*How ya doin?* I nodded at each of them awkwardly, to my left, to my right, in front, and in back. We sat in four parallel rows of tiny chairs that were made for kindergarteners. My knees came to rest near my chest, my legs doing an accidental hamstring stretch. Everyone fidgeted, necks craning left and then right in an attempt to size up one another.

"This is an exciting year," Linda addressed us, hands clasped together. "Last year, we opened with a total of four students." She paused for emphasis, held up four fingers, and then repeated. "Four students."

"This year, we will grow to over seventy."

"How many students applied this year?" an inquisitive American guy a row in front of me asked, a little sheepish about whether he should be asking questions to begin with. He had nice hair from the back. Coiffed, brown, and long. Good hair. He was taking a ton of notes. *That* guy.

*Damn, that is a good-looking man.* I thought. Wow. He had sharp features but a tender set of eyes. His perfectly sculpted mouth probably burped rainbows, and his eyes could probably domesticate wild unicorns. He was my age. Jesus, I had issues.

I would come to know this guy as Ken.

"Well, seventy students applied..." Linda answered.

"One-hundred percent acceptance? Shit, is this special education?" a French sounding dude popped. Where was I? Three young Chinese teachers who were sitting in the front row simultaneously turned around in disbelief at this brazen outburst. Guess they must speak English pretty well. This guy had a point. One-hundred percent acceptance rate. Come one, come all.

"Being an Afghani opium farmer would have looked better on your resume," I heard my mom reminding me. *Get out of my head, Mom! Let me be me.*

"Look," Linda was defensive, "That's also a 100 percent yield. One day, I hope we can aspire to the levels of achievement of Fudan Fuzhong across the street. This was Mr. Wu's business objective. In the meantime, a lot of our own students will have plenty of room for improvement, which is why you're all here. I'm so excited that our FIS family has expanded." *Mr. Wu?*

"Fudan...Fuzhong?" I butchered the pronunciation.

"This is Fudan *International School*. We are an English language sub-division of a famous high school here in

China called Fudan *Fuzhong*. Fudan International School was created by one of the head administrators of Fudan Fuzhong. Everything here at FIS will be conducted in English."

"What's the acceptance rate at the other school, Fudan Fuzhong?" Jean-Louis pressed.

"Closer to five percent." Jean-Louis whistled.

Fudan Fuzhong was one of the premier high schools in all of China. It was founded in 1950. FIS was a shitty private school.

"Well, at least we have jobs. Better than spreading your cheeks for your next heroin fix." I heard Jean-Louis whisper too loudly to his neighbor.

Linda huffed. "This empty room here will soon be our school library. We are still acquiring books."

"Acquire a book. Acquire a book. Acquire a book," a middle-aged woman with an accent sitting next to me began to repeat to herself, rocking back and forth.

"School starts on Monday, and we have no books?" a voice rang out behind me.

"That's correct."

Another teacher, a white dude in his fifties, started to clear his throat really loudly. Everyone stopped talking. I looked him over. He looked like a guy who had come to China because he couldn't make it anywhere else—and not in the same way that I had. He looked like...hmm...let's think...he looked like a fatigued masturbator, if that was a thing. Picture that. *Better keep my eye on him,* I thought to myself. *Or not...he looks contagious.*

"Everything OK, Russell?" Linda asked, with her hands on her hips.

"Just taking stock," the teacher Russell Johnson replied, arms crossed.

"Drink some tea," a Chinese faculty member advised, missing the point.

"I think the school is very nice, very nice, very nice," the middle-aged woman sitting next to me muttered to herself, rocking back and forth with a heavy accent, accent, accent.

"So, how did you end up accepting a job here?" I whispered to her.

"Linda make one phone call, and I accept." Sounded familiar. Hadn't exactly been a ten-round interview process.

"Oh. Do you speak any Mandarin?" I asked.

"*Yī diǎn*," she replied.

"Uh."

"It means, 'little bit.' Is only word I know."

"Technically it's two words."

* * *

An hour later, Linda distributed photocopies of a handwritten roster of students, as well as our teaching schedules. My eyes scanned the list. Yurika. Kotaro. Min-Seok. Kim. Chen. Wang. Only guys missing were Bruce Lee and Chicken Chow Fun.

Some of them had English names as well. Jason. Cherry. Jerry. Mona. Louis. What was going on here?

"Where are all of these students from?" I asked Linda.

"They're from all over the world, but primarily Japan, Korea, and Hong Kong. The one thing that they have in common is that they are *not* Chinese."

"Most Asian. Not Chinese. Got it."

"Our faculty, on the other hand is American, Chinese, Turkish, Puerto Rican, Slovakian, you name it."

"So it is school in China, but have no Chinese students!" A Chinese guy in his forties wagged his finger and laughed at his own joke. When no one else did, he played it cool by wiping his glasses. I would come to know this math teacher as Mr. Lu.

I looked down at the fake wood floor. The panels stretched from my feet toward the exit from the library. If I sprinted out now, they might not catch me.

So why the hell does a white guy run away to China? I grew up on Park Avenue. Yeah, *that* Park Avenue. On paper, I'm a douche. There, I said it. I went to boarding school, then went to Duke. I graduated three months before touching down in Shanghai. My parents belong to a country club. Nowhere in this memoir do I get molested. Spoiler alert.

I grew up wealthy and white. Don't let my name fool you; my mother's pasty Irish heritage ensured my father's dark Cuban skin would have no chance at making me look remotely Latin. When you're white and you have money, as long as you don't screw up, things just sorta work out. No other way to explain it. I was aware of my advantages, but I'd never really done anything about them. I'd simply used them along the path.

The *Path*. My dad was Mr. Path. Yale. Harvard Law. Banking. Christ. Jesus...

I was technically Catholic, but in college I'd spent more time kneeling in front of the toilet bowl than the church pew. I guess you could call me a slacker, but to be honest, there were plenty of times in my life when I'd worked hard—and not just after popping a NoDoz®. I'd just done what was expected. It's a lot easier to chart a path in the world when others have already paved the way for you. But I was in China now. I was off the path.

Who was I? They say life is a beautiful struggle, but the thing was, I was twenty-two years old and I'd never truly struggled. Until now.

The steam from the rice wafted evenly, like a sauna. A rectangular plate held long, perfect slivers of oiled cucumber that looked like vegan dildos. Elsewhere, golden chunks of fresh chicken saddled up with red chilies, steamed cabbage oozed dreamily, and fried whole fish sat stacked in neat pyramids. *Oh my.*

We sat down. In front of my place setting was a pair of wooden chopsticks.

To my left was Helga, a math teacher. She was the oddly meditative middle-aged woman who sat next to me during orientation. She was pear-shaped and had sun-kissed, frizzy hair, which, coupled with her tanned skin, made her look as if she had grown up in a sand castle. Her smile was uneven, the right side of mouth remaining locked in position whenever she expressed satisfaction.

After some intros around the table and some motherly words of welcome from Linda, I turned toward Helga, as she began chatting ~~with~~ at me.

"My ex-husband, he is asshole."

"Excuse me?"

"I apologize. What I mean is, my ex-husband, he is *an* asshole."

"Oh." I had no idea what to say in response.

"I leave his ass in hole in Izmir in Turkey, which is beautiful place. So nice. But he is asshole." She shook her fist every time she said "*asshole,*" as if preparing to ram her arm up his nickname.

"So, you left Turkey and moved to Shanghai because you don't like your ex-husband?"

"Yes. And also food. I like Chinese food." As good a reason as mine for moving to China. The spread on the table in front of us sizzled with steam and spices. I was hungry.

"But I miss Turkey," she sighed.

I picked up my chopsticks and stared at them. They were thinner and sharper than I imagined, wooden precision scalpels when I envisioned miniature baseball bats. Light to the touch, almost like air. The wood was cheap and coarse, which actually seemed to enhance the grip.

I fidgeted with them awkwardly. This would require practice.

There was not a single Western utensil on the table. Across from me, one of the Chinese women from the front row of orientation wielded her sticks and deftly sniped individual pieces of chicken and cucumber from the centrally located serving dishes, like a silent assassin. Then, she seamlessly altered her grip, flattening the two sticks in their right hand into a makeshift spade, digging up a mountain's worth of sticky white rice and plopping it effortlessly onto her plate in an impressive showcase of diverse functionality. She was obviously some sort of chopstick deity.

I held both sticks stiffly in my right hand, using my left to adjust them so. I did a few awkward practice clamps before turning back to Helga.

"Helga, could you please pass the rice?" I asked.

"In the summer in Turkey, it's so nice. We do sailing, and it is beautiful."

"It's, um, right there...on the table." The haze from the rice bowl fanned toward me tantalizingly.

"My son, famous windsurfer in Turkey. He is so handsome..." She started to daydream.

"It's that bowl, right there, um, to your left."

"Turkey is so beautiful. The summer is so nice. The people is so nice."

"Can you hear anything I'm saying?"

"Turkish people is so handsome."

"I like to eat turkey."

"One day, I hope return. When ex-husband is dead." My plate was still empty.

She trailed off. I turned to my right. In that chair sat Mr. Lu. He was a Shanghai native who also taught math. He spied me looking for food on the table. This was my first conversation with a real Chinese person. Thank God he spoke English.

"You like this dish? Very delicious! Cucumber. Spicy cucumber. You like cucumber? You must try the cucumber. In China, they like the fish. Eat it with chopsticks! What do you want to eat? You have enough? Have some beer. Very good!"

"So..."

"You try the dumpling from Shanghai? Also delicious. And famous! Please eat food! Ms. Linda, she likes dumplings. It has pork. Best dumpling place. On the same street like FIS."

"Could you pass the—

"What you teach again? English? Yes. American teaches English. Of course!"

"Could you please pass the spicy cucumber?" My stomach rumbled. I don't think my request registered.

"Fish. The Shanghai people like this. And eat it one piece. Just like this." He stuck an entire fish into his mouth as I just watched. His mouth swirled as if he were gargling mouthwash. He swallowed, opened his mouth again, and withdrew an entire fish skeleton, completely intact, with no meat remaining. I felt like the fish.

"Wow," was all I could say.

The spicy cucumber, the fish, and the beer were all beyond my reach. I stood up, reached across the table, and grabbed the chicken, the rice, and the infamous cucumber. I scooped each of them onto my plate clumsily and began to eat voraciously.

"Good morning! My full name is Eduardo Mestre."

"Hi there. My name is Mr. Mestre."

"Hello students. I am Ed. Ed Mestre."

"Edward. Edward Mestre."

The person in the mirror was hardly convincing. I twisted the faucet sink and splashed cold chlorine water on my face. I needed a name.

"How am I going to do this?" I asked out loud. "I am—how do the French say it?—*le fucked*. Maybe I should have never come here." My stomach didn't feel right. I splashed water again, as if a few more drops would give me the confidence I lacked.

"It's just a conversation. Just keep talking," I kept talking.

I exited my bathroom and put on a crisp blue button down

and khaki pants. I tied my shoes, grabbed a stack of papers, and walked out the door.

"You can do this," I assured myself on that fateful Monday morning in September. "It's just a conversation. Keep it professional. Winners don't shit their pants on the first day." The sky overhead receded as I pushed open the front door to the Fudan International School building. What uncertainty loomed? The distinct cacophony of children's voices was overwhelming, audible everywhere but impossible to pinpoint, like a loud fart in a crowded elevator.

In my hand, I carried copies of a Wikipedia printout of a diagram of body parts, which, after staring at my own arm for ten minutes the previous afternoon, I figured might make for a good first vocabulary lesson on day one of class. I also wielded a copy of my student roster. Koreans, Japanese, Hong Kong natives. The only thing they had in common is that they supposedly spoke *some* English. For my Ancient Civilizations class, I had copies of another Wikipedia printout—about cavemen. Was that sufficiently "ancient"? If felt like a good starting point for world history. "First, there were people in dark caves; now, we sit in dark rooms and stream pornography over the Internet," I imagined my opening sentence.

It was my first day on the job. It was my first ever first day on *any* job. It was also my birthday.

"Happy goddamned birthday," I whispered to myself twenty-three times.

My watch read 8:00 AM. *8:00 PM back at home,* I thought. My first ever class. Ancient Civilizations. Seventh and eighth graders. English language beginners.

As I ascended the stairs to my classroom on the third floor, I racked my brain to recall the name of a single ancient civilization besides Rome. Mesopotamia? Atlantis? Disco? I hid in the stairwell for three minutes, until the exact moment when class was set to begin.

I stepped into my classroom and took in the—let's call it sparse—environment. The previous day, I'd found a crumpled poster of Norwegian fjords and a ripped photomosaic of Martin Luther King gathering dust in a closet in the teacher office one flight below. No questions asked. I hung them on my classroom wall with tacks that I stole from the school bulletin board—it's not like there were any announcements posted.

Otherwise, there were desks, chairs, chalkboards, teachers, and students. That's it. My first six pupils were already seated and staring at me, beady-eyed with wonder at the tall foreigner now eyeballing each of them. It felt like a meeting between the cowboys and Indians. It was just unclear who was the cowboy and who was the Indian.

I had heard that a number of our students had spent significant time growing up in English-speaking countries. I crossed my fingers, hoping their base comprehension level was pretty solid. I squeezed my arms tightly against my body, defensively.

"Good morning!" I mustered, with a mix of trepidation and false enthusiasm. Their cold faces looked fragile with apprehension. They all dipped their chins and silently tried to summon an invisibility spell.

I slid over to the blackboard and grabbed a piece of chalk. My hand trembled as I wrote in all capital letters, "MR. MESTRE," with questionable chalk penmanship. Aren't all teachers Mr. Last Name? I thought so.

I enunciated it sloooowly: "Miiiiiiiister Meeeeeeeestre" (MEH-stray). I turned around and was met with blank, empty stares. One kid's mouth was hanging open. A droplet of drool escaped from the corner of his mouth and landed on his sleeve below. He didn't notice. Linda had warned me that these kids might struggle to pronounce foreign sounding names.

"Can anyone repeat? Miiiiiiiiister Meeeeeeeestre."

A girl in the front row muttered something to her neighbor, in Japanese. Or Korean. Or maybe Mandarin? I wasn't at all sure. *Do I say something to her?* I let it slide.

"Can anyone repeat? Miiiiiiiiister Meeeeeeeestre. Anyone? Anyone?"

Silence. *Shit.* I could feel the tension rising throughout the room. *Or was it just me?* I tried one more time. After a minute's effort to elicit a single sound from my six students, I made things a little bit easier. I erased the chalk using my sleeve (there were no erasers), and wrote a new name: Mr. Ed. "You can call me Mr. Ed. Please say again."

The same girl who was chatting a moment earlier yelled out: "Miiiiista Edo!"

Me: "No. It's Mister *Ed*. There is no 'o' at the end. Please repeat: 'Mr. Ed.'"

Girl in the front row: "Miiiiista Edo!"

Me: "It's Mr. *Ed*. Can you please try one more time?"

Girl in the front row: "Miiiiista Edo!" *Have I entered the Twilight Zone?*

Now, a second girl in the front row chimed in: "Miiiista Edo?" She repeated "Mista Edo" like more of a question rather than a statement. She started giggling. I saw her face bowl up, her cheeks about to pop as she struggled to hold back the laugh creeping over her face.

"Miiiista Edo?" She repeated, laughing. I was on the outside of an inside joke.

*What the hell was going on here?* Why was a thirteen-year-old Japanese girl with a bowl cut and a sweater vest laughing at me?

I bolted over to my class roster and thumbed through the six names.

Yurika Takeshita. That must be the girl laughing. Takeshita? What was her middle name? Wipemyass-a?

"Yurika." I snapped. She sat up in her chair. "Why is my name funny? Why do you keep saying 'Mr. Edo?'"

She paused. "'Eto' in Japan. Is like 'um.' 'Eto' mean 'ummm.'" *Umm what, Takeshita? Finish your thought.*

"Excuse me?"

The girl sitting next to Yurika chimed in. "Yurika mean your name sound like 'um' with Japanese. Mr. Um."

*OH.* "So, Mr. Ed sounds like Mr. Um in Japanese?"

"Um, yes."

It was ridiculous. And just like that, Yurika Takeshita christened me, "Mr. Edo." I was flustered.

Now that we established what would be my lasting legacy as "Mr. Um," I carried on with my lesson. Glancing around the room from pupil to pupil I asked, "What is your name?" "Where are you from?"

"Kate Mizuki. Japan."

"Wayne Ling. Taiwan."

"..."

One student didn't have a name. He just offered silence, tilted his shaggy-haired head to the right, and scratched his head. So, I reiterated my question: "Whaaaat iiiiiiis yoooooooooouuuur naaaaaaame?"

"..."

A panicky look washed over his ghost-white face. His eyes darted to the left and then to right, as if his name was written on the wall next to the Norway poster. *Look harder, kid.*

Yurika turned around and mumbled something in Japanese to this student. Realization suddenly dawned on his face like the glorious morning sun over Kyoto.

"*Eto, eto, eto,* Kotaro Sato."

Really? I wondered. Did she just translate for him? I hope not.

Kotaro wore an anime t-shirt depicting a decapitated samurai warrior holding his own bleeding head. Guess we didn't have a dress code.

"Where are you from?" I ventured.

"..."

Yurika rattled off another translation to Kotaro.

"*Eto, eto, eto,* Japan," he answered, nodding.

I paused in wonder. Kotaro tilted his head once more and continued to scratch uncomfortably. I would come to learn that this head scratching mechanism was Kotaro's way of signaling that he did not understand what was happening. It was going to be a regular thing.

"Japan. What a wonderful country. Welcome to my class, Kotaro." I offered, self-soothingly. Half a class complete, and Mr. Um was already in search of a floatation device underneath his seat.

I somehow slogged through forty-five minutes of caveman vocabulary. I was sweating profusely, when out of nowhere the Happy Birthday melody started blaring through loud-speakers everywhere in school.

"What the—!" I looked up and down. Did someone know that it was my birthday?

"It mean end the class," the student named Kate calmly told me.

"Oh." I was disappointed.

The students filed out. Wait a minute; the class bell at our school was an electronic rendition of the Happy Birthday song? Really? If once a year wasn't already enough, I was going to be blowing out candles every forty-five minutes. My eyes glazed over as the students filed out of the room.

I huffed.

Linda popped her head in and offered some velvety words of encouragement: "How is it going? How was your first class? I'm sure you're doing great."

"Um."

*Flashback.*

"You might as well sell your possessions and become a yak herder in Kazakhstan."

"Mom."

"Feels like I've spent forty years raising you the right way, and you want to run away to China."

"I'm barely over twenty," I said. Classic Mom Math. Divide or multiply by two in order to help your argument.

"I found a school over there," I continued. They offered me a job."

"You couldn't have found something...closer?"

"I was rejected by Teach For America...and every other job I applied to."

"You could keep looking."

"I want to do this."

"But...China? I'm not wild about this."

"I am." I was.

"What about Riley?" she asked.

"We're, uh, taking some time apart."

"I feel like you barely looked for a job, and now you're moving to China."

"I got rejected all over the place..."

"Well, you can keep trying. Your father has done very well in banking. That's not a bad path."

"I don't know what to tell you."

"Your family has all sorts of connections, and you decide to pack up and move to China."

"It's my choice."

"Tell me why you're doing this."

"Doing what?"

"Tell me why you're going to China."

I closed my eyes.

I was in an open-air, mountaintop shrine at dusk. The surrounding deep green, ancient forest was my lone companion. A cool breeze rustled a wind chime in the rafter overhead. I approached an ornate wooden railing overlooking the jade earth beneath me and took a deep solitary breath. The clouds rose up from the ground way below, my perch above an unreachable mantel.

My heart calmed, and I drifted off to sleep.

The truth is, no one in China knew my name. No one in China knew my background. No one in China cared. It was the perfect canvas to prove that I could make something out of nothing. I felt as if I literally had to travel to China to start over, with a clean slate, and truly discover who I was. Such is the rich kid's dilemma. Scoff as you wish, but in Shanghai, I was no better than anyone else. And turns out, I wasn't qualified to do anything in China. Except become a teacher.

"My treat," Linda insisted, as we opened the glass front door to FIS's building and stepped onto the concrete court-yard in front of our building.

"You're paying me a salary already. There's really no need."

"Ed, the noodles cost 5 RMB. Less than a buck."

Ed. *Mr. Ed.* My new workplace identity. I thought of Yurika.

"Fine. Next time, I'll return the favor."

"You're too kind," she said, halfway between sarcasm and appreciation. Linda's pace was brisk but measured as we stepped outside our building. On the basketball court out-side, we saw middle school children from another school lined up silently in tight rows, spring loaded.

I turned to Linda. "What's about to—" They answered my question for me.

At once, they launched into a combination of yoga and army boot camp marching. *"Yi! Er! San! Si! Wu! Liu! Qi! Ba!"* (1! 2! 3! 4! 5! 6! 7! 8!) blared rhythmically and repetitively over a loudspeaker.

The students, some younger than ten years old, wore red uniforms and moved in perfect synchronization. They kicked out a leg (*"Yi"*), raised a fist in the air (*"Er"*), put the leg back down (*"San"*), raised the other arm in the air (*"Si"*), retracted both arms in a humping motion (*"Wu"*), rotated ninety degrees counterclockwise (*"Liu"*), brought their right hand to their forehead in sharp salute (*"Qi"*), and then whipped their hand back down once again (*"Ba"*). They repeated this again and again, as the Chinese flag fluttered approvingly overhead in the morning breeze. Holy shit, these kids were already on the Path.

"So, *this* is communism?" I asked Linda.

"This is middle school," Linda corrected. "Midday aerobics."

"Looks like their instructor snagged himself a couple of 1987 Richard Simmons exercise videos."

"Ed, if you think this is culture shock, wait until you've been here awhile."

"So this coordinated high speed yoga cheerleading ranks low on your list of China head-scratchers?"

"Eat some crickets and get a foot massage. Then let's talk." She spoke calmly, with years of experience, like someone who had eaten a lot of crickets and gotten a lot of foot massages.

We walked through our school courtyard's front gate, discordant two and four-wheel street traffic now lurching right to left in front of us. Bicycles, mopeds, a taxi or two. Pedestrians in rice hats, others in jeans. Students with books and imitation brand backpacks (e.g., "Noth Face," "Gansport," "Swoosh"). It smelled like carbon monoxide— which, I'm well aware, does not in fact have a smell, but if it did, it would be this. Not quite car exhaust, but car exhaust mixed with bus fumes mixed with freshly laid asphalt mixed with a dash of day-old garbage.

We stopped and looked up. Across the street, a massive, cream-colored building towered into the gray sky, its chin up and arms crossed, looking down upon us disapprovingly. It was set back a few hundred yards from the road, guarded by a high, automatic security gate—the kind of thing that could keep out fire-breathing dragons as well as pesky loiterers. The building's crest rose in a perfect triangle to a perfect point, symmetrically above the gate, not by accident. Above the structure's zenith, a white orb, probably a water tower, reigned on high, like the Eye of Sauron. In front of the building, a statue that was the spitting image of the Cornucopia from the Hunger Games idled alone in a patch of tidy grass.

"Is that—"

"Famous Fudan Fuzhong. One of the most competitive and high-achieving schools in all of China."

"Well their school tower looks like it could mow down failing students with a massive laser. No wonder it's so competitive."

"The majestic Fudan Fuzhong," Linda took a longing and envious breath and crossed her arms protectively. "There is work yet to be done."

All the local Chinese students filing through the front gates of Fudan Fuzhong wore orange and blue tracksuits.

"Are they all headed to gym class?" I asked Linda. A few of them scurried by us on the sidewalk and giggled.

"That's their school uniform."

"The uniform of the best high school in China is a *tracksuit?*"

"I know," she conceded. A couple more passing Fudan

Fuzhong students smirked at me condescendingly. *You think you look smart in your goddamned tracksuit? Think again!*

Linda's determination was contagious. I think. Maybe I was just hungry. I had something to prove but no idea where to begin. I couldn't tell if I was inspired or complacent and inadequate. One thing was clear: FIS was no Fudan Fuzhong.

"Well, what do you say, Ed, shall we grab our noodles?"

The cool stone under my bare feet was a trip. My Reef sandals idled two feet away, and the sun breathed hot air onto my pale legs. On my lap was the book *Beginning Mandarin*. I'd yet to open the cover. I gazed up at the sky. I thought about removing my shirt, but didn't. The bench underneath me was oddly comfortable, and the FIS school grounds were sleepy on this September Sunday. I checked my phone. No missed calls, which made sense, because no one had my number. I closed my eyes.

"Ed, right?"

I opened my eyes. Ken stood in front of me, hair swooshed back in a tidy comb. He was tall. Like really tall. I swear to God a halo formed around his perfectly formed face.

"Yeah. Ken. Hey."

"Miles, Jean-Louis, and I are swinging downtown to central Shanghai. You in?" He had a sweet voice, really inviting, the kind you could confide secrets to. Like a therapist.

"Definitely!" I answered reflexively. "I mean, yeah, sounds cool."

FIS was thirty minutes north of the city's epicenter, so a visit to "central Shanghai" was actually a thing. I'd been in China a couple weeks, and without realizing it, I'd barely left the FIS school campus.

The guy named Jean-Louis butted in. "Miles, he speaks the Mandarin, so we probably won't wind up in a dumpster somewhere."

"Right."

"Unless we want to."

This was Jean-Louis, the guy who questioned FIS's acceptance rate on our first day of orientation. He was stocky and unfiltered, like a half-smoked cigarette.

I turned to Miles, who simply nodded confidently.

We hailed a taxi outside of our school grounds. A Volkswagen with a baby blue tint crept toward us and stopped abruptly. The car looked as unsteady as the driver, who too-closely resembled a Chinese version of the 1976 Robert De Niro titular role.

"The Chinaman stopped! *C'est un miracle*," Jean-Louis said, opening the door before the driver could change his mind.

"Don't tell him you're Canadian," Miles chided.

"French Canadian, *mon petit fromage*," Jean-Louis winked as he held the door open for us.

"Let's be nice to each other in front of our new friend, guys," Ken coaxed. I blushed a little.

We climbed into the taxi. Eager to not seem difficult, I offered to ride bitch (middle seat in the back). My head touched the ceiling, and my hips were smushed against my new friends. Ken had to angle his head to the left to fit inside.

"What is this? A miniature model of a taxi? AMIRIGHT?" I asked.

"As small as the laugh from your shitty joke," added Jean-Louis.

Um.

"Sometimes it's best to ignore him."

Miles, resident smart guy, sat shotgun with our Chinese

driver and calmly fired off directions in what sounded like near-perfect Mandarin. Or total gibberish. I couldn't tell the difference.

I caught another glimpse of the driver in the rear view mirror. His cheeks were pockmarked and his hair needed a wash. He looked tired. One corner of his lip furled upward.

Miles turned around to the three of us in the back.

"Guys, buckle up."

"What do you mean?" I asked.

"This driver has a really high license number—254,189." Miles pointed to the cabbie's visibly displayed license number on the dashboard by the meter. "That means he is a new cabbie, and he's probably craz—" Miles's head slammed against the divider as the cabbie dropped a brick on the accelerator, ran a red light, and knocked over a street-side trash bin.

"Whoooooaaaaa!" we all screamed.

I felt my breakfast surge back up toward my mouth. Turns out, Shanghai taxi license numbers are granted in order, meaning the lower the number, the more experienced the guy. The higher the number, the greater the likelihood of your impending doom. The new cabbies always got lost and ran over small children.

We slalomed through a series of tight one-way roads, narrowly dodging the hundreds of people overflowing at each crosswalk. I quietly gripped the underside of my pants. Locals on bicycles and mopeds surrounded us on all sides. At almost every street corner, construction sites with bamboo scaffolding shot skyward. Out of nowhere, our driver flung the wheel right, directly onto a highway onramp. We climbed so quickly it felt like an airplane takeoff.

The car rose onto an elevated highway that shot through the city like an earthquake fissure. We continued to accelerate quickly. The roadway was filled with four-wheeled, flimsy tin can missiles, hurtling downtown at a terrifying velocity.

All along the highway were giant new towers, adorned with product billboards hocking ramen noodles and prominent brands of green tea. The spokesmen on all the billboards appeared to be making sex faces. One guy in particular looked like he was going to ejaculate his brand of grape soda all over the highway.

Slotted in between these new towers, you could occasionally glimpse old shanty streets, with tightly packed dwellings and lean-tos, clothing lines and wires dangling precariously above the dirt and stone below. These shanty streets were packed with people in raggedy clothes. Little glimpses of old China hidden in between the shadows of the new era.

* * *

Jean-Louis swung the rear passenger door open just in time. Two more minutes of lurching and swerving in the back of that taxi and I would have painted my three new American friends in a fresh coat of regurgitated breakfast. My head was spinning as I stepped out of the taxi and looked up. Hello, central Shanghai.

We were on the Bund, Shanghai's most famous water-side street. With our thankfully-still-attached limbs, we ascended a set of stairs to a bustling riverside promenade overlooking the Huang Pu River. It was like being dropped inside of a slot machine. Women in robes danced in unison with fans. A guy peddled RC helicopters with flashing neon lights. Nine different aromas of fried noodles wafted toward me. It was total chaos. We started walking.

"Welcome to the Bund," Miles opened his arms wide and gestured broadly.

"Wow." I muttered.

"Well fuck me right in le ass," said Jean-Louis.

"If you keep calling it 'le ass,' one of these vendors might try to do exactly that," Ken offered a legitimate word of caution. I reflexively squeezed my butt cheeks.

As I tried to enjoy the casual stroll, I was being grabbed by a vendor every three steps. "Watch? Bag? DVD?" "Hello! Hello! Hello!" "Take a look! Take a look!" The street salesmen smelled blood.

"Please, I don't want to buy anything!" was my futile plea.

"OUT OF MY WAY, KUNG FU MAN," Jean-Louis brushed aside a guy that knew zero kung fu.

"*Qǐng bié dǎrǎo wǒ. Wǒ chuánrǎn xìng,*" Miles told a group of vendors. They immediately scattered. *Nota bene:* traditional Mandarin Chinese is written in those crazy characters that you can't read. Pinyin Mandarin Chinese is spelled out phonetically in that comfy Anglican alphabet we all love to sing about.

"Whoa. What did you tell them, Miles?" asked Ken.

"I told them we had bird flu," Miles replied, matter-of-factly. *Brilliant.* This guy knows how to survive in China.

He continued, "The easiest way to get vendors out of your hair is just to tell them '*Bù yào*,' which means 'I don't want.' You guys should try that."

"*Bù yào*," I repeated. A new vendor ran up to me.

"Watch! Bag! DVD! Hello hello hello!"

"*Bù yào!*" I yelled defensively. He shrank. I flexed my biceps.

Another guy ran up to me holding bags of water filled with live goldfish.

"*Bù yào!*" I yelled again, and made an accompanying ninja move with my arms.

It was working! As we walked, still more vendors abounded, touching, grabbing, howling, desperately trying anything to take some of my money. But Miles had effectively armed me with a verbal shotgun, which I blasted at every single vendor who approached me. It worked best when I yelled it: "*BÙ YÀO!*"

We continued our walk along the promenade. "*Bù yào! Bù yào!*" My eyes were quickly drawn away from the classy, European-style facades behind me, and the ravenous salesmen in front of me. Across the river I saw Pudong, the massive new financial district on the eastern side of the Huangpu river.

I saw the famous Oriental Pearl TV Tower, a fifty-story space needle outfitted with enormous glowing bulbs at varying intervals, all flashing like a tacky Christmas tree. There were glass towers, among which were some of the tallest buildings in the world. To the right was the forty-story, solid gold Aurora tower. The outline of this monstrosity enveloped an enormous television. Put quite simply, the building itself was a giant TV. I could barely take my eyes off it. Directly across from me was a boat hauling yet another gigantic television. Check that—the boat itself *was* a giant television. *I'm sensing a pattern here.*

I came to learn that Pudong in its entirety had been erected in the last twenty years. A "special economic zone" declaration by Chinese government officials had made foreign investors' eyes light up with dollar signs. Prior to this development binge, the area across the river had been little more than farmland. Two decades later, it had sold its soul for billions of dollars in skyscrapers, gigantic malls, and glamour. Pudong was the *Rosemary's Baby* of the Chinese economy.

That is not to say, however, that the west side of the river (on which we were currently standing) didn't have flashing lights. You couldn't walk four inches without seeing blinking neon signs affixed to buildings that probably housed underground discos for cats.

To me, the west side, called Puxi, had more appeal because it had the history—the museums and distinct districts with unique character. The influx of extra-terrestrial looking development in Puxi was interspersed among the traditional, colonial-era buildings of old Shanghai.

At first, meandering the insanity of the west side of the river made me tingle in anticipatory revelation. It was as if Buddha had sprinkled speed upon the entire metropolis. Taxis whizzed through the streets like they were leaving the scene of a hit and run. Pedestrians were so densely packed that their movements could only be seen as ebbs and flows.

I took in the sites of the Bund with my three new American friends.

"So the three of you knew each other before coming to China?" I asked them. We passed a group of shirtless, inebriated men playing dominos on a street corner. They needed deodorant.

"Sorta," Ken said. "Weirdly enough, we all went to Brown University but hung out in different social circles. We made the decision to come here separately and reconnected before jetting across the Pacific. Now you could say we're buddies." He put a friendly arm around the shoulder of Jean-Louis, who was a little squeamish. A local guy dressed in pajamas passed us on the sidewalk.

"Miles has spent some time here before," Jean-Louis gestured.

"I studied abroad here and have also been taking Mandarin for a number of years."

"I've got about ten hours of lessons under my belt," I admitted to Miles.

"Probably just enough to say your name."

"Barely. *Wǒ jiào* Ed."

"Not bad! You'll do fine here."

"If my students don't stuff me into a dumpling and eat me."

"So what's your deal?" Miles probed further. "You don't look like much of an *Eduardo*."

"How do you know—"

"Teacher roster."

"Right."

"So, *Eduardo?*"

"Correctamundo. But, uh, call me Ed. I have a cool name but I'm pretty pale. My parents were hoping for Benicio del Toro but they got Jim Halpert."

"Yeah you definitely wear SPF-50 at the beach."

I felt weirdly at ease. Like no one was judging me.

"That's not the half of it. Growing up, my Argentine cousins used to call me *litro de leche.*"

"What does that mean?" Miles asked.

"Liter of milk."

"How's your Spanish?"

"A little rusty."

"More *Ed* than *Eduardo?*"

"That's fair. Though all the Japanese girls at school call me 'Mr. Edo.'"

"This is China. There are some things that you just have to roll with. Don't fight it. Just accept it." Pretty sure this guy Miles led a religious cult on the weekends.

"Mr. Ed!" Jean-Louis jumped back into the conversation now. "Sounds like you know as little Chinese as Ken and me."

"Guess you guys are noobs as well?" I asked him.

"Yeah we're all pretty much fucked here. Might as well enjoy it. Should we eat some food before cabbing back up to school?"

We stopped at a crosswalk. Next to us, a toddler stationed himself between his parents, gripped their hands, and then squatted.

Ken looked concerned. "Miles, what is that kid doing?"

I opened my eyes and tried to look closer.

"Looks like he's about to pop a squat—Oh! Oh god! Oh that's gross." The kid took a shit on the sidewalk, stood back up, and continued walking, never letting go of his parents' hands. I could see that his pants had a permanent gaping hole in the back.

"Does that kid's outfit have a shit hole?" Jean-Louis asked.

"Yeah we used to call those Baby Butt Crack Pants," Miles reasoned.

"Nasty!" Jean-Louis hacked. No one turned around. "File that scene under Can't Ever Un-See."

"Here's lookin' at you, kid." I muttered. Admittedly, I wasn't grossed out. I laughed. *This place was crazy.* Such are the streets of Shanghai. Bright lights, big city.

On a sturdy column opposite my seat on the booth side of our long table, a framed alpine landscape painting hung proudly. In it, lone trees protruded from sheer rock faces. Thick clouds breathed over the scenery, nestled into mountain crevasses as if poured from a gravy boat. The washed out color palette gave the whole thing a dream-like quality. At the bottom of the frame, a gold placard read, "HUANGSHAN—YELLOW MOUNTAIN." I filed that one for later.

Without prompt, our waitress brought out a dozen large green beer bottles. On the side, they read, "*Tsingtao*" brand. Following everyone else's example, I poured the beer into a glass. The light foam and thin color made Bud Light look like Guinness.

"*Gan bei!*" our Puerto Rican Dean of Students—a really furry guy—yelled to the table, lifting up his glass. *That must mean 'cheers.'*

"To Shanghai!" Linda added. We all took a swig of our beers.

It was an odd thing to cheers. Our school? Our students? Our jobs? No, it was *Shanghai*. This state of being. This place. My first drink in China went down smoothly, as a confluence of emotions washed over me: liberation and camaraderie, youth and adulthood, nostalgia and optimism.

The drinks kept coming.

"Teaching is hard work," I leaned over and told Linda, a little too honestly.

"Funny how quick you finally realize that when you're the guy holding the piece of chalk."

"Yes." I gave a big nod.

"And our school—" she began.

"—is kind of a crock, right?" I finished her thought.

"—is on the right path..." She trailed off, eyes locked into mine, as her face went ashen white.

"I just—"

"You just—"

"I'm sorry," I said finally. "That's not what I meant."

"Look, Ed, on the surface it might not look like much, but this is what we've got. There is a lot we're trying to do here." She twirled the stem of her glass of red wine.

I felt small.

"Sorry, Linda, again, I didn't mean that."

"Look, you're young. But you don't know everything. I'll give you a pass. I know in my heart you're capable of wonderful things, *Mr. Ed.*"

"Why are you in China?" I asked. Topic change.

"Divorce, Mr. Wu's numeracy, and great dumplings. But most of all, our students." *Numeracy?*

"Shots? You guys want a shot? Shots?" asked our Dean of Students.

"Yes! We shoot!" Math teacher Mr. Lu cocked his hands like pretend guns.

\* \* \*

At 4:00 AM, back up at the school, we recapped our adventures out on a terrace in the teacher dormitory. Gold lettering, mirrored ceilings, leather couches, and lasers galore. Luke Skywalker attacking the Death Star. Chinese people sweating all over each other. Pools of Johnny Walker Black. What the hell just happened?

It was a balmy night, one where summer and fall were still wrestling for attention, but summer was winning. All was quiet on the school ground three flights below.

All other teachers had since passed out except for Miles, Ken, and Jean-Louis. This was the beginning of a pattern. With whiskey and vodka Red Bulls still coursing our veins, we had unknowingly turned up the volume on our conversation.

"I can't believe you lost your cell phone. Again," Ken looked at Jean-Louis in disbelief.

"It just happened," Miles defended him.

"Still got my wallet though. I'll buy another one," Jean-Louis seemed unfazed.

"Did you even own this one long enough to memorize your cell phone number?"

"Nope. But on the bright side, did you see how hot those two girls were?" Jean-Louis was hopping from one foot to the other, waving a piece of paper with a phone number.

"Make sure not to store that number in your phone," I said.

"Dude, we saw!" Ken, eyes bulging, gave Jean-Louis a playful shove. Ken, usually the nice one, appeared to have a clumsy, physical side when he drank.

"No, no, no. I mean did you *see* how hot those two girls were? Like did you *see them see them?*"

"Dude, we *saw them saw them!*" Another shove. Jean-Louis seemed immune.

"Shanghai *Shanghai,* alright *alright,*" Miles bobbed his head, holding court.

I turned to the three of them. "Guys, I have to ask. Why the fuck did you come to China?"

"*Duardo,* you were on fire tonight. Sick moves, *mon frère,*" Jean-Louis slowly began to approve.

"Same reason as you. To get away." Miles stated, matter-of-factly.

"How did you—"

"You think you're a pioneer?" Jean-Louis said.

"Didn't Hemingway write about this?" Miles said.

"The. Sun. Also. Rises." Ken wobbled. "Great book."

"Thesis of a high school English paper?" asked Jean-Louis.

"'Plot summary,' his teacher probably circled in red at the top," I laughed.

"What did they read in Canada—*The Moose Also Rises*?" he fired back.

"We read *The Temperature Never Rises*," Jean-Louis corrected.

"I have some history papers to grade tomorrow," Ken mumbled to no one in particular.

"So Mr. Edo," Miles turned to me. "Who or what are you running from?"

The question gripped me to the bone.

"I dunno. Guess I just wanted something different."

The three of them were silent. Jean-Louis raised an eyebrow incredulously.

I continued, "It wasn't just a lack of job prospects."

"What's her name?" Miles downshifted.

"Riley."

"Was she—"

"My parents are both lawyers in Montreal," Jean-Louis opened up, out of turn. "I don't want to be a lawyer. At least not yet."

"Aha," I understood. "Just like me." We all looked at Ken.

"I just got tired of the rat race. Screw it—off to China went *this guy*." Ken pointed at himself with his two thumbs. "I'm a history major. What the hell do you do with a history major?" His drink spilled a little.

"Dude." Miles guided him. Ken sobered up for a second.

"I applied to twenty-eight jobs. Every kind of job. This was all I could get."

I felt guilty. Here I'd had the insider track, the Path, to what Ken wanted. And I'd still failed.

He trailed off, pensively. "I figure if I do some solid work here, I'll eventually be granted entry to corporate America and live a normal life. Sometimes all I want is to raise a family in the suburbs and barbecue sausage on the weekends. Honestly I've always had this gnawing fear I was gonna die young, so I always played it safe."

"Sausage?" Jean-Louis asked.

"Ken, calm down and look around once in a while. It won't kill you," Miles said. That settled that.

"What about you, man?" I asked Miles.

"Sometimes it's about the journey and not the destination. Speaking Mandarin also helps." He winked.

The next afternoon, several glasses of water and multiple Advil later, I was in the faculty lounge of the teachers' dormitory, staring down at a homework assignment turned in by Kotaro, the head scratcher and my weakest student. He was clearly an English language beginner:

1.   What is something that you wish to learn this year?

Read good

2.   What is your favorite class in school?

中国类

3.   What job do you want when you grow up?

Rich man

I slowly banged my head down against the table just as my new buddies walked in.

"That bad, eh?" Ken asked. "Should have prepped them better."

"It's an abomination on so many levels, and I just don't care." I immediately felt better.

"Talk to me, Ed," Miles sat down and propped his head up on his elbow.

"This kid Kotaro aspires to be a rich man when he's older, as if being rich were a profession."

"That's discouraging," Ken shook his head in sympathy.

Jean-Louis countered: "I think this kid is a genius. I also want to be a rich man."

I banged my head on the table again.

"Careful not to break that thing with your forehead, or vice versa." Jean-Louis warned. "PS: that wimpy little desk there makes Ikea look fit for the Prime Minister."

"Prime Minister...such a Canadian reference," Ken goaded in a friendly voice, clearly back to his sober personality.

"Shut up. This is China. They have a Prime Minister here too," he shot back.

"They do? What's his name, huh?" I tested Jean-Louis.

"Bang bang dong."

"I meant his *name*. Not your fetish wish list top ten."

"You guys don't know either," Ken jumped in.

"Yao Ming?" Jean-Louis guessed.

"Now that's just racist," Miles scolded.

"There was a *Ming* Dynasty."

"Yao there was. In Houston."

"Actually, guys," Miles interjected. "They have a 'Premier' and not a 'Prime Minister.'"

"Oh shut up, Miles."

✳ ✳ ✳

"What else you got?" Miles finally asked. Our real estate agent, a young Chinese woman in her late twenties who spoke perfect English, told us that there was one last apartment we should see. We started walking down Tibet Road (Xizang Lu).

Xizang Lu was one hell of a street.

The aroma of greasy cooking oil.

"Smells like chicken!" Ken yelled over his shoulder and careened into some bamboo scaffolding. A packed sidewalk. Ken's head stood out like a periscope. Shrill voices. Whizzing bicycles.

"Don't get flattened, Mr. Ed!" Miles yelled from a few rows back in the pedestrian swarm.

"Miles, help! Some guy keeps touching my hair!" Ken yelled. "*Bù yào! Bù yào!*"

"Pretty sure an old man grabbed my ass," said Jean-Louis.

"Don't flatter yourself," said Miles.

Nearby, an old alleyway. Dark, Old Shanghai. Clotheslines. Two-story shanty houses. A woman leaned out of a window and banged a rug, the dust cascading below. An abandoned rickshaw. Back on the main drag, a bootleg DVD store. Neon lights. A bald guy with a briefcase of fake Rolexes.

"Take a look! Take a look!" he said.

"*Bù yào!*" I yelled.

A pet marketplace. Insects, birds, and fish. Metal cages with squirming crickets. A local guy bought a dozen.

"Why is that guy buying so many crickets?" I asked our real estate agent.

"For cricket fighting. Popular Shanghai sport. Men bet." she answered.

"Right."

Finally, an apartment complex gate. A quiet courtyard. A glass building door. An elevator. Floor thirty. A marble-laden hallway. Door open. Apartment 3006. Glorious.

Fake dark wood. Ikea furniture. Flat screen TVs. A master suite with a small balcony. Unparalleled views of the Shanghai skyline and all its flashing lights below.

Two bathrooms.

"This one is *le pooper*," Jean-Louis declared prematurely.

Just one problem.

"It only has three bedrooms," Ken mumbled dejectedly.

"Well, hold on a second here," I said. "There has to be

some way to make this work. I mean, look out the damned window."

We all looked over. Times Square in every direction. Marvelous. There was a construction pit a block away below, directly adjacent to our living room window. Hmm.

"OK hear me out," started Miles. "The agent says that that extra futon in the living room turns into a bed."

"So...who would sleep in the living room?" Ken sounded nervous asking.

"Well, theoretically we could rotate."

"You must be joking." Jean-Louis wasn't biting. He glanced around the room at the crisp new furniture and then gazed again out the living room window.

"Actually fuck it, I'm in." He stuck his hand out in the center of our circle, palm facing down. One by one, the other three of us followed suit.

"WoooooooooooaaAAH!" We rumbled together, throwing up our hands in the air in unison.

We turned to our agent, who had her hands on her hips.

"You dum dums want apartment, yes?"

We signed some papers and drew (chop) sticks to see who would spend the first month on the futon.

"FUCK FUCK FUCK FUCKITY FUCK FUCK FUCK!" Jean-Louis yelled when he pulled the shortest.

"Grammar. Students, it's time to learn some grammar. Everyone needs a little grammar. What is a 'noun'? Can anyone tell me?"

Silence.

"It's a person, place, or thing," I said, with a casual perspicacity. "This desk is a noun. This chair is a noun. I am a noun. We are all nouns. Life is a noun. Shanghai is a noun. Who else can give me an example of a noun?"

Silence. I was tired. I thought of Linda, my parents, and the crisply washed tracksuits of Fudan Fuzhong students across the street. But mostly I pictured an ice-cold draught Carlsberg beer in place of each of my students' heads.

"Silence. Silence is a noun. Guys. This isn't that hard. This is the most basic part of grammar. It's a part of speech! I was like eight years old when I started to learn the parts of speech."

"Mr. Ed," a sheepish but golden-hearted girl named Jin Mon Rho began. "I no understand."

"Words. Jin Mon. English has a way of classifying words. There are nouns, verb, adjectives, adverbs, the whole deal."

"Why important?" Jin Mon observed.

"It's what you learn when you learn English. This is what I learned when I learned English. It's what you learn. You have to understand the words to make sentences. So now we are going to talk about which words correspond to each *part of speech*. So, we are starting with nouns. These form the basis of a substantial portion of our language. Things. Things are everywhere. People. Places. A noun is all of these things. That's why this is important."

Jin Mon bit her pencil and looked to both sides. Her peers looked everywhere except at me.

"Guys, why is this so tricky?"

Silence.

"Is it prank-your-teacher day? Did Jean-Louis put you up to this? Sign of premature teenage rebellion? None of you is a teenager yet, right? Puberty's gonna be a bitch." I repeated it and shook my head.

"Bitch." Jin Mon giggled.

"Bitch," a vertically challenged student named Valiant copied, this time with better pronunciation. "Bitch." He said it again, giggling.

"No. No. No." I immediately saw what was happening. "Guys, we are learning nouns today. Speaking. English. Speaking English."

They were quiet again.

"Your parents are gonna revoke their future tuition payments if they see what a charade this place is," I muttered under my breath. "American hegemony doesn't seem to work this far east."

"Mr. Ed, we no understand," Jin Mon said again.

The happy birthday song rang. Before I could assign any homework, the students flipped open the classroom door. Through the doorway, I saw Linda's silver hair out in the hallway.

"How was class?" I heard Linda ask to Jin Mon.

"Bitch."

Linda shot me a bullet of a glance through the open class-room doorway. I looked down in shame.

October. National Golden Week holiday. A popular expat bar called Zapata's.

"Contain yourself, Mr. Ed," Miles scolded.

A tasteful outdoor patio '80s music, bar top dancing, free tequila, multi-chromatic flashing lights. Stale beer. Abundant foreigners. White people.

"Guys, we're home," I declared.

"I feel like I've been here before," pondered Ken.

"You *have* been here before," Jean-Louis put his hands on his hips, like a teacher scolding a student who has forgotten a basic lesson. "It's called college. You've spent four years at this bar."

Miles closed his eyes, inhaled deeply through his nose, and looked up at the night sky above the bar's courtyard. The aroma of stale beer was a nostalgic potpourri that time-warped us back to simpler days, a veritable Rosebud, nestled here in Shanghai's French Concession district.

My heart slowed and I relaxed my shoulders. For the first time since I had arrived in China, I knew what to do. The pervasiveness with which people exalt "new experiences" would lead you to believe that in a given day we never do the same thing twice. Here, everything was new, and I had spent several weeks struggling to relearn how to live. And finally, here was this thing, this place, this faintly Mexican-themed bar, which oozed familiarity. Where the other people looked a little bit like me. Where I opened my mouth and had the confidence that people would understand me.

It was my turn to order a round of Johnny Walkers for the fellas. The bartender was a young Chinese girl.

"Can you spot me?" Jean-Louis asked. "Can't find my wallet."

"*Wo men yao...*" ("We want...") I began.

"Dude," she rolled her eyes, "I'm from LA. What do you want?"

"Oh thank God." I paused.

"Tick tock."

"Four Johnny Reds."

"Now you're talking," she nodded.

"Bada boom shake-a-boom," I shanked my nine iron into the water. She looked at me funny, then went to fix the whiskeys.

"300 RMB," she demanded casually, thirty seconds later. *Shit, that's like $40. Half the money I took out of the ATM.* Whatever. I paid, handed off three of the four drinks to the fellas, and left them to meander the pulsating dance floor inside, drink in my hand and head bopping, looking for potential prey. I eyed a very fine-looking specimen with long straight hair and some silky dance moves to boot. She looked scrumptious but in need of some steamy accompaniment—the sort of gal you want to dip into tomato soup and take a bite.

She was dancing with a similar looking 8.5/10 when I first approached. Both of them were Chinese. *Two* girls. Okay! Chinese? Why not.

"Hi, beautiful," I leaned toward the first girl. Her perfume smelled cheap and fruity, like a 7-11 Slurpee. The techno music made it difficult to hear.

"Hello, handsome." Wow, she speaks great English.

"Care to dance?"

"Yes." *This is surprisingly easy.* Our interaction quickly evolved into some rhythmic hip swaying on the crowded dance floor. Her friend continued to move to the beats in enticing, stationary twists. Every thirty seconds or so, I pressed my luck and inched closer to the first girl, and each time she was surprisingly receptive of my advances. *This is a little too easy.*

I brushed my hand against her cheek, and she responded by offering a light kiss on the side of my neck. Somewhere beyond the polluted sky, the stars were aligning.

We'd been dancing for ten minutes or so when I looked over at her friend, who had graduated from her simple twists and stepped somewhat closer towards me as well, projecting her pelvis out ever so slightly toward me. The music bounced overhead. *Oh yeah?*

"You're pretty," I ~~breathed slowly~~ yelled loudly into the first girl's ear.

"You like me?" She ~~whispered innocently~~ yelled back.

"Yes." I casually continued. "But I also like her, too," as I blatantly took my right arm and rested it upon the shoulder of the second girl. I now had an arm around each lady.

The first girl turned to me and suggested, "You want me?"

I pondered this. *Um...*

"Yes..." was my all-too-logical response. "But I also want her, too," I ventured.

"You want her, too?" She teased like a kitten. *Meow!*

"Yes..." was again my logical response. I became increasingly entranced and obedient toward this kitty's every suggestion.

"2000 RMB!!!" She fired at me like a shotgun.

*She wants me to pay? She's a prostitute! Shit!* That explained a lot. Several glasses of whiskey had blinded me from the fact that these two lovelies were ready to do the hula for some moolah.

"I'll be right back," I fumbled, and wandered off. That was it. Door closed. Today, part of me wonders if this was one of those forks in the road—in the Path—that change a man. Despite having a puffed up chest as a twenty-two year old in Shanghai, I was nowhere close to pulling the trigger.

I regrouped with Jean-Louis, Miles, and Ken, and recounted my failed negotiation.

"Wow that is hectic," Miles admitted.

"You should have done it. A threesome with two Chinese girls for 2000 RMB? That's an amazing price!" Jean-Louis exploded, shaking his head in disbelief.

"You should've negotiated back with '1000 RMB!'" Ken fired off, beaming at his own wit as he stood a foot above the masses. You bargain for everything in China; I guess it makes sense that sex is no different. Maybe I could have negotiated down to 1000 RMB ($150), but the doctor's bill for the subsequent STD treatment probably would have brought that price back up to market value.

Jean-Louis looked down. "Guys, this is probably an appropriate time to tell you that I bought some Chinese condoms the other day."

"No way."

"I have some in my pocket."

"*Some?*" questioned Ken. "Were you banking on multiple sexual encounters tonight?" His intoxicated frame listed dangerously to one side.

"They came in a three-pack."

"You have to show us."

Jean-Louis started to reach into his back pocket.

"Okay, don't judge..." He slapped the condom pack into my hand.

I flipped the pack over: "*Jizz Bone*?! The brand is called *Jizz Bone*? What!" I keeled over laughing. It had a golden wrapper, scaled like a dragon.

"Amazing! There is absolutely no way that these Jizz Bones work," Miles chuckled.

"Do they breathe fire out of the reservoir tip?" I asked.

"Reservoir tip? Jesus, Ed," Jean-Louis replied. "Not sexy."

"Crouching Tiger Golden Condom," Miles added.

"How big are they?" Ken furrowed his brow and examined the packaging, reading the back as if he understood a word of Mandarin.

"Let me see those again," Miles asked, reaching his hand out.

Jean-Louis started gyrating while aggressively hip-thrust-ing: "It's the Jizz Bone dance." I couldn't look away fast enough.

"These are expired." Miles burst the bubble.

"Dammit China!" Jean-Louis looked skyward and cursed God...or Buddha, or whoever.

"Dude I can't believe you almost bought two prostitutes," Miles course corrected.

"He would have needed two Jizz Bones," Ken said.

"It's not like he has two dicks," Jean-Louis rationalized.

"Two dicks? My cousin has two dicks," an inebriated Southern guy, clearly American, butted into our conversation. He wore a button-down shirt, jeans, and cowboy boots. He had short curly hair, a wry smile, and a toothpick dangling from the corner of his mouth. We opened up our circle and looked at him.

"River, who you talkin' to?" A buddy called out to him. *River?*

Three other guys approached from the bar and stood behind River. They were all American and in their early twenties. It was like an episode of the Twilight Zone had sex with an episode of Dukes of Hazzard.

"Four other drunk-ass white boys by the look of it."

Suddenly, I felt conscious of my unoriginality. I looked at my watch.

"Well, it's almost midnight," I gestured to my three musketeers.

"What happens at midnight? You turn into Cinderella?" River asked. Everyone laughed.

"I don't think she turned *into* Cinderella," I shot back.

"You lecturing me on Disney? I am the Disney *master*. Aladdin went to my damn high school." One his henchmen made an expression that assured us River was full of shit.

"Did you play *Ja-far*sity sports?" I asked.

Another henchmen butted in: "Yeah, he's right, River. She was Cinderella *the whole time.*"

"So what the fuck happens at midnight?" he asked.

"Something about a slipper?" I offered.

"I thought she left the slipper," Miles said.

"If the shoes don't fit, you must acquit," Jean-Louis went OJ.

"Is Cinderella the one with the frog?" Ken entered the fray.

"Well, shit! If this tall guy isn't a *Ken Doll*," River laid his eyes on Ken.

"Yes! Yes!" Jean-Louis was beside himself laughing. "We are going to be friends with this guy!" He gestured to River.

"Round of shots?" one of River's henchmen ventured.

Turns out, River worked in finance, two of the other guys were teachers, and one dude was a bartender. We exchanged numbers and vowed to party with them soon. So much for being original.

\* \* \*

The next morning on the couch, I turned to Jean-Louis.

"I think I smell like 'weekend,'" I told him.

"Today is Thursday."

"Does 'weekend' mean that you smell good?" Ken asked innocently, entering the living room, carrying a small stack of homework papers to grade.

"No. No, it doesn't," I hung my head. "How in the name of Buddha almighty are you grading homework right now?"

"Let's see how you sme—oof. Yeah, you smell bad. You're gross."

Jean-Louis looked out the living room window.

"That fucking construction pit below is turning into a building. It's already two stories tall."

"God, this place grows fast."

"Ed, you've been *Shanghai'ed*," Miles yelled from the kitchen, matter-of-factly, chipper as always, fixing himself a coffee with no milk. In China, "dairy" is a four-letter word.

"Shanghai'ed. Yep, it's a word. Google it."

"Sounds like the past tense of a verb," I said, surprised at my ability to form a sentence.

Suddenly, our conversation was interrupted by the sound of glass exploding.

"What was that?!" Ken sounded panicked.

"Oh shit." Jean-Louis stroked his hand through his hair and gazed up at the ceiling.

"What? What is it? What was that?" I asked hurriedly.

"It's just...it's just that I might have forgotten to take all the beer bottles out of the freezer last night before we left.

Miles calmly yelled from the kitchen: "Confirmed. Glass shards and beer icebergs splattered in here like a hit and run."

"Nice one," I turned to Jean-Louis. He shrugged his shoulders, nonplussed—such an obvious oversight hardly warranting an apology. A couple exploding beers felt like below-average destruction.

"Remind me why we left bottles of beer in the freezer," Ken was still wary.

"We bought 'em warm from the supermarket. Had to cool those brews, *mes buveurs*! Got drunk and then forgot."

"Cold Tsingtaos do taste less like urine," I offered.

"Though nothing says Wednesday night in Shanghai like drinking urine," Jean-Louis misfired.

"Um," was all I could say in return.

"Jean-Louis, you ever call that girl from our first night at Muse?" Miles yelled.

"Nope, lost her number."

"Define *Shanghai'ed*." Ken yelled to Miles in the kitchen.

"If Ed's smell were a word. That's what Shanghai'ed means."

"Yeah, take a shower." Jean-Louis waved a hand in front of his nose. "And go find a gym." He poked my beer belly. I looked down.

How did that get that there?

"I think I've grown a pair of tits," Jean-Louis began. He squeezed his chest together to form some cleavage, supporting his argument with two B-cups.

"The Fitness Facility," read the sign on the building. God-damned genius marketers, these Chinese people. The lobby, with gold leafing, black paint, and gargoyles, looked like a Victorian mansion...occupied by Rick James. In three quick minutes, Miles had negotiated a flat, per-person fee of 500 RMB / $80 for an entire *year*. This guy.

"You fat fucks ready for this?" Jean-Louis smiled.

"Blow yourself."

"I can never reach. Ken, can you reach? That's a long torso, Sgt. Dick Licker."

"I'm six-foot-seven but not a pervert. I definitely can't reach. You guys are gross."

"So you've tried."

"No. I haven't tried."

"You've definitely tried."

"How did I become friends with you numb nuts?" Miles interjected.

I placed my hand on my chest, where my pectoral muscles were supposed to be. There was a soft jiggle.

Elevator up to the third level. Wet floor. Scent of BO and chlorine. The locker room.

We turned a corner and immediately saw two old Chinese men standing butt naked in front of a giant mirror, facing away from us. Their legs were spread shoulder-length apart, revealing their flabby, old-man assholes.

"*Merde*! Look away! Old guy poop chutes. Twelve o'clock." Jean-Louis whispered loud enough for the whole locker room to hear.

My eyes glanced sideways to a full mirror, where I was then treated to a generous view of the front side of each old man.

Each man was armed with a blow dryer in his right hand and was blow-drying his cock and balls with gusto. I suppose that is the only way one can blow dry his genitals. With gusto.

The naked men looked at me through the mirror, and didn't move or blink an eye. There was no hint of embarrassment or concern as they held unbroken eye contact. My eyes were drawn in one direction: down.

There it was in the mirror. An old Chinese man's penis, and, as Jean-Louis would say, his *accoutrement*. Stereotypes about Asian endowment aside, these guys needed a trim down there, because it was hard to see the tree through the forest, if you know what I mean. The two old men continued operating their blow dryers. We tiptoed over to another area of the locker room and began to change into our gym clothes.

I asked the guys: "Do those dudes realize that all that hot air is not going to make their dicks any bigger?"

"If it helped even a little, blow dryers sales would go through the roof," Miles analyzed.

"You mean they would *blow* up?" Ken smirked gently.

"Blow yourself Ken," said Jean-Louis.

"I told you I can't reach."

"So you *have* tried."

We strolled out of the gym, and Ken said: "Hey, you guys want to go get massages together?"

"Talk about your all-time top ten most heterosexual comments," said Jean-Louis. Miles chuckled.

In the distance, I saw a middle-aged white guy emerge from the frosted glass massage parlor. *Frosted glass...* He looked vaguely like an older teacher from our school, Russell Johnson. *Is that...* I started to think aloud. *No, it can't be.* I pushed the thought out of my head.

I jumped in. "Sure. It's about time a Chinese woman rubbed her hands all over my body."

"Someone has to de-virginize that pale skin of yours," said Jean-Louis. I thought of Riley, my sorta-ex. Down the block, the old white guy entered the massage parlor.

The gravity of my hedonistic vortex grew stronger. I was gleeful. Well, gleeful on the surface, I suppose. I thought of my parents. Maybe it was the mutual reinforcement from my new buddies. Maybe the fact that I was in this exotic place that somehow justified this—let's be honest—gross behavior. Future me is a little ashamed. Future me wishes he could FedEx a chill pill back through time and tell Duardo to swallow.

Maybe this was a continuation of my college don't-give-a-fuck self, coupled with a dash of worldliness and a modest paycheck. Was this "me"? Weirdly, it didn't feel like a phase. It kinda felt increasingly like *me.* This was probably the closest I came in my life to believing that I would forever be a crazy party guy, living life through the frosted window.

To wit, a few weekends later, I was sweating. A lot. So was the glass in my right hand, the residual ice from my vodka soda barely clinging on to its solid state. My Hawaiian shirt was completely unbuttoned, and it was hard to make out the pattern of my floral bathing suit amid the crowd under the strobe light. The bass from the music was cranked up so high it made my nipples vibrate. If I had a nickel.

Through a window, I saw four baby pools, out on the club's terrace. The lights inside were dimmed, and the entire club had a red glow. There were expats everywhere, all caressing red bulls and beers and whiskeys, relieved to talk to each other in English.

I'd had between two and eleven beverages when I declared to my friends, "I want to wrestle," and I wandered off.

"You're on your own, Mr. Edo. Good luck," Miles spoke for the group. I waded sideways through the sea of humanity, with drink in hand at shoulder level to avoid spillage, and made my way to the outdoor terrace with the small inflatable pools.

Now outside, I looked around the club at the other carousers and wondered, *who would NOT want to wrestle?* I simply could not comprehend why other people wouldn't want to jump into a vat of dirty water with a stranger and have a wrestling contest. When in China, you wrestle. That's what you do. Because it's crazy and it's fun, and when you move to China they revoke your visa if you don't do the crazy and fun thing. I am Ed, and I am crazy and fun. *It makes perfect sense. I'm doing it.*

So, I began to assess—how does this process work? Do you just step into an inflatable pool? Was there a sign up sheet or something? Did I need a raffle ticket? Even in my semi-lucid state, I quickly concluded that there was no semblance of a process to wrestle at this club. So, I just stepped into an empty inflatable pool, which was barely large enough for a single person. The lukewarm water went up to about knee height. No other partygoers around me seemed to notice or care that I was standing in a baby pool.

Now what? Was there a referee? How do you pick an opponent? I had barely considered how to solicit a challenger when two female Chinese combatants stepped into my baby pool, almost reflexively. One had short hair, with bangs. The other boasted a ponytail. Both wore wife beaters. They nodded at each other, as if to give a secret signal. I smiled at them: "So, now what hap—AAAGGGHHH!"

Out of nowhere, the first girl swept my legs out from under me, knocking me backwards into the pool. The other girl jumped on top of me and pinned my arms back. One of them shoved my face downward into the pool, forcing about a gallon of water up my nose. For a brief second, I thought I might drown. *This is how it ends...here in this baby pool, while wrestling two Chinese girls at a rooftop club in Shanghai.*

I managed to get my head above water and caught my

breath. The next fifteen seconds were a torrent of limbs as I finally got back onto my feet, huffing and panting, in obvious defeat. My Hawaiian shirt was shredded. The girls were standing opposite me, giggling. The match was over. And I lost. Hard.

I received a conciliatory peace sign from the victors and stepped out of the pool, looking for the flip-flops I had laid out by the side of the tub before entering. Of course, they were gone, and I was left sauntering around the club, soaking wet with a shredded Hawaiian shirt and no shoes.

In an undeserving moment of pity from God or Buddha or whoever, I spied someone else's flip-flops near another wrestling pool. I thanked the Lord, and then I stole the flip-flops. There would be time for forgiveness later. It's entirely possible that I started a shoe robbery chain reaction, or that my own footwear was a casualty of a pre-existing series of shoe robberies. This is China, after all, and if you don't lose your shoes on a Saturday night, it's probably because you stayed home to watch a movie.

I later located Jean-Louis, Miles, and Ken elsewhere at the club. They took one look at me and insisted that we leave immediately.

"Dude." I told them.

Ken was confused: "Dude?"

Miles was unimpressed: "Duuude."

Jean-Louis was impressed: "Dude!"

"Dude." I sighed.

*Ten minutes.*

A 600-second breather. The third of my back-to-back-to-back classes was beginning in *nine minutes and thirty seconds.* A room full of advanced English middle schoolers was going to trample through the doors to my classroom, and I had no idea what I was going to say to them. An open lectern, a blank chalkboard, but not a word.

*Nine minutes. This job is work.*

I flipped open the laptop in my office at FIS and fired up Google. "Seventh grade English lesson plans," I typed. 700,000 results. I started clicking. Vocabulary. Parts of Speech. Poetry. Composition. *Story Elements. Hmm.* I clicked.

*Eight minutes.*

"Mr. Ed, you have the furrowed brow of someone searching for answers on the Internet," Miles leaned against the frame of the door, twirling a pen.

"Not now."

"So that's a 'yes.'"

"Yes."

He paused for a second and looked around. "Well, whatcha searchin' for?"

I scanned the screen. Plot, characters, arc, drama, conflict. *Perfect,* I thought. I clicked print. *Shit, what story would we analyze?* Back to Google.

*Six minutes.*

"Miles, I'm lookin' for an answer to my prayer."

"Asking God to do your job for you?"

"Yeah, except 'God' is spelled G-O-O-G-L-E." I scanned the search results. *Aesop's Fables.* Perfect. Print.

"Feeling lucky?"

"Not all of us are fortunate enough to be able to follow a chapter-by-chapter high school biology syllabus. Teaching 'English' is a little more abstract."

"Perhaps," said Miles, who was FIS's lone biology teacher. He thought about it for a second. I dashed out of the office to go retrieve my printed papers from the room next door.

Four minutes. Please let them be sitting on top of the printer. They were. I thanked ~~Google~~ God and retrieved my salvation. Back to my office. *Three minutes.*

"So is this a day-to-day battle for you, Mr. Edo, as an English teacher here at FIS?" Miles interrogated playfully.

"More like a siege."

"That's why they call it 'work,' my man." *Two minutes.*

"I'd rather be at the bar."

"I guess Jean-Louis also has the same issue," Miles pondered.

"Yup, he teaches English, too."

"While Ken is more in my camp," he concluded.

"American History follows a tidy chronological pattern."

"I'd hardly call American History 'tidy.'"

"To be continued. Gotta run!"

*One minute.* I grabbed the stack of printouts, clutching them close to my chest like a newborn baby, and ran out the door to class.

"*C'est la vie.* You will survive, Ed," Miles's voice trailed behind me. "As long as you know how to love, you know you will stay alive!"

"Disco's dead, Miles!" I yelled over my shoulder.

I burst through my classroom doors.

*Zero minutes.*

"Good afternoon, students! Today we are going to read some fables and discuss what makes each one of these a 'story.'" I used air quotes to emphasize the theme of today's class—*stories.* One kid checked his watch. Another looked out the window longingly.

Halloween night. Shanghai. Zapata's. World spinning.
My Superman cape, actually a red bath towel, fluttered
in the evening breeze in the bar's patio area.

"Will one of you guys text Ken?" Miles asked. He was
wearing a toga.

"On it," Jean-Louis, also in toga, started tapping on his
phone.

"And?"

"Uh-oh," Jean-Louis sounded concerned.

"Uh-oh?" I asked.

"Ken just replied, 'Jizz Bone.'"

"You guys don't think..." Miles wondered.

At that moment, we saw his head pop above the crowd. Ken, also in, uh, full toga, gallivanted toward us.

In his arms was a woman. Not metaphorically in his arms. He was literally carrying a woman in his two arms, like a bride on her wedding night. From afar, I could see that she had short hair and wore a long blue dress. Her arms were lovingly draped around his neck.

He triumphed through the crowd holding the damsel in arms, her smile now free from lifetime confinement atop some medieval stone tower. He now stood in front of the three of us, still holding this strange woman. Was he going to put her down?

Ken flicked his head at Jean-Louis, a secret signal. I saw Jean-Louis reach under Ken's robe and slip a Jizz Bone into his back pocket. I got a closer look at the woman. The deep wrinkles by her eyes held at least five decades worth of secrets. She must have been fifty years old! The expression on her face, though, told us that she had met her...Ken. Her eyes gazed longingly at her handsome savior in his toga.

In one fluid motion, Ken nodded to us, carried this woman outside of the bar, tossed her into the back seat of a cab (like, he literally threw her), slid in, and drove off into the darkness, perhaps never to be heard from again—future king and queen of some forgotten Polynesian island.

Miles, Jean-Louis, and I turned and stared at each other. For a good three seconds, no one said a word. A night gust ruffled my red cape. Their togas were black on the bottom, dirtied by sidewalk detritus after yet another Shanghai night out.

I broke the silence. "Good thing he's not on the futon this month."

"Hi Mom, hi Dad."

"Our very own Marco Polo."

"How's home?"

"Good!" Mom chipped in exuberantly. "Cold though. Was thirty degrees the other day."

"It was sixty," my dad corrected. Multiply by two. Mom Math.

"How's Shanghai?"

I was on a Skype call with my parents.

"Things are...good. This place is nuts."

"Nuts how?" my mother ventured, calmly.

"Just...nuts," I explained in zero detail.

"Might as well get our China updates from the newspaper," my mother harrumphed to my father.

"Care to elaborate?" My father asked. Fact gathering. In his mind, a lack of details was a bad thing. He relished specificity. He had an unofficial policy against using pronouns.

"Everything. The place just feels hectic. From the crowds on the street to the bars. The whole thing."

"The bars?"

"I'm twenty-three years old."

"With a job."

"That's right," I inserted indignantly.

"Expected?"

"Daily?"

"My friends and I go to bars. We also have jobs."

"Mmm-hmm," my father concluded the line of questioning, giving me the benefit of the doubt. Despite my giving him every possible reason not to, he always shelved his skepticism and reserved judgment. He's a hardass, but he will forever be in my corner.

"And how is Fudan International School treating you?" My mother asked, genuinely intrigued.

"It's good. The school is a little schizophrenic. We don't have enough books, so we pull lesson plans from the internet. There are no rules, so we simply rely on the pillars of decorum."

"Pillars of decorum?"

"Our Dean of Students fancies himself an academic."

"Aren't you all technically academics?" my father asked.

"Academics?" my mother interjected, a little incredulously. "It's not like he's tenured at Harvard."

"Things can be a little deceptive on paper. I don't know too much about ancient history, but the school somehow thinks I'm the guy to teach it. I've got one kid, named Kotaro, who doesn't speak a lick of English."

"How's your Mandarin by comparison?" my mom asked.

"Touché."

"Are you doing anything to help *fix* the situation? Developing the curriculum, holding extra study sessions, helping the school acquire books?" my father pressed on.

"Well," I stammered, "Not really."

"I see," was his icy, impartial response. No judgment yet.

"Have you traveled at all? Wasn't that part of the appeal of this whole thing?" My mother saved me from further interrogation—only I didn't have a good answer.

"To school and back every day."

"Because you rented an apartment with three American guys." My mother sounded a little turned off by the thought of it.

"The price was right."

"So let me get this straight," my father reasoned, "Your school has no books and your students seem to be floundering. You haven't traveled at all because you've been supposedly busy at school. And yet somehow you've found the time to rent a second home downtown and go from one bar to the next."

"Well, when you sum it up like *that*—"

He cut me off. "I don't think Shanghai was a good decision. In all honesty, I'm disappointed."

There it was. His judgment rendered. It stung. A lot more than I thought. I'd had to travel to the other side of the world to get a job, and in the process I'd lost sight of what I was. Had I ever really known? I guess there are some things you can never really run away from. What did they know, anyways? They had never taught in China. They weren't my age. They didn't know what it was like to be me. I cocooned.

"Well, I don't know what to tell you guys. You're over there and I'm over here."

"Maybe you should come home," my mother pleaded.

"No."

"No?"

"No. Period. I like it here."

"Look, Edward," here came some uncharacteristic fatherly wisdom. "There comes a time in every parent's life when they realize they can't tell their kids what to do anymore. At some point, you're going to have to start to make some decisions. A career is a long time, but maybe it starts with thinking about what you want. You're never going to accomplish anything until you figure out what you want."

"I don't know."

I felt farther away from home than ever. Those two adult voices that oversaw all my formative years made me feel self-conscious and ashamed of who I currently was. Too much *Duardo*? Not enough *Ed*? Certainly in my parents' eyes I'd hardly ever step into the shoes of an *Eduardo*.

My eyes jolted open, dry and crusted from what was no doubt a toxic evening out in Shanghai the night prior. I had forgotten to take my contact lenses out. They burned like the desert. I burped quietly. I was lying on my back. The ceiling swirled after another raging night with a bunch of expats. The results from my Chinese culture experiment had clearly come back negative.

The vision in front of me came into focus. Jean-Louis's face was two feet from mine; he was leaning so close I could smell his morning breath. I felt queasy. His facial expression was one of gleeful wonder. He looked like he had just gotten an underwater blowjob from a mermaid.

I opened my mouth to slur some expression of confusion, but he immediately whipped his right index finger to his lips.

"Shhhhh."

*What the fuck?* As my IQ crept slowly northward, it dawned

on me that I was asleep on the futon in our living room. *What happened last night?*

I propped myself up on my elbows to watch Jean-Louis, wearing a gray t-shirt and white boxers emblazoned with red maple leaves, pass by the foot of the futon and escort a girl toward our front door. The girl wore a black cocktail dress. She was barefoot, carrying a pair of stilettos in her right hand. Jean-Louis held her left hand, tugging her quickly toward the front door with get-the-fuck-out speed.

The girl released Jean-Louis's hand and turned to me. I saw her face. She was Chinese. Our eyes met. She made an "eek" face, one part surprise and one part nice-to-meet-you, and flashed her slightly yellow teeth. She had smooth features and a symmetrical face. Her hair was disheveled. She gave me a peace sign with her left hand. *What was this alternative universe into which I had regained consciousness?*

I met eyes with Jean-Louis, who had a shit-eating grin. I watched as they tiptoed swiftly toward the front door. Why were they being so quiet? I felt naked. I dipped my hand below the futon sheet to confirm the existence of my boxers. They were not there.

Over by the front door, I could see Jean-Louis give his mysterious temptress a quick peck goodbye. The door closed quietly.

*CRAAAAAACK.* I heard the unmistakable sound of a forty-ounce beer bottle exploding in the freezer of the kitchen.

"Uuuuugh," someone groaned next to me. A bare arm emerged from the tangle of sheets and fell toward my body like the slow motion collapse of the leaning tower of Pisa. The arm smacked me across the face. A woman's arm.

"What a rager," she mumbled dreamily. In a flash, it came back to me, like a recorded DVR playback. A dance floor. A taxi. A girl.

I turned to her. She turned to me.

"Well. Hello you." She said. Our faces were no more than six inches apart. She had dark-as-night hair covering part of her freckled face. She was *white.* Not just by race. Her skin was pale. She had brown eyes and a wide nose.

"Hi," I mumbled at long last.

"We suffering from a little morning-after shyness?"

"Well—" I started.

"Was that *another* exploding beer bottle?" Miles yelled as he walked down the hall from the master bedroom, wearing nothing but his boxers.

"Miles, please don't yell," I could hear Ken plead as he opened his bedroom door. They both walked toward the living room, and stopped at the foot of the futon.

"Well, well, well. If this isn't a scene straight out of a romantic comedy." Miles put his hands on his bare hips. Ken joined him on one side, wearing a white t-shirt and a pair of boxer briefs.

"Guys, this is..." I began, only to realize I couldn't remember her name.

"Hey ho! Jean-Louis's awake," Miles interrupted me, as Jean-Louis strolled over from the front door. The three of them now stood over the foot of the futon, nothing but a naked sheet separating my new friend and my penis from the prying eyes of my three roommates.

"This is, uh," I stammered.

"Tanya." She sat up, covered herself in the sheet with her left hand, and extended a hello wave with the other.

"Tanya from Toronto!" I belted awkwardly. It came back to me.

"Mr. Ed, alleviated by alliteration," Ken had a big smile.

"Barely," said Jean-Louis.

"What these guys mean to say is, nice to meet you, Tanya from Toronto," Miles rescued me.

"It's a pleasure, gents," Tanya from Toronto began. "Extremely awkward, but still a pleasure." Funny enough, she looked pretty comfortable covered in just a bed sheet surrounded by three strangers and one almost stranger.

"Bad timing for Mr. Ed's month on the futon."

"*Mister* Ed?" Tanya from Toronto looked at me and cocked an eyebrow. I shrugged my shoulders.

"So this is where you disappeared to last night," Ken bobbed his head slowly.

"Seems that way," I answered.

"Whelp, I'm going into the other room, where it's less uncomfortable," Ken said.

"Yep, I have to go check the, um, thing, in my room." Jean-Louis followed. He winked at me. Only I knew *his* little secret.

"I'm going to get dressed and let you lovebirds talk things out." Miles was more direct.

I took her to breakfast at our favorite American diner. I told her I'd call.

That night, the four of us were at it again. The nod to the bouncer. The four-drink signal to the bartender. The dwindling wad of 100 RMB notes in my jeans pocket. The spastic overhead spotlight. The head snap, the dip, the backward roll. The obvious flirtation. The look. The DJ's rhythmic beats slowing down each distinct moment into a singular, smooth and infinite oasis of memories you'll never remember. Laughing like you only can when you're young. Young and possibly on a bender.

It was easy to not think about my parents by just not thinking about my parents. Somewhere right now, Riley was probably braving the Boston cold to go to work, my Shanghai students were asleep in their beds, and Duardo was on the prowl.

\* \* \*

*Knock knock knock knock.* I awoke to the sound of a fist pounding a door. I lay in bed and looked up at an unfamiliar white ceiling.

"租金是由于明天!" A voice yelled. *Where am I?*

"安静。我在睡觉!" A hoarse voice right next to me answered. *Egad! Have I gone native?*

The banging stopped. It was the next morning. I turned over in a strange bed and saw the familiar face of an expat girl. *Molly.* I remembered this one's name.

"Sorry about that," she turned to me. "Apparently rent is due tomorrow."

"Some alarm clock," I conceded.

"On a Sunday, no less," she chuckled.

"Totally."

"The Chinese are assholes sometimes."

"YES." We laughed. *Molly from Minnesota.* She had wavy brown hair, a big mouth with a kind smile, and small eyes. Twice in a weekend? I smiled to myself.

"Your Mandarin is pretty sharp," I told her.

"Was one of the pre-requisites for my Department of Agriculture job."

"Right, you mentioned. Kinda badass."

She blushed. "Shit," she looked at her watch. "I have to kick you out."

"Wham, bam, thank you, sir."

"It's not like that," she laughed. "I have to get to a meeting!"

"On a Sunday? No rest for the weary."

"No worm for the tardy bird."

"Nice."

I got dressed and looked around. Molly lived in a cramped studio in a run down looking building, but it was clean.

"Call me," she said.

"I will." I meant it.

I closed the front door to her apartment behind me. In front of me lay a rickety set of wooden stairs leading down. Overhead, a single light bulb illuminated the dirt walls of the building staircase. A rake, a shovel, and a wooden bucket lay on the landing below. *I am a long way from my fancy apartment complex.* Is this where she lives? It all looked vaguely familiar from the night prior.

I walked down eight steps, then turned around on the landing to descend the final stairs to the ground floor. I arrived at a long, dark hallway. I squinted to see. There was detritus scattered throughout. I could see daylight down the hallway to the left. I started walking. At last, I passed through a wall of fresh air and sunlight onto a cramped side street. There was cobblestone beneath my feet and clotheslines overhead. Three roaming chickens strutted right in front of me. Overhead, a woman leaned out of a window and dumped a bucket of water onto the ground. I scurried to one side to avoid getting wet. *I had gone native!*

"你并不住在这里。" Some old Chinese guy said to me in passing. *Huh?* He was barefoot and missing a tooth. I thought through my Rolodex of mental Chinese phrases.

"*Bù zhīdào,*" (I don't know) I replied. I had no idea what the guy said. I jogged out of the old Chinese alleyway, and emerged on a modern, main street in central Shanghai. *Woah.* I hailed a taxi. I flipped through my phone and found last night's new contact entry. I rolled down the back window, and thought of the women in my life. I wondered about Riley and ~~who she was sleeping with~~

what she was doing. I clapped my hands together. One cookie with two fortunes.

"I'll take a double vodka martini, extra olives."

"Don't you mean a *dirty* vodka martini with extra olives?"

"Right! Thanks." Tanya from Toronto turned back to the waiter. "I'll take a *double dirty* vodka martini, extra olives."

"Thirsty?" I asked her, nervously. I'd met my match. The young Western waitress at the empty Irish Pub aptly named "Irish Pub" exhaled purposefully, turned to me, and waited. It's weird to be on a first date with someone once you've slept with them.

"Carlsberg draft."

"Yawn," Tanya let her opinion be known. We sat next to an old dartboard. Across the room, a jukebox begged to be used. The faded green décor made it look like there hadn't been a St. Patrick's Day in a decade.

"Saying 'yawn' doesn't make it a 'yawn.'"

"Oh yeah?" She yawned for real.

"*That* makes it a—" I yawned.

"You two are a couple of snoozers," the waitress yawned.

Tanya turned to the waitress, "Then best be telling my date here to grow a pair and order something cooler than a Carlsberg." The waitress tilted her head toward me. I turned to Tanya. Her black dress made my blue button down look like a Walmart Black Friday door buster.

"It's a Tuesday."

"More like Snoozeday. Let loose, Mr. Ed," Tanya cackled.

"Something like that." I felt outsmarted or annoyed, but couldn't tell which. The waitress walked away.

"A teacher who drinks beer. You're a real thrill."

"And remind me what such a luscious Canadian lady such as yourself does in a such city as this place here?" I winced when I heard the sentence coming out of my mouth.

"I work in PR," she opted not to reference the foot in my mouth, "But mostly I Shanghai."

"And if I asked Shanghai, would it say that it Tanyas?" I beamed, back on track.

"Not sure I follow."

"Nevermind."

"You're a little awkward, Mr. Ed." She leaned in toward me, almost as if turned on by my inelegance. Women are vexing creatures.

"Not sure what it is. Think you just have a way of derailing my mojo."

The waitress brought our drinks. We cheers'ed.

"*Gan bei*," we said to each other, glasses clinking.

"You remind me a little bit of another guy I'm seeing."

I poured some of my beer down the wrong pipe and began to cough.

"Are you al—" She started. I lifted up a hand and made the give-me-a-second signal.

"Sorry. Another guy you are seeing *now*?"

"Maybe," she said, not sheepishly enough.

"Well," I pondered the information for a moment. Here lay two pathways. On the one hand, I could casually drop Molly from Minnesota's name and see Tanya's all-in wager that I would be comfortable with the concept of playing second fiddle (or first?) in her orchestra of two or more men, by offering her a seat within my own.

On the other hand, I could veer left onto Hypocrite Avenue, not divulge my tasty treat from Minnesota, and hold my cards to my chest. However, this would mean either that in Tanya's eyes I was OK with being another guy on the side, or that I would have to make an indignant plea that we see each other exclusively, which would mean either goodbye to Molly from Minnesota, or maybe that I would also keep her around but take up permanent residence along Hypocrite Avenue. Women.

I looked at Tanya from Toronto. She flexed her neck muscles in anticipation of my response, revealing her bottom row of teeth. Her jet-black hair fell to shoulder length, and her lipstick was a little too rouge. This didn't feel like chemistry. I suppose she was pretty, but let's be honest, her face could hardly launch a thousand ships.

"So you like olives?"

* * *

Two nights later I planned to meet Molly at a Starbucks near my apartment. Chilly evening air. Hands in pocket. Eyes scouring the sidewalk for my Minnesotan. Checked phone eleven times. No texts. Heart racing.

At last, I saw a friendly wave approach me steadily among the factory conveyer belt of Chinese pedestrian faces. Her smile alone added a few extra dates to our ledger. She cleaned up good with her hair strung back in a ponytail, a fall coat, and jeans that looked modestly fashionable. I think. I don't know anything about fashion. Riley always told me my clothes were too big. Molly's stride had a comfortable-in-her-own-boots tempo.

"Starbucks, huh?" I asked as she approached. "Authentic first date in China?"

"You've already seen me naked. Call it a second date?"

"Deal."

I grabbed the metal handle of the glass door and pulled it open, motioning Molly in ahead of me. Overhead the freaky, familiar green mermaid smiled at us from within the comfy circular glow of the Starbucks logo. Inside, it looked like a Starbucks. It smelled like a Starbucks. I couldn't believe it. Another Western bubble in the Chinese hurricane.

We snagged a couple of grande drip coffees with milk and took a seat. For a second, neither of us said anything.

"Hi," we both said, awkwardly in sync.

"So do you come here often?" I asked in a purposefully obvious voice.

"Girl needs her caffeine kick," Molly winked.

"There's *milk* in this coffee. Can you believe that? Dairy in China. Sometimes it's the small things."

"Do you remember strawberries?" she countered.

"YEAH. What happened to those? Feels like I haven't eaten fruit since I crossed the Pacific." We both shook our heads.

"Have you ever tried a durian?" She asked. "Those will blow your mind."

"What is that?"

"Southeast Asia's finest fruit. It's the size of a volleyball, looks like a landmine, and smells like a rotten onion."

"Some delicacy."

"Acquired taste."

"Let's get this party started," I began. "So what brought you to China?"

"That's your pickup line? The same guy who just waltzed over and told me his middle name was 'Danger'?"

"Really not sure what came over me."

"Who introduces themselves by their middle name, by the way? There wasn't even a dangerous situation. Isn't the danger-is-my-middle-name thing usually in response to threat?" She laughed.

"You do realize that 'Danger' is *not* my middle name."

"I grew up on a farm."

"Excuse me?" I asked.

"What brought me to China."

"Your story is missing the middle part." I tried to connect the dots.

"It would have been really easy to never leave. Most people that I grew up with never did. I guess you could call me the black sheep. I mean, if I hadn't dreamed of seeing the world, I'd probably be milking a cow right now."

"Sounds just like where I grew up," I grinned.

"An *Eduardo* from New York City. Just like my parents dreamed." She shook her head, with a touch of astonishment.

"What's crazy is that a farm in Minnesota feels farther away from home for me than an apartment in Shanghai."

"You don't know the half of it."

"I gotta ask," I paused. "What's it like to milk a cow?"

She furrowed her brow in reply.

"Is it a little bit like giving a miniature hand job?"

"Have a little experience in the matter?"

I laughed, "Well, this is probably a good continent to find a willing recipient of a miniature hand job."

"It's like giving four miniature hand jobs."

"Huh?"

"The cow has four teats."

"Four tits?"

"Teats."

"Why do you keep saying 'tits' in an accent?"

"The teat is the thing that shoots out milk."

"It *shoots* out? Like a gun?" I smiled.

She shook her head again, with a giant grin. "We should eat some strawberries together."

"From cow hand jobs to strawberries in one breath. That's gotta be some kind of record."

"You should see me with a can of whipped cream," she winked at me. I fanned myself with my right hand, in deference to her sexy comeback.

"So you live solo."

"And you have three roommates."

"You ever get lonely?" I asked, conceding that I would probably not be long for the Shanghai world if I were here solo. I'd come here to make it on my own but spent my time hanging out with three guys like me.

"Yeah. I do." She took a sip of her coffee, and put her elbows on the table. She clasped her hands together into a ball and rested her head on it for a moment.

"Maybe that's why every expat here drinks so much," I offered. "Loneliness."

"Maybe!" she laughed again, spreading her arms wide. "I think that's also a sign of alcoholism."

"Worked for Hemingway."

"Didn't work for most other people."

"Do you ever marvel how the second you meet an expat here, it's like you're immediately friends? You could literally have nothing in common, and it doesn't matter."

"Oh my God. Totally. Like you pass a remotely white looking person on the street, and you just want to hug them. And you know that they want to hug you, too."

"Hug a stranger in America and you'll probably get stabbed."

Molly was reinvigorated: "But isn't that what's amazing? We live in this magical place. Every day is such an adventure, so much so that you relish these little glimpses of your old world."

"How's that coffee?"

"Touché. Strong." She rubbed the back of her neck, briefly cooling her rhythm.

"You speak Mandarin," I tacked.

"Yup." She pronounced the *p* with a little extra pop.

"Do I need to ask?"

"Everyone else wanted to study Spanish," she continued. My poker face turned sheepish. "Right, *Eduardo*?"

"Claro que sí," I gave her some obligatory *Español*.

"It sounded exotic. And four years later, here I am."

"So you wanted to be different?" I'd hear this story before.

"I suppose you could say that."

"Chart your own path?"

"Escape from the Western World."

"Seems you've torn a page from the Book of Ed."

I kissed her goodnight under the ~~snow-covered mistletoe~~ blinking neon lights of a counterfeit DVD store.

"Want to come up?" I asked her.

"This moment is too good to spoil."

"We can kick this pace back a notch."

"I'll see you soon, Mr. Ed."

* * *

I think middle school was the last time that a girl gave me butterflies. I felt like I could be all of myselves around her. Minnesota charmer in China? That didn't match any more than my checkered history fit together tidily. Maybe everyone here was struggling with some version of the identity crisis that had landed me here in the first place. She didn't feel like one thing any more than I did.

It was like a courtship in reverse, which I guess is how it works these days. Consummation is the prologue and not the conclusion. The chase was on. Backwards.

"That's great, Ed," Ken was genuinely happy for me. We were sitting on the couch in our apartment. "Must have been the coffee."

"What about Tanya from Toronto?"

"Compatibility. Negative."

"And by compatibility, you mean she's not hot enough to deal with her other shortcomings."

"Yeah, I mean—wait, what do you mean by 'shortcomings'?"

"Don't take this the wrong way, but she seemed pretty comfortable in just a sheet. Methinks she may be a lady of the night. Not to mention, she's Canadian."

"Methinks you think right."

"Huh?"

"During drinks on Tuesday, she casually mentioned that she's seeing another guy."

"Sloppy seconds."

"Unclear how many courses she's been enjoying," I said.

"Time to send her packing."

"Jean-Louis and his countrymen may be a little offended."

"Methinks he'll be alright. Not the first time Canada has played second fiddle to America," Ken countered.

"Are we pirates? Is that what we're doing here?" I was confused.

"I thought 'methinks' was more like Shakespeare."

"Seriously, though," I continued, "she was just too *loose* all around, if you know what I mean."

"Mr. Ed! Inappropriate," Ken countered.

"So I guess I'm going to break up with Tanya. Ugh, I hate conflict."

"Haven't you only been on like one date, man? I'd hardly call this divorce."

"I think I just don't like to deliver bad news. Phone call?"

"Text message."

"If Mr. Nice Guy says text message, we're going text message."

I waited a few days, and got a text from Tanya from Toronto before I could break it off.

"Art show this weekend. You want to be my plus one?" It read.

I began to type a reply, politely declining. While fumbling over wording, I put the phone back in my pocket. With each passing day, it became harder and harder to conjure up the magical series of words to end things. If you could even call what we had a "thing." So I never replied. And neither did she. Our fleeting non-relationship vanished into the ether. In a way, it was easier, but I knew it was wrong to say nothing. No matter. Silence is golden. Sometimes it's easier to run away from your problems.

Molly and I continued to see each other sporadically. Two dinners, one round of drinks, even a swing through the Shanghai museum. We ate strawberries. Slow but steady. We weren't dating, and neither of us even brought up the "d" word. No one wanted to define the relationship and ruin what was, at the moment, a pleasant and casual courtship. I couldn't tell if we were moving backward or forward.

A few weeks later, my two older sisters came to visit.

Pretty sure I mentioned them earlier. For like a second. My family. Right. Them.

Well, I'm the youngest of three. Laura's the oldest, and Cristina's the monkey in the middle. She's not actually a monkey. I round out the trio. Last guy to the party. Although, sometimes we forgot to invite Cristina. Middle child syndrome. Once, my father stared at the place settings at the Thanksgiving table, baffled why his numbers didn't add up. One seat missing, who could it be? He had forgotten Cristina. Poor, neglected middle child. She fought her short straw through feats of athleticism and relentless positivity. To her friends, she was the garrulous All-American athlete who never complained about anything. To us, she was our sister.

Laura, by contrast, always wore the oldest sibling badge loudly. On our meanest days, we tell her that she peaked socially in high school. The freshmen girls at her boarding school used to fear her. One time, she kidnapped thirty of them during the night and hid them in the upper campus squash courts for twelve hours. All without getting in trouble.

By college, she'd channeled all of that decisive energy into studying and life planning. Now, she is most feared by her Google Calendar. She does the little things to such an impossibly high standard that it's not even worth competing. On a hunch, Laura once spent days reading the footnotes of the Irish citizenship process, and lo-and-behold, two months later my sisters and I wielded European passports.

Once, when we were younger, Laura brought home *The New Birth Order Book*. She read one page on the chapter about oldest siblings before getting annoyed. She flipped the book to Cristina.

"Three-hundred pages of sibling confrontation. Um, no thanks!" she declined.

"Let me see! Let me see!" I'd asked eagerly. I found a chapter about being the youngest of three siblings. I opened to the page and began reading.

The chapter began: "If you're the youngest of three siblings, I bet you opened the book right to this page and began reading." I shrieked, threw the book up in the air, and stormed out of the room. None of us ever read another word.

They toured around Shanghai for a few days, and we tacked on a short trip to Beijing for the weekend. I was finally going to get out and travel the country. Take *that,* Mom and Dad.

\* \* \*

I stepped out of the taxi. Tiananmen Square. The patterned gray stone underfoot extended endlessly in every direction. There were no benches, trees, or shrubs—just cold gray concrete that matched the sky overhead. Armed police patrolled every inch with darting, suspicious eyes, seemingly ready to un-holster their firearms at the slightest disturbance.

"Good thing we aren't here to protest," Cristina said. At the far end of the square, an absolutely enormous portrait of Chairman Mao Zedong adorned the front wall of the red-walled Forbidden City. Hello, communism.

Opposite us, a drab building adorned with large columns beckoned. The mausoleum of Chairman Mao Zedong.

Inside, Chairman Mao's embalmed body sat underneath a clear crystal coffin, facing skyward, his chest adorned with a crisp Chinese flag, the yellow star and sickle boldly telling the world to go blow itself.

From there, we trekked across the endless expanse of Tiananmen Square to the Forbidden City, the ancient city of red, a maze of Chinese history inside.

Stone courtyards. Red walls. Treasure. More red walls. Oh yeah, and red walls. Mystical figurines.

In the Ancient City's Palace of Earthly Tranquility (Huh? Yes), I stopped and breathed for the first time.

* * *

The sky cleared overhead in the distance. There it was. The Great Wall of China.

We waded through a gauntlet of souvenir vendors (*"Bù yào! Bù yào!"*), climbed a small ridge, and emerged on top of the wall itself. The Great Wall of China.

The wall was about twenty-five feet wide. Large slabs of flat stone made the whole thing surprisingly pedestrian friendly. There were turrets every few hundred yards, and the whole thing had the feeling of a medieval castle that had been stretched out like silly putty and plopped along a mountain top ridge. It was great! It was a *great* wall.

The views stretched so far you'd almost believe the earth was flat. The dirt-brown rolling hills and leafless trees went on endlessly to the north and behind us the south. The three of us leaned against the thick stone guardrail, staring off into Mongolia in the distance. For once, tourists were sparse.

Apparently, most builders of the Wall spent their entire lives toiling and lugging stone up the ridge top to fortify China's defenses for a Mongolian invasion that never occurred. When a builder died of exhaustion, he would be rewarded by being tossed into the wall with the rest of the dirt and stone, his skeleton forever stuck between a rock and hard place. It sounded to me like the banking job of the era, but without the pay, prestige, or pressed suits. OK, maybe it wasn't the banking job of the era. Thankfully, times had changed a bit.

"So, this is where you live," Laura turned to me.

"Yep, I live in China."

"China, man," Cristina shook her head in disbelief. "You're a Chinaman. What are you doing here little bro?"

"I guess, I don't really know. Working. Having fun."

"How old are you again?" Laura asked. Siblings have a hard time remembering these small details.

"Twenty-three."

"Dad said you're too busy partying to give a shit about anything."

"You weren't supposed to tell him that," Cristina gave Laura a look.

"He said that?" I asked. It just sounded so un-Dad. He was the information gatherer, the lawyer-slash-banker. At long last, I think I'd turned him into the disappointed father. My stomach fell.

"Yup."

"Well, I've got my whole life ahead of me," I said defensively.

"Are you at least learning stuff at work, or learning Mandarin?" Cristina asked, gently.

"Sorta."

"Sorta?" Laura rolled her eyes. I noticed.

"It's hard," I sighed.

"I'm sure bro," Cristina sympathized. "I mean, we're only a few years older than you. But we've both found something we like to do, and we're running with it to see where it takes us."

"I guess sometimes I feel like I don't have anything to grab onto," I admitted.

"So you ran away to China?" Laura cracked a smile.

"Not really sure I could be any farther away at this point."

"For your next job, you could become an astronaut," said Cristina.

"Do you like teaching?" Laura asked.

"There are definitely parts that I like, but it's still work. It's not like I've found my calling in the universe."

"You think my marketing job is my calling in the universe?" she asked. "It doesn't work like that."

"Then how does it work?"

"You just...you figure it out. You move forward. You decide stuff," Laura was unsympathetic about my millennial problems.

"Maybe you should chill out on the partying. Just a *little*. Travel. Learn something," she offered some obligatory oldest sibling advice.

"Life awaits, little bro. Better start swimming." Cristina put an arm around me. It was an oddly placed, mountaintop swimming metaphor.

And for a moment, I felt as if I'd figured it out. I stood atop the Great Wall. My sneaker kicked loose a small flat stone. I picked it up in my right hand and curled the thin edge along my index finger. I cocked my arm back like a baseball shortstop and flung the rock northward as hard as I could, skipping the stone with a wispy pitter patter along the invisible ocean below.

Well, la-de-da.

"Holy shit, Ed, you went to *Duke?*"

"Damn right," I yelled to River.

"I went to Carolina. *Fuck Duke.*"

"Right back at ya, Old Man River." So much for that authentic China experience.

I looked down. I was wearing white pants, a white shirt, white socks, and white shoes. My sushi plate was half finished, but my cocktail glass was empty.

I'm not sure what came over me at that moment. I looked down at my plate and decided that I was going to throw a piece of sashimi at another person at the table. Why did I decide this? It felt like the right thing to do. That's all that I can explain. *It's what this "Me" should do*, I thought to myself. Crazy Me would do it, so I did it.

So, I picked up a piece of tuna in my right hand. I turned

to throw it at River, but that would be too obvious. So, I re-aimed and tossed it at our friend Ding, a Chinese girl of American descent. The piece of tuna thwapped her on side of the head.

"What the fuck, Ed?!"

"Ding Dong, Ding."

"Knock knock."

"Huh? Who's there?" Weird time for a knock-knock joke, I thought.

"Spy."

"Spy who?"

"Spicy salmon, you piece of shit," she threw a rebuttal piece sushi my way, battering my right arm, leaving a massive soy sauce stain on my white button down and landing between my empty beer glass and the remnants of my sushi plate, now an ammunition dispenser.

Next, Jean-Louis grabbed a yellowtail roll and heaved it at River. And so began the Great Sushi Skirmish.

It escalated quickly, as every member of our table joined

in. Fancy pieces of sushi were flying everywhere. One piece struck me right in the eye, blinding me for a second.

"I'm hit!" I yelled.

"Incoming!" River lobbed a couple sushi grenades at Ken.

People were ducking, squirming, and blocking in order to avoid fish projectiles.

Within one minute, it was over, and all of the ammunition was spent. The table looked like France in wartime.

There were pieces of sashimi stuck to the walls, globs of wasabi all over everyone's white clothes, and pools of soy sauce on the table, which quickly turned into soy sauce rivers. There are no victors when it comes to sushi wars. I'm told that the next day, Ding found two pieces of tuna sashimi inside of her purse.

Amazingly, when the waiter opened the door to make sure that the screams he heard were not the sound of a ritualistic donkey sacrifice, he barely blinked. Like it was par for the course. He calmly started to clear plates and pick up sushi rolls from the floor. He paused and then asked us if we wanted dessert. What did we have to do to *not* get offered dessert? Have an orgy and light the building on fire? Which, coincidentally, to my at-the-time mind, sounded kind of awesome.

That's just how "Me" was operating at the time. The default lens through which I viewed the world was to ponder ways in which to creatively destroy it—not-nuclear-bomb-hurt-people destroy it, but steal-traffic-cones destroy it. Ruffle its feathers just a little bit. The new me consistently sought out ways in which to be annoying without truly pissing people off. I wasn't an anarchist; I think it just made me interesting. And I swear to you now, I was thinking less about what others thought of me and more just about ways to have fun. Lobbing that first piece of sushi was exhilarating. It made me feel alive. It tickled me. It kindled the gentlest of fires inside me.

I didn't want to commit crimes or hurt others. I wanted to throw sushi. I was a mini-rebel, a rebel Jr., Eduardo Jr., really—like I couldn't actually commit to a full-on rebellion, and in some ways this should have been my hint that I wasn't *really* a rebel. That maybe I was tiptoeing into another identity without fully committing; that this was a phase, and my recognition of that phase probably would have made me feel a lot dumber for throwing sushi. But I didn't. I felt great. This was Me, I was convinced.

We arrived at the official "White Party" at a bar in the

French Concession district. My phone buzzed. Molly from Minnesota was two minutes away. She was going to join us in line. *This is not going to end well,* I thought, as I took one good look at myself. She soon approached with an emphatic wave.

"Wow, Ed. Looks like you've already had yourself an evening."

"And it's not even midnight."

"You're starting to look like a true Chinaman." *She didn't care?*

"China, man." I shook my head.

"China, man." She laughed easily. I guess this country recalibrates your sense of what is socially acceptable.

We went into the bar and danced like wrecking balls. Our friend River later announced to everyone that he was hosting a champagne late night party at his apartment. *Kindred spirits?*

We stumbled out of the bar. Molly had a morning meeting and bid the group adieu.

"You work too hard," I told her.

"I know," she admitted, and got into a taxi.

"That girl is cool, Mr. Ed," Miles put a hand on my shoulder. "You should keep her around."

"Do you think she likes me?"

"Are you asking about Ed or about Duardo? Or Mr. Ed?"

"Shit."

"I think Duardo is pretty sweaty from busting a move in there." My shirt was soaked, and a gust of evening wind made me shiver.

"Yeah."

"On the bright side," he grinned and put an arm around me, "the night is young and so are we."

Back at River's sprawling apartment, I emptied my second? third? fourth? champagne flute. Hours passed. At one point, I walked into the bathroom and caught sight of my reflection in the mirror. I leaned in closer to it and took a good, hard look at myself: the disheveled hair, the glassy stare, my mouth hanging open slightly. It was time to leave. I felt dark. Anguished. I wanted it to end. I had to get out.

I dashed out his apartment door. I stumbled down a hallway, into an elevator, to a new landing area, to another hallway. I opened a heavy metal door, which opened to an unfinished building roof deck fifty feet above the street below. I walked slowly toward the edge and breathed in. I tiptoed clumsily toward the edge. I didn't think about it. But I thought about thinking about it. For a fleeting second. You can't help it. Like when someone tells you not to think about something, it sticks right into your head. I felt alone, but I stepped back.

I could see my three roommates down on the street below. They were running in a circle around a taxi, putting a number of items into the trunk. What the?

"Guys! How do I get down?"

"Jesus, get down!"

"My name is Ed!" I screamed back. It felt good. I was no longer alone.

Back at 555 Xizang Lu, the cabby popped the trunk, and in it were four traffic cones, a Chinese flag, a framed photograph of some random Chinese guy, and a large metal Chinese letter/character, all items that my roommates had pilfered during the ten minutes that I was lost in River's building. Jean-Louis actually pried the Chinese character off of a wall across the street from River's place. I hope we gave the guy a big tip.

A couple of policemen lingered outside our apartment complex. "Don't mind us, our white clothes, or our new traffic cones," I thought. We passed through the gate and were walking down the path to our building when Ken dropped his new cones and decided to tackle me.

"HUG ATTACK MR. ED! GAAAAAHHHH!" The impact hurtled me sideways. I smashed through a small fence and ruined a neatly manicured bush. Ken stood up with ease. I tried to move but was completely stuck in this bush next to the path. I couldn't really see anything, but I could hear the policemen yelling and sprinting over to where I was stuck at the scene of the crime.

"*Courir!*" Jean-Louis yelled, and my three roommates jetted as fast as their legs could carry them. What happened to "leave no man behind"? The policemen yanked me out of the bush and started yelling in Chinese.

I wrestled my arm free and un-holstered my wallet from the front right pocket of my white pants. At the sight of this, the policeman clutching my left arm unhanded me. There was a moment of stunned silence between the two of them as I took out a single 100 RMB note (about $14) and handed it to the two of them. They looked at each other in thoughtful consideration.

"*Hao ma?*" (OK?) I asked them.

"*Due, due, due*" (Yes, yes, yes) they both eagerly repeated.

I looked back over my shoulder as I walked away, half expecting the policemen to come running or Ken to blind-side me again. The two policemen, however, had coolly iced their step back to the street. I probably just doubled their day's salary in five seconds. They warily gave me one last look over their shoulder to check which building I entered. *I wonder what that means.*

I flung our apartment door open.

"Ken! Where the fuck are you!"

Miles and Jean-Louis were giggling on the couch. Ken had face planted on the futon. He was stone cold passed out, already snoring.

"You guys see what this giant did to me out there?"

"Ummm, yup, we were there."

"Hi-la-rious."

"That tackle cost me 100 RMB in bribery money. This tall nincompoop owes me."

"You paid too much." Miles shook his head.

"Yeah, even I wouldn't have gotten ripped off like that," Jean-Louis nodded.

The doorbell rang.

"You idiots!" I yelled. "It's the police. They're gonna want more money."

I tiptoed over to the door and creaked it open.

There were no police. A pint-size man in a bike helmet struggled to hold up a large number of shopping bags in each arm.

"Mac. Don. Ards." He enunciated the three words using harsh syllables.

"Huh?" I gaped at him, totally confused. He tried again.

"Mac. Don. Ards?" He tried again, this time less confident.

"Huh?"

"Mac. Don.—"

"OOOOOH," I looked down at the ten bags he was carrying. Each bag sported the familiar golden arches. McDonald's. This was a McDonald's deliveryman. Or as this guy pronounced it, "MacDonArds."

"Oh maaan," Miles slapped his hand to his forehead. "I forgot that we ordered McDonalds."

"Jesus, guys."

"Yep! Miles heard from River that you can phone order McDonald's for delivery here."

The delivery guy continued to stand there, his arms trembling from the weight of his ten delivery bags.

"*Xie xie ni!*" (Thank you) I told him, and sweet relief swept over the guy's face upon his realization that he was indeed in the right place. *I wonder which of these ten bags is ours?*

The guy promptly dropped all ten bags at my feet and stuck out his hand to receive payment. *All ten bags are for us?*

"What the shit," I turned around, "How much did you guys order?"

"A lot, I guess," Miles mumbled hazily. Nearby Ken kept snoring.

I proceeded to hand the guy 100 RMB notes until he put his hand away. 100 RMB...200 RMB...300 RMB...400 RMB...500 RMB...600 RMB...700 RMB. His hand went away. Miles had ordered us $100 worth of McDonald's. And mind you, McDonald's is much cheaper in Shanghai.

The delivery guy turned around and skipped on his merry way toward the elevator bank. I bent down to pick up our ten bags of McDonald's. I caught a glimpse of the clock. It was 6:00 AM. A good time as any for the largest McDonald's feast ever consumed.

"Says the Big Macs cost only 20 RMB each," Miles looked at the receipt.

"Bargain," I mumbled, face full of food.

I think I ate four Big Macs and twenty-five nuggets. To answer your question, yes, McDonald's tastes exactly the same in Shanghai as everywhere else in the world. Together, the three of us barely made a dent in our fast food pile. It was time for bed. Ken kept snoring, face planted on the futon.

"Tall fucker." I mumbled. I promptly took the remaining

Big Macs and erected a burger pyramid directly on his chest, placing each one carefully in order not to wake the sleeping giant. Next, I dumped all of the remaining nuggets and French fries all over him. As a crowning achievement I stuck two French fries up his nose, which coincidentally stopped the snoring. A true bed of roses. Jerk.

In one night, I started a sushi food fight at a restaurant, danced with a homeless guy, buffered a sidewalk, almost jumped off of a building, went through a bout of klepto-mania, bribed two policemen, and bought out an entire McDonalds restaurant. All while dressed in white. The harder I luxuriated, the less I wished to look myself in the mirror. I wondered how the rest of Molly's night turned out.

My voiced sounded like twenty years worth of Marlboro Lights. I started having doubts. If this was truly Me, wouldn't I not care? I hated that I cared. I wanted to not care. Crazy Me would have worn a dirty hangover across his shoulder like a Boy Scout badge—an affirmation that this was my Path. And yet, I wanted the feeling to go away.

It was a hangover of the conscience that was suddenly starting to eat at me. I hadn't been a great teacher to my students. Check that—I hadn't even *been* a teacher to my students. I destroyed more than I constructed, and as fun as it is to blow things up, eventually the little voice deep down tells you that you should chill out. *Ugh, get out of my head!*

With each incremental morning stupor, I could see my miniature parents, one parked on each shoulder. My miniature mother held a miniature buttered English muffin in her miniature right hand, her pinky in the air. Sushi fights and stolen traffic cones yielded her insufficient cocktail fodder. On the other shoulder, my miniature father wore a miniature baggy suit with his miniature hair parted tidily covering his miniature bald spot. His face betrayed nothing. His miniature arms were crossed. He didn't have to say it.

On Monday morning, Miles, Ken, Jean-Louis, and I sauntered out of our apartment and hailed a taxi.

Miles was his chipper self: "Gonna be a great week." In my Monday morning, zombie-like state, I hadn't noticed that he was carrying a large box with holes in it until a Volkswagen Santana 3000 pulled over to grab us.

Jean-Louis was in a sour mood because he somehow lost his apartment keys: "I swear they were in my pocket."

"Miles, what is in that box, and why does it have holes?" I mumbled, with one eye still closed.

"Shit, my pocket has holes," Jean-Louis said.

"I got a great deal on a bunch of frogs."

"That box has frogs in it?"

"Bullfrogs—20 RMB a pop. We're going to dissect them in biology lab today."

"Why am I not surprised?"

Miles popped the trunk and tossed the box in casually. My other two compadres didn't bat an eyelash.

Ken hit his head on the way into the taxi: "Shoot! Ow!"

I slid into the middle seat between Ken and Jean-Louis, while Miles was awarded shotgun.

"So what are you non-frog-dissectors gonna teach today?" I asked once we started rolling.

"Ed. No talking. Silent reading time for all my students today," said English-teacher Jean-Louis.

"US Revolutionary War," said history-teacher Ken, sleepily. "In a dorky way, I'm actually sort of excited."

What was I going to teach? I thumbed through a small notepad. More Parts of Speech to the English beginners, and five-paragraph essays to the advanced kids. All lesson plans drawn from the internet. I still didn't know what I was going to do with Kotaro and the history students that morning...

First period was history class with my beginning English students. Yurika the Rugrat, Kotaro the head scratcher, and the rest of the gang wandered into class. I walked over to the blackboard and stared at my students. I was utterly unprepared. For an instant, my brain flatlined—I had forgotten English, my native tongue. *Ugh, why did I come to CHINA!!!*

Thankfully, a portion of last week's teaching was still unfinished, so when I remembered how to talk, I instructed the kids to pick up where they left off. We passed the first twenty minutes of class reading the remainder of the story of Medusa and Perseus out loud, culminating with the victorious decapitation of Medusa's head by a heroic Perseus. Everyone remembers this story, right? I stole this lesson plan from Wikipedia.

Yurika struggled through the final sentences, and then that was it. No discussion, no questions. Nothing came to me. I wasn't even sure how well they actually understood the story.

I ran out of things to say. Twenty-five minutes of class remained. How to kill the time? Hmm. An idea. I instructed my students to write their *own* story, implementing some of the characters we learned about in Greek mythology. *Sure, that will keep them busy.*

"For example, you can write a story about Hercules. What if Hercules was your friend? What would you do together? Or, you can pretend that you are Theseus and you must fight the Minotaur. What will happen? You can write about anything. Just write *something*. Or, you can write a new story. Make sure to stay quiet while you write. Mr. Ed's head hurts."

Kotaro's face froze, as if he had just taken a good long look into Medusa's eyes. No signs of comprehension yet. *I'm tired.* They began writing.

Thankfully, the Happy Birthday song blared. I collected my students' stories, grabbed a black coffee from the teacher's office (no dairy in China), and crawled back to my office to embrace a free period.

There was a mountain of ungraded homework papers on my desk. *Nope, not getting to those any time soon.* I brushed the homework pile aside, and took a look at the mythology stories that my students just submitted. First on top of the pile was a story from Kotaro. *Oh boy, here goes:*

*"One day there was grandmother and grandfather. Grandfather and grandmother took a shit in the neighborhood."*

That's it. That was whole the story.

Then again, the grammar was actually pretty good. "Took a shit." That was simple past tense, correct subject-verb agreement, with an irregular verb tense construct. Then it dawned on me: this grammar was *too* good.

I ruffled through the rest of the papers, and found one from another student in the exact same handwriting. It dawned on me that the other student wrote Kotaro's story for him. Kotaro had somehow cheated on an ungraded in-class writing exercise. *Maybe he was smarter than I gave him credit for. How did I miss this?* Meanwhile, I couldn't believe that my worst student had plagiarized a story about grandparents shitting everywhere.

For a minute, I felt alone. I missed home. I looked down at my watch. 9:45 AM. That meant 9:45 PM on the East Coast.

I thought about it for a second. Then, I fired up Skype, and called Riley, my ex/ex? girlfriend. I never knew what to say around her.

"Wow, hi," she answered.

"Hey."

"I'll be honest, I didn't expect a call."

"Well, I was having a nostalgic moment," I admitted.

"Oh," she said. "Well how's China?"

"~~China is tough. Sometimes I get lonely. I miss college. I miss us. Times were simpler. Why didn't they tell us that real life is complicated? I love this place, and I hate it. I'm so far, and yet I'm SO FAR, you know? I can't tell if I'm running away or running to something. Like, am I really going to be a teacher for the rest of my life? Am I going to live abroad? What comes next? I've been with other girls. What has been your...situation on that front? What are we? Why do we keep talking? Is this a relationship? Are we just friends? This is sort of like relationship purgatory. Is this normal? I'm having a tough day...~~" "Good," I lied. At the moment, it was not good.

"Tough day?"

Part of me wanted to vent, to unload the truth. I hadn't been unfaithful. There was no longer something between us to break, but here we were talking, a world away. Did I miss her? Sure. Would I tell her that? Never. Her voice was a rush, which stifled me; its force bottled up every emotion I had inside. This is why we could never be together. Did I have a tough day?

"You could say that. How's Boston?"

"It's...fine."

"Tough day?" I reciprocated.

"I feel like all I do is work."

"I miss home sometimes." I eked out an emotion.

"Are you saying you miss home or you miss...*me*?"

Emotionally outmaneuvered again. I wanted to tell her my secret. *I've started seeing other people.* Was it even a secret? I mean, she had to be too, no? It had been months. We were young. Could I finally tell her I missed her? Did I even miss her? I had to say something.

"I don't know. I guess I—"

"I've been sleeping with another gu—"

Silence. She cut out.

"Riley? Riley? Riley? Are you there? Hello?"

I re-dialed. Connection failed. I went to click re-dial once again, and then I didn't. Did she say what I thought she had said? *Sleeping with another...pillow?* Everyone knows how that sentence ends. Maybe I didn't want an answer. In a sense, if she gave it, my hand would be forced. I would have to tell her, right? Oh man, you know what would be easier than all of this? Not re-dialing again.

The timing was dark humor. We routinely lost internet connectivity throughout the day at FIS. I once asked Linda why, and she explained that sporadically the government becomes over-zealous about censorship and shuts the entire internet off. I thought of a small Chinese guy pulling a giant lever.

Had Riley moved on? Ugh, I felt sick. My angst was unfair territoriality, given the physical distance between us, but it stung nonetheless. I shuddered at the thought of her with someone else, even though I knew deep down I had no right. I was truly alone here now. No strings tying me back the US. This was my life. Here, in this new place. I thought about Molly. I wondered if she thought about me.

I needed a small victory. A distraction. I looked down at my shirt. *Laundry!* Yes, I had clean clothes to pick up across the street from the Fudan Fuzhong laundry lady. That should be easy. I made for the elevator and pressed "1." On the ground level, a gaggle of students clad in tracksuits from Fudan Fuzhong bull-rushed the elevator before I could exit.

"Out of the way, you track-suited maniacs!"

I elbowed a teenage student in the rib cage and snuck out before the elevators doors clanged shut. For some absolutely illogical reason, the Chinese will pack into smaller areas such as elevators, subway cars, buses, and building entrances before letting people out.

I started to cross the main street near school, Guoquan Lu.

*EEEEEEEEEEK! CRASH!!*

A speeding motorbike swerved violently to avoid splattering me across the sidewalk, spun out, and smashed to the pavement, sliding fifteen feet past me, but leaving me completely unscathed. The driver, wearing jeans and a helmet, did multiple barrel roles before petering to a stop. A few paper bags containing groceries exploded all over the pavement. *CHINA!!!*

The busy street scene froze in time, and dozens of pedestrians began to stare. The young Chinese motorist stood up, checked his limbs, dusted himself off, and took fifteen steps toward me. He put a finger in my face and shouted at me in Mandarin. The windshield of his motorbike was smashed, its side dented and scraped. I was alive.

\* \* \*

That night, the doorbell to our apartment rang around 9:00 PM. Molly was coming over for a late dinner. I wore a collared shirt. I even tucked it in.

"Molly," I said as I opened the door, only to see a pudgy, smiling Chinese man in his forties standing where Molly was supposed to be.

"You're not Molly. Unless this door has warped me into another dimension. Molly?" I looked closer. He kept smiling.

He handed me what appeared to be a bill for 400 RMB (about $60). I had no idea what this bill was for, or even how to ask what this bill was for. There was no way to press "0" and be transferred to a representative. Maybe if I pressed his nose?

At that moment, Molly emerged from the elevator bank in the building hallway.

"Thank God," I said loudly as she approached.

"Who's this?" She asked. I made an I-don't-know face.

"*Nǐ shì shuí?*" Molly asked this guy.

"*Tāmen qiàn wǒ de qián. Diànlì,*" he replied. I stood there smugly, like a guy talking shit whose posse just arrived to back him up.

Molly turned back to me. "He's a bill collector. This is an electricity bill."

I looked at the guy. He shook his body for a quick second, as if pretending to get shocked by electricity, in order to reinforce his identity.

I turned to Molly. "What would I do without you?" I cracked a smile after a long day.

I took out my wallet and handed this strange man cash. He walked away. Molly stepped inside and looked out the window in the living room.

"This building under construction is creeping dangerously up to your window level."

"Tell me about it."

This was my first encounter with a Chinese bill collector, but hardly my last. My roommates and I never figured out how to pay our bills all year, so every few weeks or so a bill collector would arrive and point to a light bulb (electricity) or a faucet (water), and we would hand over money. That's it. That's how it worked.

"You would not *believe* the day I had," she started. "CHINA!!!" She exclaimed, throwing her hands up in the air as she dropped her bag on the floor.

"Amen."

"You too, huh?" she asked.

"Me too."

"China."

"Sometimes I'm not sure how we do it," I huffed.

"Sometimes I no longer want to do it," she replied.

I shrugged off her comment as the final chapter of a long day. Sometimes, only an indefatigable optimist could survive this place. We cooked pasta and talked about Shanghai. The mood was adult. When her plate was empty, she sighed.

"I should really get back."

"Right. It's late." I walked her to the door. She undressed me with her small, kind eyes. I looked down. Her lips kissed me tenderly on the cheek.

"Thanks for dinner." She turned around and left.

I blamed China. Of course, my twisted state of mind and crushed sense of worth were byproducts of some external misfortune heaped upon me. Definitely nothing I could have done, right? I'm pretty sure no one under the age of twenty-five has ever accepted the blame for anything. That's an adult thing. Maybe it's because you don't have any real responsibilities until you've bagged a quarter century.

I sat down at my desk in the office at FIS. My fingernails concealed caked city grime. I ran my hands through my dirty hair. The stack of ungraded homework papers was just growing larger. I whimpered.

"Mr. Ed, you game for lunch at *The Spot?*" Sonia, the Slovakian ESL teacher, asked me. In all of China's tumult, so many times the food was its sweet salvation.

"Just what the doctor ordered. Hey Ken," I called across the office. "You game?"

*"The Spot?"* he replied. "Sounds delightful."

We walked over to The Spot, where the hostess motioned us to our usual table. I smiled at her—the kind of smile you can only give someone whose food, despite many opportunities, has yet to give you the runs. The Spot was run by a migrant family from Gansu province in Northwest China.

In typical Shanghai fashion, the kitchen spilled out onto the sidewalk, where a pair of grandmas huddled over giant woks, cooking up a revolving door of provincial delights. The customer seating was crammed into the back of the restaurant.

The Spot was the eye in the Chinese hurricane. Today, however, we were sitting in the back area of the small restaurant, quietly enjoying our spread, when we heard a plate smash in the kitchen out front. There was a great commotion, and two distinct voices were bellowing at each other. We all jumped up from our table, and as we strained our necks to see what was going on, we heard another plate smash. And then a yelp. And then another plate smashed. Through the tornado of chaos, I was able to see the cause of the commotion.

Two screaming waiters were smashing plates over each other's heads!

The first guy took a porcelain plate from a pile of clean dishes and swung it with two hands at the second guy's head. The second guy ducked just in time. The first guy's momentum was too strong, and he lost his grip on the plate, which smashed into a nearby wall. The second guy then took a fresh plate, cocked it like a Frisbee, and attempted a backhanded torso shot on the first guy. He flung the plate in a tight spiral at the first guy's abdomen and made clean contact. The plate knocked the wind out of the first guy, who fell to the ground as the plate then shattered.

Nearby, their mother (or aunt or something) could only twist her hair in suspense. I'm not sure if she was more worried about her children or her plates.

The scuffle's momentum carried it out into the restaurant's main room. The first guy, reeling from the abdomen shot, ducked out from behind the kitchen area into where the patrons were sitting. *Look out!* Patrons began to duck and cover their heads, fearful that they would become collateral damage.

The first guy grabbed four teacups as ammo and began to throw them like baseballs back into the kitchen area. Everyone in the restaurant grabbed their heads as if their plane were going down. The first cup nailed the second guy right in the elbow. Direct hit! The next three cups smashed against a wall in quick succession and rained porcelain all over one family's lunch.

The mother emerged with a frying pan and started whacking the first guy over the back. He covered his head and fell to his knees in submission. The rest of the family, and all of the diners in the restaurant, started laughing. *This is funny? This is a funny thing? What the hell is wrong with you people?*

Just like that, it was over. Everyone just resumed eating. The family that was nearly decapitated by three teacups didn't even leave the restaurant. The dad plucked a plate shard from his noodle bowl and continued slurping. *Just like our family dinners at home*, their smiles seemed to say as everyone shook it off. They probably didn't even get a discount. Unreal. In China, when people go out to eat, their lone request is to not have a plate smashed on their head. In the US, you ask for dressing on the side and set yourself up for disappointment.

To be honest, it was refreshing to finally see the pugnacious side of such a complicated people. The Chinese are aggressive behind the wheel and on the sidewalks, and the volume dials of their voices all go up to eleven, not ten. However, the drunken bar fight (an American staple) didn't seem to exist. Though I was poked, prodded, groped, and screamed at on many occasions, I had never been attacked or assaulted, nor had I feared that I would be. This day, however, awakened that possibility. *Dishware. Jesus.*

I zipped up my backpack and slung it over my shoulder, relieved at the conclusion of another week at FIS. The guys were waiting for me downstairs. I looked at the growing pile of ungraded homework papers on the desk in my office, and paused for a moment. *Those can wait until next week*, I thought. The school was mostly empty; the students had fled for the weekend half an hour earlier.

I put my right hand on the door to the office, about to push it open, when I heard two stark voices on the other side of the door. I cupped my ear to the door to listen.

"Study? You can't be serious," said a male student.

"We have an econ test on Monday," said the female student. Two FIS seniors, both native English speakers. A boy named Lewis and a girl named Guang, I recalled.

"Who cares? Nobody here cares. You know if you spell your name right that Mr. Johnson will give you an 'A.'"

"I guess," the girl was less convinced.

"Any homework we actually have to do for Monday?" the boy asked.

"Watch a movie and write a one-page summary for literature class, couple of math problems for calculus, nothing else."

"Sweet, that'll take less than an hour. Looks like I'll get to spend the weekend playing video games."

"Do you ever worry about college in the US next year?" the girl sounded concerned.

"I hear that college is even easier."

"I wish the teachers here cared more," the girl yearned.

"C'mon. Think of how lucky we are. Those kids across the street never sleep," the boy rationalized.

"I guess."

"I hear that for ESL students here it's even easier."

"Really?" she was curious. "Because they don't speak English?"

"Because all those teachers—Mr. Ed, Jean-Louis, Sonia— they're like twenty-two. They don't give a damn. They are practically our age."

My heart sank. That hurt. And yet, who was I to argue? I opened my mouth, ready to burst through the door and defend my honor, but I couldn't think of anything to say. So, I dropped my backpack and slunk down to the floor. My eyes welled up and I let out a hushed sob.

"You hear that? Let's get out of here," the boy said. "I think some kids are playing basketball right now. Let's go find them." They left. I closed my eyes and welcomed the silence.

My phone buzzed. The guys were looking for me. I stood up and wiped a glob of snot onto my sleeve. I put my hand on the door again, ready to leave. I paused. I turned around, looked at my desk, and retreated back to grab the stack of ungraded homework papers.

"Do you guys think we're *good* at teaching?" I asked the fellas from the passenger seat of the cab, en route to our luxury apartment for the weekend.

"Big question for a Friday afternoon," Jean-Louis pulled a baseball cap over his eyes and leaned his head against the back window.

"Well, Mr. Ed, I suppose it depends what you mean by 'good,'" Ken got philosophical. "Are we Andover Academy good? One could argue that unsurprisingly we are not. Are we Fudan International School good? I sleep soundly at night." Our taxi ripped onto the North-South highway, skyscrapers whipping into the corners of my peripheral vision, my wide eyes swallowing the road ahead. I turned my head over my left shoulder. My three buddies were scrunched together in the back seat.

"Ed, it works like this. I teach biology." Miles was his matter-of-fact self. "There is literally a syllabus to teach high school biology. I follow the syllabus."

"But are your kids learning? I mean, what happened when they cut those frogs of yours open?"

"One girl told me that her family eats bullfrogs."

"I believe her."

"I wasn't about to dare her to prove it," Miles answered.

I pressed. "But did they *learn*? Did you finish the class, dump the frogs into the trash, kick your feet up and say, 'Wow, I did a good job today'? Did they at least have fun?"

"It was hectic. One girl shrieked and then threatened to sue me. Overall though, I'd call it a win."

"I feel like my kids never care or listen." I conceded.

"Well, on a scale from one to China, how much do *you* care?"

"Myanmar."

"She'll always be 'Burma' to me," Jean-Louis butted in.

Miles ignored him. "Ed, it's like this. I've overheard some of your classes from the hallway as I've passed by. They sound like school. Here you're this guy who swings around stripper poles," (this happened), "wrestles in baby pools, and shoves French fries up Ken's nose—"

"I'm still annoyed about that," Ken rumbled. I stayed silent, listening intently to Miles.

"My point being," Miles continued, "You are a FUN GUY. You're fun. With a capital 'F.'"

"F...U," Jean-Louis smirked and continued spelling it.

"Sometimes," Miles continued, "it feels like you save up all your crazy energy, unleash it out on the town, and then bottle it up and switch to your work voice the second you step through the front door of Fudan International School."

"This is starting to feel like I'm in the therapist's chair."

"Well, you've sorta got a case of multiple personalities going on. You're Mr. Ed by day, and then by night you're... you're...Help me out here, guys."

"You are DUARDO," Jean-Louis said.

"You don't think we *all* suffer a little bit from multiple personality disorder?" I disputed.

"Guilty," Ken admitted.

"Yeah," said Miles, "but sometimes I think your work-voice-don't-care-that-much-Mr.-Ed personality manifests itself more strongly than all of our Dr. Jekylls."

I thought about this.

"Ed, you either have to care more because you're inspired, or you have to be yourself and make it *fun*. Sometimes I think these things go hand in hand. Like the more fun your kids are having, the more fun you'll have, and the more you'll care. And then wham-o, everything is awesome. Otherwise, things stay hectic."

Ken subbed into the seat behind the therapist's desk. "The more you think about it as school, separate and apart from yourself, the more it's going to feel like school."

"What about you, Mr. Ken? You seem to take things at school kinda seriously."

"This is the thing that's going to get me a real job. So it matters. Pretty much a desperation thing."

"Real job?"

"Like back in the real world. This is not the real world."

Miles volleyed back to me. "Who was the best teacher you

had growing up?" I faced forward again in the passenger seat and looked up at the sky through the windshield.

"Probably Mr. Stevens, high school physics."

"Why?"

"Because we shot metal balls out of canons and once measured the weight of his car within a 5 percent error margin by pushing it forward in a parking lot with our palms pressed against bathroom scales."

Miles pondered, "You used the bathroom scales to make sure you were pushing the car forward with constant force."

"Yes."

"And then measured the acceleration using stop watches or something."

"Yup."

"And then used force equals mass times acceleration."

"Bingo." Miles's scientific aptitude was multidisciplinary.

"Cool."

"It was fun," I admitted. "I still remember that. But I'm an English teacher. Science is another animal."

"Well, who was your best English teacher?" Ken asked.

"That's tougher. Maybe Mrs. Armor. Also high school."

"Why?"

"She used to lecture in these different voices. Like one day a goblin, and the next day a drunken Irishman. Her family was super wealthy, so she taught at our school for free."

"She cared. She made it fun," Miles added.

"And how do you think your current students would describe *you*?" Ken asked.

"Jesus. I don't want to know." I really didn't know. Super serious? Uninvolved? Tardy in returning homework? Unprepared?

"It's still early in the year. In your ca-year," Ken gave me the thumbs up.

"I don't know what to say, guys." I felt a little down. Sometimes it's not that easy getting negative feedback. After hearing what they said, I knew they were right. Making the mental shift is just a little harder.

"Say you'll pick up the cab fare," Jean-Louis smiled. "We're here." He swung open the rear passenger side door and got out.

I stayed up all night on Saturday and Sunday grading papers, catching up, preparing lesson plans. It might have been years since I stayed in on a Saturday. By Monday, I was exhausted.

"Ed?"

"Ed."

"Ed!"

Miles slapped me across the face.

"Huh?" I awoke in my office chair.

"Dude, it's 3 PM on a Monday. Get your shit together. We have a faculty meeting right now."

"Blooondie. I quit. China wins."

"Ed, today we get to meet Mr. Wu, the mysterious head administrator of Fudan Fuzhong and FIS."

I perked up.

"You mean the secret guy that runs this place?"

Miles began, "Oh yeah. This is *the guy*."

"The true brains behind this masterful operation called Fudan International School?" I said sarcastically.

"You're referring to the fact that we have no training, resources, guidelines, expectations, dress code, curriculum, school rules, or even basic demographic information about our students?" Miles added.

"And yet our students pay a small fortune in tuition."

"These are among the many reasons why those little tracksuit-wearing, Fudan Fuzhong shits across the street laugh at us."

"Totally," I agreed. We both looked down.

"Are you saying that you actually *care*, Mr. Ed?"

"Sure. Yeah, I think maybe I do. Maybe just a little bit."

I admitted with a sly smile, in deference to Miles's cab ride wisdom.

"Mr. Ed," Miles pretended to fan himself like an admiring fan. "Is it hot in here?"

\* \* \*

The Happy Birthday song echoed loudly throughout the halls. The class day was over, and it was time for a very mysterious all-faculty meeting.

We all walked into a teachers-only classroom and took a seat. Miles plopped himself next to me. Jean-Louis grabbed a chair on my other side. Linda stood at the head of the classroom, hands clasped together. She began.

"Good afternoon, esteemed faculty of FIS. I hope that you are all enjoying this beautiful fall day. First, a quick announcement. We are finally getting our first shipment of books next week." There were sighs of relief around the room.

"Second, today there is someone I wish to introduce to you. He's not always around, but he's always present. He's got big pockets, but his hands are rarely in them. Everyone, meet Mr. Wu." She motioned to her left, where a very plump, middle-aged Chinese guy smiled with a car salesman's authenticity. *Show me the Carfax.*

"Mr. Wu serves two roles. He is the number two administrator of Fudan Fuzhong and is also the number one administrator here at FIS. Without further ado, here is Mr. Wu." She giggled at her accidental rhyme.

All the Chinese teachers began clapping thunderously. I hesitantly banged my hands together a few times. I locked eyes with Miles next to me, who had one eyebrow raised.

*This is Linda's boss? The real guy running the show behind the scenes? And he also works at Fudan Fuzhong? He literally suits up for both teams.*

Mr. Wu stepped forward. He had silver hair and a really round face. He looked a bit like a pancake. Check that—he *really* looked like a pancake.

He opened his mouth to speak.

今天，我看到了希望教师FIS。一年前...

Well, shit. Mandarin.

He continued uninterrupted for ten minutes. I caught a few words here and there, but to me, the bulk of the speech still sounded like noise. At the end of his spiel, he took a small bow. All the Chinese teachers clapped again.

Mr. Wu had brought a translator, who stepped forward to translate ten minutes' worth of uninterrupted Mandarin. *Here we go.* The translator began:

> "Today, I see hopeful teachers at FIS. One year ago, our school had few teachers and few students. Today, we have the many teachers from the many country. I see the harmony in the classroom and on basketball court."

Then the translator stopped.

"We're being shortchanged on that hack job of a translation. What'd he say?" I asked Miles.

"Translation accurate," Miles whispered back.

"You shitting me?"

"Was gibberish."

"Unbelievable," I whispered, "Don't you think he looks like a pancake?"

"Yes!" Miles hushed excitedly, loud enough that a couple other nearby teachers turned their heads, "That's what it is. It was killing me. He is totally Mr. Pancake."

"Mr. Pancake!"

Jean-Louis butted into our hushed conversation. "You know, 'Pancake' was my nickname in prison."

"Oh shut up. You're from Montreal. You know damn well that your prison nickname was 'Canadian Bacon.'"

"Is everything OK back there?" Linda called out to the three of us, in front of the entire faculty.

"Yes, Linda. We were just complimenting Mr. Wu's speech," I assured her. "And wondering about his plans to improve student, uh, harmony this spring."

Linda nodded. The translator whispered to Mr. Wu. Mr. Wu whispered back.

"Mr. Wu says that is your job." My mouth opened to reply but no sound came out. Plus one point for Mr. Wu. Jean-Louis held back a chortle.

"Thanks, dipshit," I whispered to Jean-Louis.

"You're the kiss ass."

Mr. Pancake sat down to observe the remainder of the FIS school faculty meeting. He gave the three of us a funny look. I returned the favor.

"Next topic of conversation," Linda proclaimed.

"I think we need to institute a detention policy for bad behavior," our Puerto Rican Dean of Students declared. This was almost a weekly topic. The Western teachers began to debate whether this was a good idea. The Chinese teachers sat in silence. Mr. Pancake looked on.

"Well, is detention really the most ethical solution for misbehavior?" Linda pondered out loud. We couldn't arrive at a consensus.

No detentions until next month, kids. Students were routinely late, they didn't do their homework, and they dressed sloppy. In short, they didn't give a damn, and our school barely gave them a reason to get out of bed in the morning, let alone a disincentive for *not* getting out of bed in the morning. We had to do something about it, but we never did.

"Any other topics of conversation during this faculty meeting? Any other problems that you guys are having?" Linda opened the floor again.

Helga stood up. *Uh-oh.*

"Yes. I have a problem. Charles, who is boy in my math class, he is a bad boy. He never turns in the homeworks. I ask him why and he says, 'I don't know.' What I do about this student? In Turkey my math students always turn in their homeworks. Sometimes my students will never even hire a book from the library. What I do? What I do?"

"Do any teachers have comments for how to address this problem? There are no bad ideas," Linda gestured.

"I think we should expel all the students," Helga continued.

"OK, there are *some* bad ideas. Does anyone else have any comments?"

The silence was so uncomfortable that I stepped in.

"Helga, Charles goes to study hall every night. Maybe we can ask each study hall proctor to pay extra attention to Charles every day, to make sure he does his homework."

Helga paused. "Thank you, Mr. Ed. Is good idea."

"Nice idea, Mr. Ed," Linda gave me a professional nod, for what was—let's be honest—an obvious fucking idea.

Jean-Louis raised an eyebrow. I crossed my arms in smug satisfaction. For a moment, I felt in control.

The Chinese portion of our faculty never said a word

during these meetings. Not one, which was peculiar, considering how loud I had found some Chinese people to be. At first, I suspected it was because the meetings took place in English, but I later discovered that it was because they had all learned since birth never to question the authority of their superiors. *Dun dun duuuuun. Holy smokes, right?*

Most of our Chinese faculty were quite satisfied with the teaching jobs they had, because teaching is about 6000 percent better than becoming a coal miner or rice farmer. Interestingly, respect for teachers among in China was such that educators were given a distinct title "*Laoshi*" in broader Chinese society. Similar to how doctors get an MD after their name and lawyers get a JD. In China, you get a "*Laoshi.*" I had spent less than three drunken months in China, and I had already received my "*Laoshi*"—the Chinese equivalent of the juris doctor. In a sense, you could say I had "taken the bar," which in China doubles as a euphemism for being a gentleman who frequents libation establishments.

The Happy Birthday song rang again. Meeting over.

I picked my chin up. What are you going to throw at me next, China?

"Enjoy this curveball, Mr. Ed," China replied.

One Tuesday morning, I was lingering outside Linda's office when a courier dressed in an orange-and-blue tracksuit delivered a bound scroll with a red ribbon tied around it.

"What is it?" I asked her.

"It's a declaration."

"Of independence?"

"Of war."

"War?" I asked.

"Battle."

"..."

"Fudan Fuzhong is hosting a track meet. And they have declared battle against us."

"Um. By delivering a bound scroll?"

Because my school, Fudan International School (FIS), was an affiliate of Fudan Fuzhong, we were invited to *battle* them in a track meet. This athletic mêlée was going to consist of all of the divisions within Fudan Fuzhong and us. That's it. No other schools. Just us and Fudan Fuzhong. Suspicious? Never.

Days later, we received the list of track events for the upcoming meet, again in scroll form. Most of my international students, who largely hailed from Japan and Korea, were set to combat our nemeses across the street in running, shotput, discus, high jump, you name it. As I scanned the list of events, I nearly had a heart attack.

In the middle of the list of events, I saw my name.

"4X100 M Relay Race FIS Team—Eduardo Mestre." And the other names? Jean-Louis, Ken, and, you guessed it, Miles. Even more perplexing was the fact that our opponents were three teams of *Chinese eleventh graders from*

*Fudan Fuzhong.* Yes, the four of us American teachers were entered into a footrace against some Chinese high schoolers. Why? Let's call it a proxy battle for global supremacy.

\* \* \*

The day of the track meet, in a weather rarity, Shanghai was awash with golden rays of sunshine.

Our mass of 100 or so faculty and students was idling by the elevator entrance to our school building, preparing to walk over to the track meet across the street. Linda's closed eyelids tilted upwards to the sky. She exhaled confidently as she basked in a fleeting moment of exuberance and yes-we-can school spirit. Maybe she was just overdosing on Vitamin D. She let the elusive sun touch her pale skin. Her burgeoning wrinkles needed the light. Without opening her eyes or moving her head, she sensed my presence and began speaking.

"Can you feel that sunshine, Ed? Today is going to be a good day." Her phone rang, shattering the tranquility with a tri-tone beep. Her expression contorted. Linda rattled off some Mandarin into her handset and then snapped the phone shut like a mousetrap. The brief, luminous glory was gone.

"We have to get to the track meet immediately," she

announced to the teachers in a panicked, one-breath sentence. Apparently, we were tardy for the opening ceremony. *Opening ceremony?*

Our international students were clad in a smorgasbord of colors and styles of athletic gear and khaki pants as we jogged across Guoquan Street over to the entrance to Fudan Fuzhong's campus.

We hustled around the giant building, the Eye of Sauron on top watching eerily, past the Hunger Games cornucopia, to the open expanse directly behind, which housed an oval track encircling a green athletic field.

There were people everywhere, all standing still. It was oddly quiet. As the athletic field came into view, I saw it. The entire Fudan Fuzhong faculty and student body were tightly drawn into neat rows and standing taut in total silence. Twelve hundred people, all in matching orange and blue tracksuits.

"Twilight Zone much?" I asked Ken.

"Not now, Ed, this is bad."

Their arms were tucked behind their backs and their legs were snapped together tightly, like wooden chopsticks that had yet to be broken apart. Another thousand parents and other spectators surrounded the track with crossed arms and furrowed stares. It was dead silent. There were thousands of people waiting for us.

"Did we do something wrong?" Ken's voice trembled.

"Yeah, we didn't have a poster of Mao Zedong in our bedroom growing up." Jean-Louis answered coolly.

"It looks like they are about to declare war on us or something," I observed.

I felt thousands of narrow eyes slicing me with disapproval as our benchwarmers jostled onto our designated space on the field, where a perturbed Fudan Fuzhong school official was directing us.

All of the Fudan Fuzhong students continued to stand in perfect silence. We struggled noisily to get our students into two neat columns as the Fudan Fuzhong school official instructed us. In this moment of national intimidation, I will admit that their discipline was impressive.

"Mista Edo, what is happen?" Yurika asked me.

"Not now Yurika. Fudan Fuzhong has a stick up its ass."

"Stick? Ass?"

"Don't repeat that." We teachers poked and prodded our students into place, trying to emulate the arrangement of the Fudan Fuzhong student groups, hoping to quell this early embarrassment. The thousands of judging eyes continued to bore through me.

The moment that our students were settled, the Chinese national anthem began to blare over the loud speakers. In front of us, three students from Fudan Fuzhong hoisted the Chinese flag smoothly to the top of a tall flagpole. Their deft, coordinated pulls on the line made it clear that this was not their first flag-raising rodeo.

In tight unison, thousands of Chinese people whipped their right hand from behind their back to eyebrow level, in salute of the flag. Ken turned to me.

"I really don't think we should be saluting the flag. What if someone sees us?"

"Isn't it worse if they see us *not* salute the flag?" I reasoned.

"I don't like this at all."

"Oh relax," Jean-Louis interjected. "It's not like either of you is going to run for president. *Santé.*" He made a *cheers* motion with his hand, and then, without skipping a beat, he nestled his right hand above his brow, grinning.

I took my right hand, trembling, and in a moment I'd rather forget, I saluted the communist red flag of China, its yellow stars flapping in the faint breeze. "Fuck me," I muttered.

"Spread 'em," replied China.

The anthem forgivably waned away into silence, and I subtly darted my eyes left and then right and then forward again in an attempt to draw some visual hint as to what was coming next.

About twenty Chinese girls whizzed from various columns of the mass of students and made their way to the front of the congregation. They formed a tight-flying V arrangement in front of the thousands.

A gym teacher began to chant forcefully, "*Yi! Er! San! Si! Wu! Liu! Qi! Ba!*" ("1! 2! 3! 4! 5! 6! 7! 8!") It was the same aerobic dance routine that I'd seen local middle schoolers perform every day. *Really?*

They began the routine as the rest of us stood in silence and watched. Kick out a leg ("*Yi*"), raise a fist in the air ("*Er*"), put the leg back down ("*San*"), raise the other arm in the air ("*Si*"), retract both arms in a humping motion ("*Wu*"), rotate ninety degrees counterclockwise ("*Liu*"), bring the right hand to their forehead in sharp salute

("*Qi*"), and then whip their hand back down once again ("*Ba*").

Again and again and again. The twenty girls' jerky dance routine at best would have won third prize in a middle school talent contest. After twenty repetitions, I turned to Jean-Louis.

"You know, the definition of insanity is doing the same thing over and over and expecting a different result," I told him.

"Like waking up in Shanghai every morning pretending everything is gonna be OK?"

"Precisely."

Here was this dour flag salute followed by a gauche Richard Simmons impersonation, undermining the solemnity of the whole ordeal.

The twenty girls finally ceased the aerobics and reclaimed their places among the crowd. It was silent once again, save a faint morning breeze. At once, the gym teacher raised his arm, screamed something unintelligible, and then all hell broke loose. Every individual dashed in every possible direction as the track field erupted in noise. It was a supernova explosion of human beings. The games were underway. May the odds be ever in your favor.

* * *

An hour later, upon restoration of some semblance of order, the day's events began. Shotputs. High jumps. Sprints and distance running.

The sidelines of the running track were packed three or four students deep for each race. The crowd's inquisitiveness caused spectators to lean out onto the track to glimpse some of the races, resulting in a massive disadvantage for runners in the outside lanes, as there was hardly any space left for them to run without bowling over any fellow students. *God, I hope I'm not running in the outside lane for my relay.* I envisioned myself bashing multiple Chinese children with my heavy American frame.

I spotted Jennifer, the Chinese office assistant at FIS, who looked immensely stressed as she held a makeshift schedule of events. She waved a pen and pointed at our kids as if conducting a symphony, directing them to various athletic events around the field.

"Jennifer, where do I go for my race and how do I know when it's time?" I sounded like a six year old.

"Mista Ed, your race begin in five minutes. You go now. Over there. Win for Fudan International School!"

"Thanks, if you say so."

Out of the corner of my eye, I saw Russell Johnson, the questionable older white guy who taught Economics at Fudan International School. He put his arm around Mona, an eleventh-grade Taiwanese girl from FIS. *That's odd.*

I looked for my three friends, but they were nowhere to be found. Jennifer could sense my anxiety.

"Miles, Jean-Louis, Ken are in the place now." Jennifer pointed me to the far corner of the track. "You go there." My heart rate accelerated. *It was really happening.*

I was the third leg of the 4X100 relay, so I would have to wait alone in the far corner of the track.

I pinballed my way through the crowd and found a male Chinese faculty member of Fudan Fuzhong, complete with whistle and a clipboard with a bunch of Mandarin written all over it. It was body to body with Chinese students, and I was the only white guy in the area. No one spoke English. *What the hell do I do? Was it my turn? How did I know when my race started?*

In my finest Chinese, I offered, *"Wo chu ma?"* (I go?). He shook his head and gestured that he would tell me when it was time. Despite his assurance, anxiety began to infiltrate my bones once a few races had been completed and I still hadn't been waved over to my starting position on the track. *"Wo chu ma?"* I repeated. He shook his head. I was going to miss my race.

Finally, in the heat of the chaos, clipboard man ushered me to the second lane from the outside of the track. It was time. *Phew, not the outside lane.* At least the race wouldn't end with me unleashing a full-sprint body check on an unsuspecting Fudan Fuzhong student. I looked at my competitors for the third leg of the relay race. They were undoubtedly in high school, but they looked fit. One of them elbowed the other two and motioned to me. They all smirked.

*Am I really about to race a couple of Chinese high school kids?* Though I couldn't see anything through the throngs of students, I knew that somewhere on the other side of the mass of teenagers Miles was at the starting line, clenching the baton and waiting for the gunshot.

Now I was nervous. What if I lose? This is too ridiculous. But there are a ton of people watching. At least a couple thousand. What am I doing here?

Miles was our lead. He would then pass off the baton to Jean-Louis, who would then give it to me. Finally I would hand the magic stick off to Ken for the final stretch. *What could possibly go wrong?*

The crowd was roaring, and my heart was drumming in my chest so hard that it was making the rest of my body vibrate. I was a whirlwind of anxiety and still had a few shreds of genuine concern that I was running in the wrong race. I had no idea because I couldn't see any of my teammates.

Just as I was gathering my zen and looking back down the track to where Jean-Louis would emerge before my manic dash, I turned forward and saw Helga, the Turkish math teacher, standing on the track in front of me with a giant smile, clicking away on her digital camera. "Helga!"

"Oh, Mr. Ed, you will run the race for FIS now!"

"Yes, Helga. I'm running that race right now."

"Let me take you a picture. Smile!"

At that exact moment, the gun fired and the crowd roared. I could hear the crowd's wails enshroud the runners as they dashed from the starting line. "Helga, thank you so much for taking the picture, but now is not a good time. I have to run my race!" She kept snapping pictures.

"Helga, please, the race has already started!"

"Oh. I must go now. Good luck! Run with fast!" Helga called out, her Turkish accent as thick as glue as she waddled off the track. Though I couldn't see Miles or Jean-Louis for the first fifteen seconds after the gunshot, the rolling cheers of the crowd let me know that this race was hurtling towards me like counterclockwise hurricane. *It's on.*

In a flash, the four-team stampede was upon me. Jean-Louis's eyes looked like they had just witnessed a crime. He was in first place, slightly ahead of two wiry eleventh graders in the inner lanes. His legs churned forward like freight trains. For a fleeting moment, Jean-Louis was winning at China. There were no lost wallets or cell phones. No struggle to decipher the local dialect. No indifferent students. It was pure.

Suddenly, the eleventh grade runner on the outside track crashed into an unsuspecting spectator who had leaned into the race for a better view. The spectator flew backward in a tsunami of limbs, as if punched by a superhero. *Holy shit!* The runner stumbled, regained his footing, and accelerated once again. The team in the outside lane was now several steps behind the other three teams. Jean-Louis was in the lead, drawing near. Jean-Louis.

Every giant stride brought him closer to me, like a wrecking ball. In his right hand he held the baton. In an instant, he was upon me, half a step ahead of the two teams in the inside lanes. Our eyes locked. He outstretched his right hand and decelerated.

I grabbed the baton and turned to sprint. My muscles were spring-loaded as I snatched the baton and slammed the gas pedal. "*ALLONS-Y! GO GO GO ED!*" Jean-Louis bellowed bilingually as I took off with the baton. It was time.

My brain immediately knew that this was a moment I would remember for the rest of my life. The day of my footrace against a bunch of Chinese schoolchildren, with a crowd of thousands rooting for the home team.

I couldn't even feel my feet underneath me. They just *went*. My arms pumped like pistons. My legs grinded. I floated, light as a feather. But my breath was heavy. Between the bars and the pollution, I dragged. *This is not as easy as I remember.*

Out of the corner of my eye, I saw that I was now neck-and-neck with the second place kid on the inside lane. He had gained on me. The track in front of me curved slowly left, as we neared the final stretch, where our teammates lay waiting, ready to grab the baton and sprint to the finish line.

My engines were at maximum RPM. I came around the

turn where I would hand off the baton to Ken for the final straightaway to glory for our country.

*Timeout.* Something was wrong.

*Who is that in my lane, ready to receive the baton from me?* That was not Ken. *Oh my God. There has been a mix-up.*

It was Kotaro. Don't-know-my-own-name, grandparents-shitting-in-the-neighborhood Kotaro. He scratched his head when he saw me barreling toward him. His eyes opened wide. He knew it too.

Reflexively, I eased up my speed and handed him the baton. Kotaro yanked the stick out of my hand and jolted down the home stretch of the relay.

*Maybe he will come through? Maybe he will polish off our victory? Maybe he has secret speed that I don't know about? Ko-ta-ro?*

Nope. We finished in dead last. Even the team that crashed in the outside lane managed to catch us.

Ahead at the finish line, I could see the other three Fudan Fuzhong racers giving each other a congratulatory peace sign with two fingers outstretched. They looked at Kotaro, chuckled, and snubbed him.

We lost. I lost. In the classroom, on the town, on the sports field. This country was holding me down. Or was I holding myself down?

"Mista Edo," Kotaro approached me later and held his head down. "I am sorry." That was the most English I had ever heard him speak.

"It's not your fault, Kotaro. It's not your fault." I put a comforting hand on his shoulder. Kotaro had become confused about which race was his, and inadvertently taken Ken's place in mine. I could feel the eyes of the thousands of spectators scoffing at the insignificance of little Fudan International School.

I stood in the center field with my disappointed hands on my tired hips, and looked up at the afternoon sky. The pistons of student athletic activity pumped all around me, but I was alone.

I dropped to one knee, propped an elbow on my thigh, and rested my forehead in the palm of my hand. I shut my eyes and started laughing. I could feel the track-suited Fudan Fuzhong students disperse from my vicinity because one of the crazy Americans from the International School was having a bit of a moment.

Wasn't I supposed to be upset? World crumbling around

me? Bad at my job, kind of alone, far from home? Even in trying to reduce my life's complexities down to a simple relay footrace, I lost at that. I lost a goddamned footrace to a bunch of teenagers. My body tickled everywhere. I keeled over and howled in laughter. *What the hell was going on?*

Soon, I'd have to inform Molly of my middle name change from "Danger" to "Futility." And, you can't spell *futility* without F-U. Thanks for that, China. Eduardo Futility Mestre.

I opened my eyes and Linda stood over me, concerned. Not in a can't-believe-I-hired-this-guy sort of way, but in an I'm-actually-a-little-worried-about-this-guy's-mental-health sort of way. And then she asked the question.

"Are you alright?"

I turned to Jean-Louis. The apartment couch underneath my bum was a forgiving cradle. A Chinese game show was visible on our television, the volume on mute. A soaking-wet contestant had just won ten hamsters. For a fleeting instant, it was quiet. I stared at him to the point where he crooked an eye and felt compelled to respond.

"What?" he asked me.

"Good."

"How's it going?" Jean-Louis pressed on, as I continued to stare.

"Not much," I replied.

"Fine."

"Can I—"

"Oui monsieur."

"—ask you something?" I began.

"Mmmhmm."

"Do you ever wonder what we're doing here? In China? Did you ever think you'd come here to find yourself and pick a direction, but you still have no idea what you're doing?" I sighed. "Like where is my *Eat, Pray, Love* moment? Why is that so difficult in China? I mean, I've traveled my entire life, and yet here I have befriended like zero local people, just about every girl I've talked to is an expat, I can't speak Chinese, and I'm not even good at my job. I simultaneously care about everything and nothing. I thought I'd find something here. But, I haven't. All I do is get drunk while China eats me up and spits me out. The world spins, and I feel out of contr—"

"What the fuck is *Eat, Pray, Love?*" he questioned.

"It's a book."

"About the existential experience of Shanghai street food?"

"It's about a woman who travels."

"Let me guess. Along the way she eats, prays, and loves?"

"Something like that." I was starting to think that Jean-Louis was not the right person for this conversation.

"Sounds titillating."

"Stop thinking about tits for a second."

"Incoming lecture from Mr. Edo."

"Don't you feel like something is missing?"

"From this conversation?"

"From life."

"Didn't you just have a pep talk with Miles and Ken? Like a week ago. In the cab. This is what you silly Americans call *déjà vu*. Well, *déjà entendu*, if we're getting technical. Aren't you already at your pep talk quota?"

"I think that just got me thinking."

"Does this have anything to do with your track meet meltdown?"

"I think that day just opened my eyes. In an existential way. Like I'm trying to do some soul searching but the ground beneath me is so uneven that every time I try to take a look at myself, I see a fuzzy picture."

"You rehearse that shit in the mirror? Ed, we're twenty-three. Take a chill pill or go masturbate or something."

"My point exactly."

"Huh?"

"I don't know. I guess I'm trying to figure out what that point is. And this place isn't helping."

"This apartment?"

"This country."

"China is not helping you find a point?"

"Jean-Louis."

"Ed."

"I'm struggling here."

"I am too."

"C'mon man. Engage with me on this topic."

"Alright, Monsieur tête-à-tête. Relax."

"How do you do it, Jean-Louis? I don't mean to sound critical, but it's not like you're going to win teacher of the year. But in the face of adversity you are singularly the person who is most OK with any outcome that I have ever met. Like you believe in predetermination or something."

"Dude, you overestimate my intellectual quotient. It's not that. I just have a totally different outlook on this whole China thing than you guys do. Both my parents are lawyers. I'm down with the law. It's a good pathway for me, further along the road. I'm not going to wake up tomorrow and decide that I want to be a teacher for the rest of my life. So, this year is more like a journey rather than a destination. I don't really care about being the best teacher in the world or bettering myself as a human being or any shit like that. I'm twenty-three years old and I live in China. I'd rather get drunk, bang a Chinese girl (he winked at me), and have fun before my life gets serious later."

This was singlehandedly the most I'd ever seen Jean-Louis open up. And at once, his philosophy made sense. He had a direction in life already. A pretty decent one, at that. Not a life's calling, but a pathway. In China, he was purposefully off the Path.

"Oh." It was his most honest moment since I'd met him.

"Now, where are those other two turd burgers? Let's go buy some beers." His candor was short-lived.

Jean-Louis had already found what he was seeking, albeit somewhere else. Miles had found the place he was looking for, and China was it. Ken? I guess you could say he had found a process. FIS was his springboard to a future—his means of self-improvement toward destinations unknown.

Me? Searching for something is hard when you don't know what you're looking for.

My life kept spinning. Miles, meanwhile, was as optimistic as ever. Lost a track meet? *We'll win the next one!* Dysfunction up at school? *We'll sort it out.* The fact that he spoke Mandarin surely helped sooth the wounds from China's arrows. Or maybe it was just his attitude. Sometimes it seemed like the things that made me so crazy *in* China made him crazy *about* China.

One day, Miles spontaneously decided that he wanted to get himself a Chinese driver's license. I think he partly wanted to do it just to prove that he could. Maybe the nation of China just lit a flame under his ass. He reveled in the same chaos that tore me apart.

So how the hell do you get a driver's license in Shanghai? Miles was going to find out. Incredibly, they actually have a DMV, despite the absolute lawlessness that rules all roads and major thruways. One Saturday morning, Miles set out, determined to cut through the red tape and emerge with newly issued government identification.

"I don't think I could imagine a worse way in the world to pass a Saturday than at a Chinese DMV," I announced. Miles opened the door to leave our apartment.

"If you don't return, after how many hours should we just presume that you're dead?" Jean-Louis asked. "Like, when can I start combing through your personal effects?"

"Hmm...like ten. If I'm not back in ten hours, I probably died at the Chinese DMV," was his thoughtful response.

"Ten hours. Setting my watch."

"We've got a funeral service on speed dial."

"Who do you want to read your eulogy?"

"What sort of refreshments do you want us to serve at the wake?"

"Shut up, you idiots." And he walked out.

"Good luck, Miles!" I yelled to the already closed front door.

And he left.

"How much money could someone have to pay you to go the DMV right now?" I asked Jean-Louis and Ken.

"Probably like a year's salary," they nodded in unison. We popped in a DVD and relaxed. All of my recent failures were tiring me out.

The doorbell rang. Maybe Miles awoke from his trance?

A Chinese guy in his thirties stood at the door. He had jeans and a button-down shirt and held a clipboard in his left hand.

"Who is it?" Jean-Louis yelled.

"Chinese guy." I answered back. I turned to the guy. "*Ni hao.*"

"Bill collector?" Ken asked from afar.

The guy looked at me. Rather than trying to explain what he wanted, he simply resorted to sign language. He took his right hand, lifted it above his head, and sprinkled his fingers like a shower. *Water.* He showed me the water bill on his clipboard, and I paid him in cash. I retreated back to the couch.

"Seriously, guys," I started, "What would we *do* without Miles?"

* * *

Seven hours later, Miles returned.

"Man, we were about to send out a search party."

"You idiots wouldn't even be able to tell a Chinese search party who or what to look for," he chided.

"Probably right," I reasoned. "That's why you would have died after ten hours gone. Because we would have absolutely no way in hell to rescue you."

"So, did you get it? Are you now a licensed Chinese driver?" Ken asked.

Turned out, Miles didn't get the driver's license. He spent four hours in line and, at long last, managed to schedule a written test for the following week to actually attain the license. That took him seven hours.

One week later, it was back to the DMV for Miles. Once again, he returned after seven hours, but this time he flung open the apartment door with his arm victoriously pointed up.

He showed us the card. I couldn't understand a single word on it. His picture looked like a mug shot. In the end, all Miles had to do to score a driver's license in China was to pass a written test.

"Was it hard?" We all asked.

"No. No. No, it wasn't..." Miles trailed off.

"Many homicidal maniacs must have passed this test," Jean-Louis clipped Miles's wings.

"Many homicidal maniacs *plus one* appear to have passed the test," I corrected.

Miles continued: "One of the questions asked *how many* alcoholic drinks one should consume before driving."

"What were the answer options?" I cracked a big smile.

"0–2 drinks, 3–5 drinks, 6–8 drinks, or 9 or more drinks."

"Nine or more!" Jean-Louis was giddy. "I'd probably try to stick my dick in the ignition after nine drinks."

"Bet after twelve drinks you'd go for the tail pipe."

"Guys," Miles corralled us, "I correctly answered '0–2.'"

"Many *drunk* homicidal maniacs appear to have passed

the test. " Jean-Louis started slow-clapping sarcastically. "Brown University education, right there."

"Wow, Miles, I'm really proud of you, man." Ken was effervescent.

Homicidal maniacs. Now, Miles was officially one of them.

"Alright, so you've got a driver's license," Jean-Louis reasoned. "Now you just have to buy, rent, borrow, or steal a car."

Turned out that Miles had thought of this, too. He asked the Chinese teachers at school, before being pointed to Nina Song—the mother of one of our highest achieving students at Fudan International School. She worked in PR, and she was highly connected. I suppose you could call her a PR *guru*. She put Miles in contact with a car rental agency. We made a reservation, and the next day it was time to make like Columbus and go west. To where or to what? We had no idea. But, when your friend gets a driver's license in China, you go on a Chinese road trip. To where? Path unknown.

The next day, we walked into a decrepit, two-story, stucco building adjacent to a gas station, to which The PR Guru had referred us. The two guys behind the counter renting us the car could not have been giggling any more unabashedly at the four white idiots standing in front of them.

"Why are they laughing at us?" Ken asked me quietly while Miles negotiated the vehicle rental. "Did Miles do something wrong?"

"Besides having blonde hair, moving to China, getting a driver's license, and renting a car with a pile of cash, nope. Nothing wrong."

We signed a hundred different papers, which were all adorned with official looking red stamps. We plunked down some cash (always cash), and were shown to our vehicle, which was a highly used, yellow Volkswagen Santana 3000. The doors had rings of rust around the edges, and the tail pipe was held up with a coat hanger. It had no sideview mirrors.

"It's a taxi," Jean-Louis said, pointing out the obvious. And it was. It was an honest-to-god taxi. "It's a shitty fucking taxi."

"Shitty goddamned fucking taxi."

"Why the hell did we rent a taxi?" I asked, legitimately baffled.

"Guys, next time *you* rent the car, okay? Rent, hail, borrow, acquire—" Miles threw his hands up in the air, "—these are all similar words in Chinese. They probably thought we wanted to hail a taxi."

"And, because this is China, that is probably a not uncommon request." I nodded.

"Maybe that's why those dudes were laughing. They probably thought we had some taxi fetish." We looked at Jean-Louis. Ken scratched his chin. Jean-Louis opened the rear passenger door.

"It has seatbelts!" He started to a do an it-has-seatbelts dance.

We opened the doors and buckled up. I sat shotgun and unfolded the giant Chinese map given to us by the rental car guys. I started to sweat. Everything was in Mandarin. We peeled out onto the street ever so cautiously before coming to rest at a red light.

Immediately, someone flung open the rear passenger side door.

"Aaaaah!" We all screamed.

"Aaaaah!" A random Chinese guy screamed back. *This guy thinks he is hailing our taxi.*

"*Ni hao!*" Jean-Louis chirped.

The guy mumbled something in Mandarin, shut Jean-Louis's door, and jogged off.

"What the hell was that?" I turned around to Ken and Jean-Louis.

"He thought we were a real taxi! This is my new favorite car." Jean-Louis pressed his face against the glass and gave the taxi a kiss. "Miles, can we *please* pick up a Chinese passenger?"

"That middle seat in the back is unoccupied—we could have fit that guy!" I agreed.

"Fellas. Mission at hand is to leave the city, not scrounge up a couple extra RMB by illegally kidnapping some Chinese passengers in our illegitimate taxi."

"Well, when you put it *that* way..." Jean-Louis sounded like a kid who was told he couldn't have any ice cream.

"Miles! Highway onramp is up there on the right." I successfully navigated us to the East-West Shanghai highway, an artery to leave the city.

With a purposeful right-hand turn onto the highway onramp, Miles stepped on the accelerator.

"Here we gooooo!" He whipped around a truck and almost clipped a fellow taxi.

We all ~~shrieked like little girls~~ cheered in manly voices.

Miles settled in behind the wheel, and we drove west. Miles out of downtown, thirty story buildings were still sprouting up like weeds. Giant green highway signs directed motorists to an infinite array of roads, industrial districts, residential zones, and commercial plazas.

"Where to, gents?" I studied the map.

"To infinity and *beyond!*" Ken proclaimed, raising his right index finger into the air to add emphasis.

In the rearview mirror, I could see Jean-Louis cross his arms in disapproval.

"Hey Buzz Lightyear, do I have to pull this spaceship over and throw you out?" Miles asked.

Jean-Louis piped up: "You get one *Toy Story* reference for free. Drop another one on us and there will be trouble in the galaxy."

"Great movie. Unquotable to anyone over age sixteen," I added.

"Screw you guys," Ken harrumphed.

"Map says there's a lake like three inches away," I declared.

"Convert to miles," Miles said dryly.

"Forty-five miles."

Miles looked down at the speedometer. "Convert to kilometers."

"Like seventy."

"OK—random sketchy lake ETA, thirty minutes."

Ken did the math in his head. Average = ninety miles per hour. "Please drive slower than that," he whimpered.

"Random sketchy lake ETA, forty-five minutes."

We drove.

"Guys," Miles broke in. "A driver's license isn't all that I picked up at the DMV."

"You also picked up..." Ken started to guess. Miles reached into his pocket, took out a torn piece of paper and handed it to me.

"A phone number!" I revealed to the group.

"Miles!" Jean-Louis was impressed. "Story. Commence."

"Well, it was weird. I was in line at the DMV."

"Romance was in the air," I backseat drove.

"This Chinese girl kinda gave me the stink eye."

"She's Chinese!" Ken concluded.

"The girl was with her mother," he continued.

"It was the mother!" I yelled. "That would make you and Ken a pair of Eskimo brothers."

"Hey now."

"Will you three idiots shut up and let me tell the story?"

"Fine."

"The mother and the daughter look at me and sorta giggle to each other. I start to wonder if my fly is open or something, when the mother just waltzes over, tells me in Mandarin that I should 'date her daughter,' hands me the paper, and then walks away."

"No way."

"Yup. That was it. Now I have her digits."

"Unbelievable."

"You gonna call her?"

"It's about time I dipped my pen in Chinese ink."

Now off the highway, a sign, suspiciously in English, directed us counterclockwise around a large blue lake to the "Waterside Fun Park." *Sure, that sounds fun.* We motored towards this potential aqua paradise. What loomed? Water slides? A harbor? A puddle of water? We zoomed through an abandoned gated entrance and hummed inwards in our taxi.

It looked more like a giant industrial complex than a kiddie theme park. There was not a soul anywhere.

"Whoever designed this waterside fun park has definitely never been to Disney World."

"The designers probably grew up in a dirty Shenzhen factory."

Massive warehouse buildings popped up all around us. It was empty. This place was an old industrial park. Nothing but tin roofs, old paint, and cracked concrete.

After making a dozen turns and getting as close to the blue blob on our map as we could, we exited the car. I saw a blue lake of sorts in the distance, and we meandered toward it. We walked about two hundred feet to the water's edge and discovered a congregation of expatriates mingling and sharing laughs along the bank of the large azure lake. Green trees jostled in the wind in search of sunshine on this gray day. The water on the giant lake was calm. There must have been two hundred people, eating hamburgers and drinking Heinekens. It was a cheery atmosphere, despite the gloomy industrial park behind. Where were we?

"Who are these people?" Ken wondered apprehensively.

The group was removing small sailboats from the water. Some sort of competition had just finished. There were expat parents with expat kids, clearly enjoying their expat afternoon. Was this where expat families congregated on expat weekends? Did they really go expat sailing in this abandoned industrial park?

Out of nowhere, I heard Helga's unmistakable Turkish accent: "Oh yes the sailing was very nice." A few bystanders cleared out of our line of sight, and there she was.

"Helga! Hi! What are you doing here?" asked Ken, as he jogged up to her. She turned to us.

"Ohhhh, everyone is here! How are you? You have come to watch me do the sailing?" She was as genuinely surprised to see us as we her.

"Um, of *course* we are here to watch you sail," Jean-Louis answered before any of us could truthfully explain the coincidental encounter. I gave Jean-Louis the evil eye, as Helga was no idiot and surely realized we were not there to watch her do whatever it is she was doing, right? *Sailing?*

"I won the race!" She proclaimed, as though she finally remembered something she had desperately wanted to tell us since the moment of our chance run-in.

"That's great, Helga!" I congratulated her. *What race?* Then, a voice boomed over a microphone in English:

"Please quiet down everyone, we are set to begin the ceremony. Thank you." Jean-Louis and Miles looked at each other.

"In third place in the competition, team four!" The emcee, a Chinese gentleman with a polished British accent, read the names of the members of team number four. The four white guys strutted casually to the podium, received their small trophies, and did a mini fist pump to the polite soundtrack of third-place applause from the audience.

"Today's runners-up," he continued, "Team number one!" The process repeated.

"Now is me!" Helga giddily elbowed Ken. *No way,* I thought.

"And the winners of the race, team number two!" Raucous applause followed the reading of the four names, which, sure enough, included Helga. *What the.* Helga skipped over to the podium, grabbed the silver chalice, and hoisted it up for God to see. Her teammates were three white dudes. My jaw dropped and my head shook back and forth in incredulity. I was at loss for words, but I applauded and yelled Helga's name. She poured a Heineken into the trophy's cup and took a victory gulp.

We drove home. What a long, strange trip it had been.

"Good morning, class. Today, we are going to continue with our exciting journey through the parts of speech," I said to my students, with Monday morning enthusiasm.

Jin Mon looked as if she were about to cry. Even the impish, energetic student named Valiant glanced immediately at his oversized calculator watch.

"Today, we are up to *indirect objects*. Who can tell me what an indirect object is?"

"..."

"Well, can't really say I'm surprised by that. If you look at your printouts—"

I froze. In my hand, I held a fresh leaf of paper with a block of text written in out-of-touch, textbook-style language. *Indirect Objects: Definitions and Applications,* it read at the top. A rush of negative memories about my worst teachers growing up washed over me. Disbelief, from unmovable career educators with their empathy tanks out of gas, at why students hadn't powered through a textbook full of dull and unrelatable information about a subject matter light years away in importance from what truly mattered to adolescents.

In that moment, I just got it. This was my goddamned light bulb. I wouldn't want to talk to Mr. Ed at a party. I wouldn't want to tell my parents about Mr. Ed. I wouldn't write a college application essay about Mr. Ed.

It all changed in that moment. I saw Miles by the doorway, casually raising a metaphorical beer, his steady gaze and approving smile that this country simply could not derail warmly rushing through the room. The walls immediately flipped from the dull hue of a cubicle partitioned work place to an unassuming bar, its charming white frescos more emblematic of a local joint on a Mediterranean island, where the clock is forever stopped at 5:30 PM. Helga winked at me from the windy patio outside the bar. It was peaceful.

I saw Ken sitting down at the desk behind me, his head buried in his papers, life's answers written in invisible ink. I saw the brains of my half dozen students, waiting. This perfect and objective measure of how well I was doing and what I had achieved lay right in front of me. The totality of my work would manifest itself in my kids. I could see, hear, and feel them waiting to see, hear, and feel words emanate from my brain, to my mouth, to my hand holding the chalk, to their ears and eyes, to their pens and their notebooks, and then shot like an arrow into the deepest crevasses of their brains.

Jean-Louis sat in an empty chair in the corner of the room, feet on the desk in front of me. He peeled down his bottom lip and then gestured with two arms wide open at the entirety of the room, the school, the city, the country, reminding me not to take this all too seriously. It was so silly, this whole thing. It mattered so much, and in some ways. it didn't matter at all.

"Mr. Ed, are you OK?" The sweet-hearted Jin Mon had precocious empathy. She tilted her head down in concern and waved her right arm slowly back and forth, checking that I was still conscious.

"Why you smile, Mr. Ed?" Valiant was preoccupied with my vitals.

"Grab your handouts with two hands, like this." I instructed them coolly.

They looked at each other, and then picked up their handouts with two hands gripping the paper together on one side.

"Now, rip the paper in half." I demonstrated with an emphatic tear of my paper. Then, I threw the two halves in the air and yelled, "WOOP!"

They followed. Every student in the class threw their shreds sky high, the paper raining down like confetti. "WOOP!" they all yelled, in exactly the same pitch and volume as I had. We all laughed. Suddenly, I wanted to hang out with me again.

"OK, leave those papers on the ground. I'll clean them later. Today. we're gonna try something new. All this grammar stuff...guys, it's actually important! But, it's not important *just because it's important*. It's important so that you don't embarrass yourself at a cocktail party. So that you can speak and understand. That's it."

With their limited English vocabularies, they caught my gist.

"We know what verbs are, right? I *walk* to school; I *play* basketball; I *like* dumplings. I want everyone in the room to yell an action verb, any action verb. Ready?"

"Valiant!"

"Shoot!" he yelled, howling with laugher and turning his hands into guns.

"Jin Mon!"

"Love," she said dreamily, giving herself a mini-hug. The others followed in quick succession.

"Kick!"

"Sing!"

"Give!"

"Bake!"

"Yes!" I held my two hands up high. "Everyone of you is *exactly right*. You are all a bunch of geniuses." They giggled.

"Now," I continued. "Remember the boring classes last week about 'direct objects'?" They all made a vegetable face. "I want you to add a direct object to your verb." Remember that a direct object *receives the action* of the verb. I did a karate chop to signal a green light.

"Shoot the alien!"

"Love the boy."

"Kick my brother."

"Sing a song."

"Give a present."

"Bake the cake."

I gave each of them a high five as I bounced around the room. This was fun.

"Now, Lee and Kim," I gestured to two students, "You bring up two great examples," which are important for today's lesson about indirect objects. I grabbed a piece of chalk and turned around. On the board, I wrote, "I gave my friend a present."

"What's happening in this sentence? Am I *giving* my friend?" I held my arms out and pretended to carry an enormously heavy human being. I even feigned the strain of the weight of my imaginary person. I lumbered toward Lee's desk, feet spread wide to channel the weight of my fake friend down into my quads, and promptly dumped the "friend" onto Lee's desk, wiping off a bead of fake sweat in the process.

"I gave my friend," I proclaimed to the class, as they struggled to contain their giggles.

"Is this what's happening? I am 'giving' my friend?"

"No!" Lee interjected confidently. "You gave gift *to* your friend."

"Yes! Lee is absolutely right. In this sentence, 'friend' is what's called an indirect object. The indirect object is affected by the action of the verb, but it does not receive the action." I wrote another example on the board: "I baked my mother a cake."

"What's happening in this sentence?" I asked them. "Am I baking my mother?"

Santa Clause has never heard of Asia, but FIS still gave us a two-week Christmas break from teaching. In the spirit of Rudolph, Donner, Vixen, Blitzen, Prancer, and all the other reindeer whose names you forget once you turn six, the Fudan International School faculty decided that we should throw our students a Western-style Christmas party before the break. It was a haphazard arrangement that teed up a fascinating cultural clash.

We decorated a large classroom with the usual Christmas nonsense. Where all of these items came from, I have no idea. Helga had somehow managed to obtain a full-size fake Christmas tree. In retrospect, every single fake Christmas tree in America is probably manufactured in China, so I guess it can't be that hard to find one in Shanghai if you shake a few...trees.

In the corner of the room were several cardboard boxes containing a shipment of books destined for the FIS school library. Its shelves were slowly filling up.

The party began. Within fifteen minutes, the entire FIS student body was assembled in the extra-large classroom. Within sixteen minutes, the boys were standing on one side of the room and the girls were standing on the other, an empty chasm between them. Some things never change. Christmas music adorned the room at a modest volume, pumping through a pair of computer speakers with insufficient bass.

Mr. Pancake, the head administrator of FIS, was present, and was bopping (this is what pancakes do, they bop) his head in delight at what an apparent success his pet school had become. We exchanged mutual nods.

Things at the party were a bit stiff. "Jingle Bell Rock" proved to be the tipping point, however, when the highly suggestive eleventh grade student named Mona and another Taiwanese girl suddenly burst into the chasm between the lads and the ladies and began to groove suggestively. Russell Johnson, the wooly, older FIS teacher, looked particularly keen on the sight of Mona dancing.

All the boys stared. A seventh grader dropped his can of soda. It was a revelation. The twisting dips, sways, and thrusts of Mona and her female dance partner aged the male student population by six years in the span of six seconds.

After a jaw-dropping minute of Shakira-like swagger, these

two little ladies began to beckon and even taunt the boys to join them, at some points even attempting to physically grab the arms of some instantly petrified boys in an attempt to secure a dance partner. Though mesmerized in a hypnotic trance, the boys and their arms recoiled as soon as Mona tried to snatch an appendage with her serpentine lunges.

Mona and her buddy, however, had the effect of encouraging some of the other girls onto the dance floor to experiment with some shy, subtle, dance maneuvers. The gender interaction thermometer still read zero degrees, but at least a few groups of girls were now giggling and gyrating. By comparison, Mona seemed to swing her hips a tad too suggestively. *That's not good...*

Slowly but surely, some of the boys wormed their way towards the center of the classroom to unshackle their inner John Travoltas. It was Tuesday Afternoon Fever. Mr. Pancake's head was now bobbing so emphatically it looked as if it were going to snap off and roll across the dance floor.

Shortly thereafter. I was witnessing a full-fledged high school dance party—in China. Our shy little misfits were dancing. I couldn't believe it.

After twenty minutes, our Puerto Rican Dean of Students

and our Slovakian English-language coordinator grabbed a broomstick and began a perennial party favorite: the limbo. It was a huge hit. Later came the Conga line, led by Mr. Pancake himself. Half an hour after that, the Macarena.

There was no booze, but it was magical what a little bit of sugar and caffeine could accomplish. Despite our many failures as a school, this was the first moment at FIS when I looked around and saw smiles everywhere. For a fleeting moment, I thought, "It's *working*." We were all paddling our oars in the same direction. Our little startup international school had all of this promise—I could just feel it.

Linda was in the corner clapping her hands rhythmically. Mr. Pancake's head was bouncing like a bobble head doll. Ken, Jean-Louis, and Miles were leading another Conga line. Helga was in the corner repeating, "Very nice" again and again. The math teacher Mr. Lu was double-fisting two open cans of Coca-Cola.

Miles looked at his watch, winked at me, and darted out of a corner door to go meet his new Chinese girlfriend for a cup of tea. I smiled and shook my head at him in disbelief. And the world kept turning.

Maybe we can make something of this place, with our merry band of misfits on the other side of the Earth.

* * *

Over the next few days, our makeshift educational operation held end-of-semester exams. Desks emptied and chalkboards were erased. Doors closed.

I had been living in Shanghai for almost five months now. I hadn't drowned, but I wasn't swimming. I could have been a better teacher, sure. But my outlook felt different. And my kids were learning. A little bit. Some were spoiled and some were lazy, but others were exemplary. Getting up in front of a bunch of students to lecture about English grammar and writing was no longer the worst thing in the world.

I taught. I put together lesson plans. I watched my students grow, just a bit. I wanted them to learn more. I wanted to do better. I finally admitted to myself that I was having a little bit of fun. After handing in their final tests, a number of students had even smiled on their way out. Things felt lighter.

It was now mid-December and I was alone in my classroom, having just finished grading the last of my heap of student exams. The results weren't an abomination. I guess sometimes you have to call that progress. My pupils managed not to fall on their faces. I'll take it.

The next day, I had a flight back to New York to see my

family for a few weeks. To recap my adventures in the Orient. To show them how I had matured. To tell them what I had learned. To "say something in Chinese."

I closed my laptop, put the cap back on my pen, and packed up my backpack. I walked toward the door of my classroom and turned off the light. I peered back at the dark room.

Four tight walls to call my own in a small school in a big country. One little nook of control in an oasis of insanity. Miles away, our giant apartment yearned for its over-privileged occupants. Down below, the streets teemed with momentum. This was a country where things happened, whether you wanted them to or not.

I looked up toward the classroom window. The undressed glass framed a cold gray sky atop the futuristic metropolis. This was China. Somewhere, the naked old men were blow-drying their balls and then heading to an underground cricket fighting circuit. Somewhere, the prostitutes were twirling their hair and practicing clientele negotiation tactics. Somewhere, poor Kotaro was scratching his head. Up above, the stars twinkled faintly, China's gray polluted haze cloaking the night's majesty. I took a deep breath.

# Part Two

I stood atop the open-air viewing platform of the Oriental Pearl TV Tower. The erect antenna shot up into the night sky above. Hundreds of feet down below, the frenzied twinkling of the Shanghai Pudong skyline didn't sleep. The usual audio hullabaloo from the streets was drowned out by a cold winter wind, which made me shiver. I looked left and then right. I was alone.

The platform had no railing. Through the metal grate under my bare feet, I could see down to the street in the distance below. I turned around, my back to the edge of the platform. Inch by inch, I nudged my heels back toward the precipice. Despite the cold, I now felt warm. Or I couldn't feel the temperature. I closed my eyes and continued edging backward. At last, I felt no force under my heels, just the strength in my toes now keeping me grounded on the mantel of Pudong. I spread my arms wide, to maximum wingspan, bent my knees, and leaned back. As I felt the pull downward, I extended my legs straight, my body lurching outward from the platform into a backward swan dive, falling.

I opened my eyes, the façade of the tower rushing upward in front of me. The open-air standing platform began to shrink, but before it collapsed to a speck, I saw myself, donning a crisp pinstriped suit, standing atop it calmly, waving to my falling self. Something was wrong.

The gnawing beep of my cell phone alarm jolted me from jetlagged slumber.

*Where am I? Is any of this real?*

My eyes crept open. For real this time. I was back in Shanghai. 7:00 AM Sunday morning. It was January. It was cold.

My exam. I had an exam. My heart pounded. A test? Yes. A medical test. Yes. Something about my visa. Was everything all right? I rubbed my eyes. I needed a medical examination to renew my visa. The exam was this morning.

\* \* \*

Two weeks prior, I'd had "the talk" with the parents.

"So, how is your job?" they'd both asked.

"Honestly, the school is kind of a mess. The problem is we don't have great standards. The leadership doesn't feel present, and there is a sense of mistrust between the Chinese teachers and the Americans. We don't have the right supplies, books, or anything. And our students are all at such a mix of English language skills that the strongest students feel underwhelmed while the worst feel left behind."

"That's a thorough assessment," my father was taken aback. "And are you learning?"

"I guess. I mean, my job is hard sometimes."

"Is this is what you want to do with your career? Teach? Abroad?" My dad's fact-gathering was earnest.

"I honestly don't know."

"Would you consider looking for jobs here in New York?"

"I honestly don't know."

"It can't hurt," my dad reasoned.

"I honestly don't know."

My mother squished her face pensively. "Do you think that the school can change?"

"I do," I responded. And I believed it. I really did.

"I think you're ready to apply for a job at a New York bank. The big leagues," my dad started. "With this China thing, I think you've got the resume."

The Path.

"Dad, for once I actually have a job."

"I know, but maybe you'll see things differently in a few months," he said ominously.

"OK. Fine."

It got me thinking. What lay beyond China? Maybe I liked the idea of working, of having a steady job, of being like everyone else. I thought about Independent Me, building a life on the other side of the world. Maybe things weren't so bad here in NYC. What the hell? I applied to some "business" jobs. I'd heard some friends glow about their business jobs. Maybe that was also something I could figure out, could conquer. China had instilled in a new confidence in me.

I got an interview at a place called Monitor Group, a business management consultancy. Yeah, that's a mouthful. I studied up for the business case interview a few days later.

I studied hard, but I wasn't sure why. This was something that I theoretically didn't want, but I still felt compelled to do well, like doing well at this would prove that I was good at my other thing. My job. So, I gave it my all, reading and practicing. The teacher became a student.

The day of, I grabbed an old hand-me-down pinstriped suit of my father's and took a yellow taxi to midtown Manhattan. I felt...I don't know what I felt. I guess I hardly thought about it. It didn't feel that abhorrent a process (are there degrees of abhorrence?), and some of the interview questions were pretty...stimulating, even. They invited me back a few days later for another series of interviews. I studied more. They told me they'd be in touch. My dad was satisfied. Oddly, so was I.

In a cab en route to the Sunday morning medical examination, I reflected back on the fall. All of our wild nights floated through my cave of memories like a schizophrenic mist. I got dizzy just thinking about them. The mist evaporated, and the striking images that remained were the faces of all of my students.

Six of the FIS American teachers were due for the examination. We walked into the nondescript building in a nondescript neighborhood. We checked in at the nondescript desk and, almost immediately, four medical assistants in lab coats emerged from behind a door. They proceeded to talk very loudly at us, gesticulating wildly, as if recapping a story at the family dinner table. *Do I look like I understand Mandarin?*

Even Miles seemed vexed by the proceedings.

We sat down in the non-descript waiting room. One by one, we were summoned.

Then it was my turn.

"Mista Eduardo Mestre?"

I followed the nurse to a medical examination room. She sat me on the paper rollout atop the familiar doctor's office patient chair. The room featured the usual doctor's office staples. The out-of-date standing scale, a hanging stethoscope. Still sleepy, I let out a big yawn, turned my head right, and covered my mouth so as not to be rude.

There it was. On the desk in the examination room. My QUARANTINE form from the airport in August.

*Holy fuck.*

It still had the checkmark next to every single disease known to man.

"Mista Eduardo Mestre, this is your quarantine form, yes?"

"Um."

"OK. We must do testing."

"No, no, no, that was a mistake. When I returned to Shanghai a week ago I filled the form out correctly."

"We do standard testing Mista Eduardo," she smiled at me as she slapped on a pair of rubber gloves. *Oh my god.*

I was brought from medical room to medical room. There was poking and there was prodding. All I could do was smile and nod. I gave four vials of blood. I got the stethoscope treatment, and I was photographed and x-rayed.

Then I entered the final room.

"Please, Mista Eduardo, you go backward." The nurse gently instructed, in English.

Please don't let this last test have anything to do with my ass. I turned around so that my back was facing her. *China, I will never ask for anything again—please, no butt stuff.*

"No, no, you go on the back."

"Oh, you want me to *lie* on my back. Got it." *Phew.*

"Your shirt, Mista Eduardo."

"Uh."

"Up the shirt."

"Lift my shirt?"

She then proceeded to rub cold jelly all over my stomach. Agh! I gasped at the temperature and the freaky sensation.

"Cold?" She smiled at me. Yes, your alien jelly is cold, you devil woman.

Next she grabbed a device that looked like a giant vibrator, and proceeded to rub it all over my stomach. Wait a minute. This was a sonogram. A sonogram!

I could see the little image flickering on the screen beside me. There was no fetus. I think. The mess of green lines on the screen was harder to decipher than the TSA X-ray scanner.

In the end, I was NOT pregnant, even though if I stuck my belly out just a little extra from a side angle it kinda looked like I might be expecting twins named "Bud" and "Weiser."

God, I loved this place. CHINA!!! It was good to be back.

"Guys! Inbound missive from Nina the PR Guru!" Ken thundered.

"Missive? Jesus, *c'est un email,*" Jean-Louis cackled. "What does it say?"

"It saaays..." Ken stroked an index finger down his laptop screen as he digested the contents of Nina's email, "that we are invited to dinner with her and a few friends from a Shanghai Buddhist temple."

"Huh?"

"We are invited to dinner with her and a few friends from a Shanghai Buddhist tem—"

"We heard you," Jean-Louis interrupted. "I meant 'huh,' as in 'Why the fuck is she inviting us to dinner with people from her temple?'"

"Her group from temple? Is that like her church group?" I asked, genuinely unsure.

"Yep, except they are all vegetarians." Miles coolly interjected, as he popped a potato chip into his mouth.

"Check this out," Ken continued, "Among the attendees, she mentions a Buddhist monk. Also, she says that she wishes to dine with us in order to 'meet the esteemed educators of her son,'" Ken put air quotes around this last part. Her son was a fifteen-year-old at our school. *Uh-oh.* Royce.

"And a monk? God, this is a bizarre country." I shook my head.

I'd seen a number of monks wandering around the streets of Shanghai. I had never engaged one in conversation. Passing one on the street was sort of like passing a blind guy with a cane. You deliberately jump out of the way.

"I feel like if you turn down dinner with a Buddhist monk and God is actually Buddhist, you will be reborn as a cockroach."

"Draconian, much?" Ken pondered.

"You do realize that Buddhism recognizes lots of gods?" added Miles.

"MULTIPLE angry gods then."

"I do realize. We *have* to attend the dinner."

We felt obliged. Are you even allowed to RSVP "no" to a Buddhist monk? What is proper monk etiquette? I grew up on Park Avenue with my mother touting Tiffany's Table Manners, but there was no chapter on monk etiquette.

We RSVP'd yes. Next question: what to wear?

"Something between a t-shirt and a tuxedo," Jean-Louis ventured.

"Helpful."

"Very helpful." Miles concurred.

"You're welcome."

"What I meant by 'helpful' was 'not at all helpful,'" I clarified. "Is it racist to just assume that the monk will be wearing an orange robe? Is that a race thing?"

"Pretty sure it's a religion thing," Miles shook his head at me.

"Well, you could say it's a *color* thing," Jean-Louis beamed. He had a point.

Was the monk's closet just full of nothing but orange robes, the way Superman's closet has only blue spandex and red capes?

The night of the dinner, Miles, Ken, Jean-Louis and I all debated the topic. We all settled for slacks and a button down. Respectful, but not attention-grabbing. We threw on our winter coats and walked out. Our extended wardrobe debate made us late for dinner.

"The rest of your party is waiting in the back room," the hostess informed us, in impeccably crisp English, as we entered Jendow Vegetarian Restaurant. "Please follow me."

We entered the private dining room. A woman with soft features, jet-black hair, and a don't-fuck-with-me pantsuit stood up from her seat. This was undoubtedly Nina the PR Guru.

"The esteemed educators of my first-born son, it is a great honor to have your acquaintance."

"Damned glad to meet you," Jean-Louis dove in for a handshake, as though Nina the PR Guru were his bro. We all gave him the stink eye.

"Lovely to meet you, Nina," I offered her a dual-hand shake, plus something in between a bow and a curtsey. Her hands were limp and cold, her gaze steely.

"Please allow me to introduce Master Hui Ming."

"Nice to meet you, Mister Hui Ming," said Jean-Louis.

"His title is *Master* Hui Ming," Nina the PR Guru gently corrected him.

Not to propel stereotypes, but the monk had a shaved head and an orange robe. He was undoubtedly *Master Hui Ming. Master?* I wondered.

Almost as though we rehearsed it, Ken, Miles, Jean-Louis, and I lined up horizontally, clasped our palms together as if praying, and offered a synchronous quarter bow. Master Hui Ming responded with a gentle nod, the subtlest affirmation of our existence.

Some sort of Chinese-English translator sat to his right, and Nina Song sat to his left. We four amigos took up the other end of the table, directly opposite the monk. We were the last of the group to arrive.

"Sorry that we are late. We had a little trouble finding the eight-fold path to the restaurant," I jested. *Where did that come from?*

Total silence. Not just total silence—people froze when they heard my off kilter joke. Everyone froze except Master Hui Ming. The translator leaned over and whispered into Master Hui Ming's ear. Then Master Hui Ming also froze and stared at me. *Real smooth, Ed.*

I zoned out for a little. What was I thinking with that comment? We chatted and ordered food. Vegetables for everyone.

The monk looked graceful with his chopsticks. The way you'd expect a chopstick-wielding monk would be. He flaunted the wooden tongs as if they were his sixth and seventh fingers, nabbing vegetables with the dexterity of a surgeon. And that robe. *Does that thing have pockets? Where does he carry cell phone? Is his cell phone made of gold?*

We dined mostly in silence. It made me nervous. *Are we meditating? What's happening here?* My eyeballs darted left and right, and I mimicked the pace at which others were eating and drinking. I tried to breathe silently while

I chewed my cabbage purposefully, with extra chomps to measure my pace.

Out of nowhere, Nina the PR Guru turned her head to the four of us and projected across the table in English, "You now may make questions to Master Hui Ming."

Make questions? We all looked at each other cowardly before Jean-Louis bravely ventured, "Are there many Buddhist temples in Shanghai?"

One of Master Hui Ming's minions translated, received his master's answer, and then translated back into English: "There are three."

Right. There was a lengthy pause before Ken timidly stepped in.

"What are some of the unique qualities of the form of Buddhism practiced around Shanghai?" At the dinner table, Ken was always the accidental academic.

The translator did his exchange with Master Hui Ming. "Buddhism is one."

Right. What to ask the monk? Think of a question, Ed!

"What is the role of Vishnu in the Buddhist belief system?" I finally blurted out.

"Ed, that's Hinduism," Miles whispered into my ear. *Gulp*. "Shit." The translator flipped my idiocy (and possibly my swearing) into Mandarin, and Master Hui Ming then replied, translated into English:

"Master Hui Ming thinks you made a good joke."

*Phew*. I dodged a bullet with that one.

The end of dinner mercifully arrived, and the translation minion handed us the business card for Master Hui Ming. It was brightly colored gold.

We also received Nina the PR Guru's business card. It said that Mrs. Nina Song was the CEO of a major Shanghai consulting firm. It appeared that simply being a white person in China quickly finds you friends in high places.

"Whelp, that was a medium-sized embarrassment," I moped as we walked out.

"Yeah," Jean-Louis pondered. "If this Buddhism thing is for real, you're probably gonna get reincarnated as a medium-sized lump of turd."

A few weeks later, my mother came out for a visit, to take a dip in the veritable pot of boiling water I called home. She was set to spend two days in Shanghai, watching me teach during one of them, before we jetted off together to the ancient city of Xi'an (SHEE-ahn) for the weekend.

My mother was always, uh, efficient. Growing up, she balanced a full-time private practice as an allergy MD and raised three children in the city that never sleeps. She was always the only mother to routinely show up at my soccer games with Snapple and Dunkin' Donuts, not to mention she can roast a mean Thanksgiving turkey. I think the only time she sits down is to go to sleep.

She is also one hell of a traveler, routinely roaming the world's remote tourist spots with the zest of a fifteenth-century European explorer. She has an uncanny ability to adopt the local accent of each country she visits, fitting in like a rainforest frog that changes color depending on its environment. To this day, she's still mad that my friends and I once drank a bottle of Chinggis Vodka from Mongolia gifted to her by a leading local doctor in Ulaanbaatar.

That said, she's not without her faults. She has mediocre balance, and she is the last remaining person on Earth to still confuse Michael Jackson and Michael Jordan. My sisters and I sometimes call her "O.R." because of her penchant for overreaction. Needless to say, despite her warmth, I always felt compelled to hide my vulnerabilities from her, to impress her. This occasion was no different.

Before she arrived, I scrubbed our apartment top to bottom using a bottle of Chinese brand imitation Windex® and six rolls of imitation Bounty® paper towels. At school, I ordered my students' desks into tight parallel rows. I had to prove to her that I had made it, that things were going great. I wanted to give her cocktail party fodder. I wanted her to be able to boast about her responsible son and all the great work he was doing in Shanghai as a teacher.

My mother opened the door to our apartment downtown.

"It does have a charming odor," she remarked after a hug hello.

"The smell of four gringos in China?"

"Think that's it."

"Check out our views, though."

"Wow. And you can afford this?" she asked disbelievingly. I nodded.

"It does look like that building is gonna lop off your view soon. Must only be ten stories below."

"Ugh, I know. It has been flying up."

"I have to say I'm impressed," she told me the next day, after the end-of-the-school-day Happy Birthday tune chimed.

We'd spent the prior class period acting out a short play about pirates that my middle school students had written together. The sweet seventh grader named Jin Mon Rho had walked the invisible plank at the urgency of the four-feet tall ship captain named Valiant. True to form, their play had more casualties than the two World Wars combined. Valiant's fictional reign of terror that day earned him the nickname, "Violent Valiant."

Four of my students flashed me the peace sign. "Have good weekend, Mr. Ed!" they said in unison.

"Mr. Ed," Jin Mon Rho said quietly to me as she exited the room, "for first time in my life, teacher is my friend." Before I could respond, she calmly walked out.

My mother witnessed the encounter and pressed two hands against her heart. I felt relieved. The teacher had passed the test. Sometimes I'd wondered if my mom was 100 percent sure that Fudan International School was a real place, with real human beings doing real work educating real students. On paper, it sounded ridiculous. My college peers were analysts, coordinators, and associates. I was an Oriental orchestrator of middle school pirate plays. The funny thing was, here it took the most imaginary of my lessons to prove that what I had was real.

"That was just so so so so wonderful!" My mother beamed in her typical, overly excitable fashion.

I felt as if my risky China bet had paid off. In the meantime, it was off to Xi'an.

\* \* \*

Before 1974, Xi'an was the unremarkable capital of Shaanxi (SHANshee) province. That year, however, peasants made a remarkable archaeological discovery: thousands of life-sized terracotta clay warriors buried underground, dating back to the third century BC. Sheltered by four medieval style city walls, Xi'an was a shrunken anachronism compared to Shanghai.

Our first evening there, my mother and I headed to the

Muslim Quarter. The night air was chilly, and you could see your breath. I shivered. We passed a hole-in-the-wall grilling up mutton kebab and other unidentifiable carnivorous delights on a street-side grill. Sold. We entered the drab establishment, removed our coats, and took a seat.

Pointing and gesturing, we ordered a plate containing an assortment of spicy mystery meats served on sticks, as well as two beers. Quite satisfied with my savvy maneuvers at the table, I taught my mother "Cheers" in Chinese—"*Gan bei!*" (Gone BAY)—and we dug in. *Look Mom, I'm doing great in China!*

Immediately I grabbed some mutton and tried to rip it with my teeth from the kebab stick rather than delicately slide it off. This plan backfired. The meat was tough, and just as my first piece was about to spring free from the stick, it flung back like a rubber band and smacked me directly in my right eye. This otherwise would have been a minor embarrassment, but the meat was smothered in spice. I had shot chili sauce directly into my eye. *Shit!*

The pain was instant and excruciating. "OOOOOW!"

"OUCH! That looks like it hurts." My mother was a trained doctor but in this situation a terrible nurse.

"Spicy mutton projectile in my right eye. My face is on fire! What should I do?"

"Pour something on it!"

"All we have is beer!"

"Pour something on it!"

I grabbed the bottle of beer, tilted by head back, and dumped the beer directly into my eye.

"Better!"

"Told you so," she smiled warmly.

"You just wanted to see me dump a beer on my face."

"I'm your mother. I've seen a lot worse than that."

Finally the pain eased. I had lager all over my hair and clothes. I grabbed another stick of mutton, and ever so graciously slid off a piece with my teeth, and proceeded to chew.

\* \* \*

The next morning, together with a tour guide that our

hotel arranged, my mother and I taxied away from the city proper to the site of the legendary terracotta warriors. This was going to be one of those bucket list kind of days.

Apparently, 1.4 billion other people shared my dream. When we pulled into the parking lot of the terracotta warriors archaeological site, there were at least one hundred tour buses parked ahead of us, and we could not walk more than a few feet without being swallowed by a Chinese tour group mob, always in matching red hats or t-shirts.

As wealth in China had just recently begun to accumulate in many smaller cities and poorer provinces, many Chinese were now able to afford their first vacations. Can you imagine what that must feel like? Your first vacation? As an adult?

The principal attraction in Xi'an is a series of four underground pits containing several thousand life-sized terracotta clay warriors. There are foot soldiers, cavalry, generals, archers—an entire army made out of clay, situated in a cavernous warehouse. A true archaeological work in progress.

We stepped into the warehouse containing the primary excavation pit. Below us, there were multiple football fields of menacing, life-sized, terracotta warriors, each in tight formation assuming a unique battle position. Their original paint had long worn off, each now a matching dull brown hue. My mother held my shoulder for balance and looked up at the bowed ceiling way above. The place felt like the world's largest airplane hangar.

"Well, you picked a pretty impressive thing to do for your first job. This sure beats Midtown Manhattan." I gave her a hug. The day's highlight, however, occurred on our way out of the archeological complex.

"Mom, what's that over there? Looks like a souvenir shop."

"Never miss an opportunity."

We meandered the aisles of souvenirs and other trinkets before arriving at the back wall of the shop, where there were life-size replica terracotta warriors, built exactly as the originals were built.

"Wait, you can *buy your own* terracotta warrior?" I exclaimed.

"Oh my. I think you can."

"Are you interested in purchasing your own terracotta warrior?" The saleswoman interjected with impeccable timing. This wasn't her first tourist rodeo.

"It must be ten feet tall," Mom whispered to me. Divide by two. It was five feet tall.

"Sure."

"How much does one cost?" My mother asked. This wasn't her first tourist rodeo either.

"This one here, that you are looking at, costs $2,000 USD," the sales woman offered deftly, in perfect English.

"*Tai gui le!*" I blurted. My mother raised an eyebrow. "It means 'too expensive,'" I muttered to her, using my impressive, adult tone of voice.

"OK, what price will you pay for authentic terracotta warrior?" The sales woman asks.

"Well, for starters, do you ship to the United States?" My mother reasoned.

The sales lady replied her well-rehearsed assurance: "Yes of course. The shipping is included in the sales price, to any country in the world."

"Good thing, Mom, because no way you are fitting a six-foot clay statue into your carry on."

My mother thought for a moment. "OK, we will offer—"

"...$200!" I cut her off.

"$200...is too little," pouted the saleswoman, in a hardly believable voice. "Will you pay $1,000?"

"$300." I folded my arms.

"$800."

"$350. Final offer."

She thought about it for a hot minute.

"OK, you have a deal."

"WOW!" my mother shook my shoulders once the attendant scampered away. "You were so great there! Like the Michael Jackson of negotiations!" She gave me a quick hug. "That was so impressive! So totally impressive." Classic mom over-reaction. "I'm so proud of you. Sure you don't want to go into finance?"

"Thanks, Mom, but no thanks."

She looked at me. "Gosh, you've come a long ways in a year." Her eyes held an unfamiliar gaze. Like an artist who has just set down her paintbrush. Her smile was the largest she could manage without showing teeth, as if she wished to keep the source of her happiness all to herself. The corner of her eyes hid the beginnings of mirthful wrinkles.

What you actually *do* with a life-sized clay warrior statue that you bought in China is another story. For now, my mother and I looked at each other and laughed.

All in a day's work.

For a brief period of time each year, it actually gets cold in Shanghai. Over the next two months, winter winds wrapped Shanghai like a frigid bear hug. A frigid *panda* bear hug. Better analogy.

We didn't exactly hibernate. We normalized. Weekend nights were tamer, and for about six weeks, I entered into the first really adult routine of my brief existence as a human being. I buckled down and got to work. The hallways of FIS teemed with the typical shrills of adolescence, and we even had the pleasure of welcoming a few new students into our school.

Miles started dating the Chinese girl he met in the DMV. She was mute and didn't speak a word of English. On evenings out on the town, she was often just his conversation piece. A prop. A prop that he had sex with.

"Good to see you, everyone. This is my Chinese girlfriend."

That's how he started his conversations. I can't even remember her name.

Even Ken and Jean-Louis had eased off of the gas pedal. Normalcy was contagious.

What was Riley up to? I wasn't really sure. I decided that I wanted to start seeing Molly from Minnesota more exclusively. Our super-long reverse courtship had been in neutral for months, and it was time to step on it and make a big boy decision. I was ready for this.

I hate to say it, but there is something sexy about stability, about having something to grab onto. I think it's the notion of not being flung into a panic every time your alarm clock goes off. For the briefest whisper of a moment, I became comfortable with the thought of working from 9:00 AM to 5:00 PM at a steady job, in a steady relationship. The r-word. It tasted tangy coming out of my mouth.

Before you picture me with a mortgage and a minivan, recall that this was still China, where tranquility is a four-letter word.

"I think we should start seeing each other exclusively," I told Molly one night over a carefully orchestrated dinner, on a cold Thursday night in late February. I had made us a reservation at Jean George, a fancy French restaurant overlooking the Bund, with the futuristic Pudong skyline across the river roaring through the wall of windows next to our table.

"Excuse me?" She sounded surprised. Not a good sign. I was tongue-tied.

"You're the one thing I've connected to since I've been here. Hanging out with you is singularly the thing I look forward to the most each week. I think we can make this work. I'm opening myself up, and think that we could be great together. I, uh, like you."

"I'm leaving China," she replied.

"What ~~the fuck~~?"

"I just, I just can't do it anymore."

"Is it because of...me?"

"Oh lord, Ed. No. God, no. Epic misread."

"It's not me, it's you?"

"It's not you, it's them."

"It's not me, it's *them*?"

"Ed. It's not you. It's...China." She paused, took a sip of Cabernet Sauvignon, and gestured in a circle with her free hand.

"I'm just tired. This place makes me tired," she continued. She looked apologetic. But only a little.

"Tired?"

"The people, the pace, the noise, the language—"

"But you *speak* the language," I interrupted.

"I'm tapping out."

"So that's it?"

"I leave next week."

"That's it?"

"That's it."

"Well, talk about your all-time backfires."

"I'm sorry," she said.

"Guess we can skip dessert."

A week later, she left for some new government job in Washington, DC. That was it. It stung. If she couldn't make it here, what the hell was I doing here? In a way, China was a rotating door for expats. People came. They left. They returned. They were invigorated. They got tired. They left again. On this particular occasion, I was on the inside of the revolving door, looking out. Maybe it was a sign that I should be on my own.

I was stunned. I guess sometimes, that's youth. The hits come fast and hard. What next?

\* \* \*

I took the elevator to the third floor of our class building. The doors clanged opened to a stiff gust of winter wind from inside the hallway. It was chillingly cold.

FIS had a cleaning lady (called an "ayi") who would always leave the windows open. All of them. Not just a couple. Literally every single window. No matter the temperature.

Why did she do this? Our school had no cleaning supplies. So, every day the ayi would take her filthy mop and push puddles of dirty water around in circles. Her bucket had no device for squeezing the water out of the mop, so her cleaning efforts would essentially just dump gallons of dirty water onto the floor of the school, turning our hallways into a miniature water park.

She possessed no separate tool for drying the water, so she had to seek out other means to dry the floors. Maybe a little bit of fresh winter air. All this aside, to complement her swimming pool conversion, the ayi was singularly obsessed with locking all of the classroom and office doors, thereby turning lowly Fudan International School into open-air aqua dungeon. That is why the windows were open.

I finally asked Wei and Jing, the furtive Chinese teachers with whom I lunched earlier in the year, why the ayi did this stupid thing.

"She dry the floors," Wei told me.

"Solving one problem by creating a bigger problem. Like cutting off your arm to save your hand," I replied.

"Americans cut arms?" Jing asked me, quizzically.

"No no no. Forget I asked."

Every morning, when I would think to remind the ayi not to turn our workspace into a freezer, she would vanish like a flashlight in a hall of mirrors.

So, each day I would methodically walk down the hallway and close each window one by one, only to find them all wide open again within the hour. The students complained, but I was powerless to help them.

One morning, I confronted her. I began: "*Wo men yao...*" ("We want...") Then, I motioned with my arms the action of closing a window. The only problem was, pulling your arms down from above to mimic the closing of a window makes it eerily look like you are trying to hump somebody.

She interpreted my babbling as, "We want hump." She scratched her head and ran away. The windows stayed open.

This was winter in Shanghai. I blinked, and it was March.

It warmed up pretty quick. They say that Shanghai has two seasons: winter and summer. Winter ended, spring-cameforasecond, and suddenly it was summer.

One sun-drenched weekend, Ken had found himself some extra work in Shanghai teaching Advanced Placement US history test preparation to overly advantaged students from our parent high school, Fudan Fuzhong. One of those sorts of jobs that falls into the laps of white people in China.

"Guys, I could really use the money. I need to start saving."

"Tell that to your drunk alter ego. He's a big spender," said Miles.

"Truth is," Ken continued, "it will be good for me to get a broader experience teaching a different set of kids. I feel like I'm getting good at this whole preparing and presenting deal."

"You mean teaching."

"Yeah. But more than that. Near the end of college, I felt eminently un-hire-able. I think my work in the classroom has made me eminently more articulate."

"I would agree, your eminence," I teased.

"Be quiet, Ed. You guys go frolic this weekend, I'm going to earn eminently more cash and eminently refine my teaching skills."

Miles, Jean-Louis, and I, meanwhile, thought it time to emerge from hibernation and take another trip. Things at school had been going well, and for once, I felt as if I had "earned" a weekend off. So where to?

On Thursday night, we opened up our China guidebook and sought out the place within striking distance of Shanghai that had the prettiest pictures. Really scientific. In ten minutes, we had a winner—the island of Putuoshan, a "mystical religious island just a short ferry ride from Shanghai."

A ferry to a remote Buddhist island—what could possibly go wrong?

The next evening, we found the hole-in-the-wall ferry ticket kiosk in downtown Shanghai and approached the man behind the plexiglass.

"Thank God for the existence of Miles," Jean-Louis turned to me as Miles bantered away in Mandarin.

"Don't thank God yet. This is China, and God might still decide to spread your cheeks and show you Jesus."

"The ass-mmaculate conception."

"It's not like a baby comes out."

Jean-Louis quickly checked to make sure that he hadn't lost his wallet, keys, or phone.

"OK, three tickets. Check." Miles waved three red pieces of paper. "8:00 PM departure." He looked at his watch. "That's soon. Time to move."

"*Dieu, merci*...for the existence of Miles," Jean-Louis repeated.

We hailed a cab and showed the driver the tickets. He recognized the address. We sped off toward the departure port to catch our ferry.

"You want to eat your words now or later, Mr. Jean-Louis?" I asked as the driver stopped in a dimly lit shipping port, the sort of place the mob might think of stashing a body, and motioned for us to exit the cab. There was trash everywhere and shipping containers stacked three high. Through the window, I saw a rat scurry into an empty KFC bucket.

There was no ferry in sight.

"I think I'd prefer to feed my words to those rats over there."

"Judging by their size, I don't think you'd be the first."

"Guys," Miles tried to focus us.

"You think words have high caloric content?" I asked Jean-Louis.

"Mine do for sure. Lots of syllables. Mmm, mmm—giant syllables for vermin consumption." He did a giant-sylla-bles-for-vermin-consumption mini dance in the back seat.

"Guys!" Miles yelled. "Ferry leaves in ten minutes."

"What ferry? This place looks like a bad guy's lair," said Jean-Louis.

"Yeah—game over," I agreed.

We grabbed our bags from the trunk. Miles said goodbye to his Chinese girlfriend, who had actually been with us this entire time but had not said a word, and we huffed it into the sketchy shipping depot.

I spied a few locals in dirty overalls smoking cigarettes.

"Putuoshan?" I asked them.

One guy flicked his head back, gesturing that that Putuoshan was deeper into the shipping depot.

"Ten-to-one odds we get murdered?" Jean-Louis asked genuinely.

"Ferry leaves in five minutes."

We turned around a corner and saw it. *It couldn't be.* This boat was the size of an aircraft carrier.

It had a giant smokestack and must have been half a kilometer in length and at least fifty feet high. It looked like a turn-of-the century beast—the kind of thing that used to lug immigrants across the Atlantic. It must have held five hundred passengers.

A crewman overhead began to unmoor the behemoth, the thick ropes landing with a thud on the concrete dock below. Another guy on the boat started to wind in the passenger gangplank.

"WAAAAIT!" I screamed...in English.

We sprinted, flashed our three red tickets, and the crew-man calmly let us onboard. We made it.

We stepped into a narrow hallway. The boat smelled like cigarette smoke. I looked right, and there was a group of eight Chinese guys staring at us, smoking cigarettes. *Well, that makes sense*, I thought. *There are a lot of Chinese people on this boat.*

"*Bières de fête?*" Jean-Louis said immediately.

"Beers sound great," said Miles.

"You don't want to head to the bow and scream, 'I'm the king of the world!' first?" I asked.

"Pretty sure we're still moored."

"Random *Titanic* reference, Ed."

"Yeah, really random." Miles and Jean-Louis both paused and stared at me for a long second.

"Really random, or really obvious? Heh, heh...Whelp, I think we earned a couple *Tsingtaos.*"

We wandered down a series of halls. Chinese families and young adults were lingering everywhere. Metal pipes ran along the corridors. The interior gray paint had started to peel. We clambered up a utilitarian staircase, opened a heavy door, and met a wall of fresh air once again.

Finally, sitting on an outdoor bench up on deck, *Tsingtao* beers in hand, the boat was now in motion. We were wrapped in a cool evening breeze. I looked up at the night sky. For a fleeting second, I saw stars. I checked my phone. 8:30 PM.

"So what time you think we'll get into Putuoshan tonight?" I asked.

"Dunno—couple hours?" was Miles's guess.

"Lemme see that guidebook again." Miles flipped me the book. I opened it. Miles and Jean-Louis exchanged a couple of laughs. I started reading about Putuoshan. *Fuck.*

"It says the ferry is twelve hours."

"WHAT?" Jean-Louis's head exploded. Miles froze.

"But it had such pretty pictures."

"You win again, China."

"This is hectic," Miles added his catchphrase.

"Guys, it's 8:30 PM." I told them. "That means we don't arrive till morning."

"Where are we supposed to sleep?" Jean-Louis whimpered.

"This might be a night where we cuddle for warmth on a hard metal floor somewhere," Miles started to look worried for once.

"Or, this is a sleeper ferry, and there are some beds somewhere with our names on them," I put my index finger in the air.

"Please be right," Jean-Louis whined. "Please be right."

We gently prodded open the heavy metal cabin door and met a wall of darkness. Inside, not a creature was stirring, not even a...except eleven Chinese guys all snoring rancorously in unison. The smell of cigarette smoke hung in the air. This was going to be lovely.

"Smells awesome in here," Miles proclaimed.

"Smells like weekend," I added.

"Smells like cancer," Jean-Louis corrected.

I blindly fumbled through the mass of people and personal effects to locate my empty bunk, stubbing my toe in the process. I yelped loudly, but the chorus of snores was already at a sufficient decibel to ensure that no one woke. It sounded as if each guy in the room had a kazoo jammed up his nose.

I lay down on my bare mattress. No pillow or sheets. I curled my arm into a nook for my weary head, cursed God, and closed my eyes.

Sleep came fleetingly, and the lone dream I can recall involved a gun with silencer, a muffler, a rope, and air freshener.

\* \* \*

Saturday's daylight invaded our porthole at the tidy hour of six in the morning, earlier than I used to go to sleep after a Friday night out in Shanghai. The rest of our cabin was now a frenetic shuffle. I bid unconsciousness adieu and joined my roommates in the morning dance. I sat up and put in my contact lenses to see two shirtless guys just staring at me. I stared right back. It was too early in the morning for a staring contest, so I relented and looked away first. *Yes, guys, there is a pasty foreign dude in your bunkroom on your sketchy ferry to the holy Buddhist island of Putuoshan.*

I loaded my toothbrush with Crest® and stumbled across the hallway to the communal bathroom. The other guys in the bathroom had to do a double take to ensure they were not still dreaming in their bunks as visions of sugar plums and crazy white people danced in their heads. Indeed, I drearily shared the same reaction that the scene before me was a practical joke played by my brain. It was, however, all very real. Every Chinese guy hocked a huge loogie both before and after brushing his teeth. Lovely.

Upon gathering the meager smattering of possessions we had brought for the journey, we strapped on our backpacks and bolted for the deck to see what alien universe was now surrounding us.

"Fresh air!" I shrieked giddily as we reached deck.

"Makes me shudder thinking what we breathed the past eight hours," Jean-Louis cringed a little.

"Can't be much worse than what we inhale every day in Shanghai."

"Yep, I think I'm already developing emphysema," Jean-Louis agreed.

"You don't even know what emphysema is," Miles shot back.

"It's a *disease*."

Miles rolled his eyes.

Our steamer was now in the center of an archipelago. There were mostly ~~desert~~ deserted islands surrounding us, though some had a few sporadic dwellings here and there. Each island was lush and hilly and no more than a few square miles in size. Our vessel was plowing straight ahead to what appeared to be the largest of the islands and the most developed.

"Developed" out there, though, was a relative term, and even the island of Putuoshan had only a couple of structures. Our hunk of steel eventually maneuvered its way into a small port, and we disembarked.

We hailed one of the three awaiting automobiles and rolled to the central area of our island, which consisted of about five small hotels and a number of tourist shops. We found an available hotel room and dropped our things.

"Now what?" Jean-Louis asked.

"Let's go explore," Miles motioned.

"Absolutely." I literally skipped out of the hotel room. It's not every day you're on an island like this.

Our guidebook said we should head to the base of the tallest hill on the island, about a thousand feet in height. Taxis were sparse, but the island had a reasonable bus system to chart tourists around.

At the base of the giant hill was a set of stairs. An absolutely endless set of stairs. Locals seemed to be coming down it, but few were ascending. We consulted the one-page description of the island from our guidebook.

"I guess there's no elevator," said Jean-Louis.

We started climbing.

The path of stairs zigzagged its way up the crag, and we followed its every swerve. This was without a doubt the longest single staircase I had ever seen. It was about five feet wide and a billion feet long.

We passed a few dozen people during our thirty-minute ascent.

At about 11:00 AM, we summited. Being an American, I thought there might be an American flag planted at the top of the mountain, as if our mission had just surfaced on the moon. Instead, there were several hundred Chinese tourists madly flocking to and fro between about twenty gift stalls all hocking identical items of zero utility: flags, Buddha statues, hats, t-shirts, and green tea.

We all let out a collective sigh. The only vendor who had at all differentiated himself was a young gentleman seated on the ground with a blanket spread before him. On the blanket were a number of seashells and oranges. *Really? Shells and oranges?*

Just like the other vendors, shells-and-oranges guy peddled his wares.

"Miles what is he saying?" I asked.

"Shells and oranges here! Get your shells and oranges. All your shopping needs! Come on down! Families welcome! Shells and oranges!" Miles did what felt like a spot-on impersonation.

"This guy has done terrible market research," I analyzed.

"Because he's selling shells and oranges?"

"Because shells and oranges are not complementary products. They actually don't have a single thing to do with one another. Talk about an experiment in futility."

"So judgmental, Ed." Jean-Louis smiled and put his hands on his hips.

"Mr. Ed has a point," Miles took my side.

"What would you sell up here, Jean-Louis?" I asked.

"Sand and pineapples."

"Sensible." Miles and I nodded.

From a few spots atop the summit, we could see a green wave of trees undulating across this jungle island mountain range. The various beaches way below were so still that they beckoned discovery.

Standing atop that peak was the cathartic release that Shanghai's grip did not allow. We took a synchronized deep breath and exhaled.

It was time to retreat back down the giant staircase. About a quarter of the way down, we discovered a dirt path jutting off into oblivion across the hill. It seemed to go sideways rather than down. We followed it. Twenty minutes later, we were now bushwhacking through the woodsy hillside of a remote Buddhist island off the coast of China.

As sea level finally began to come into focus, I was swinging through branches like Tarzan in order to put each next foot forward.

"This was a bad idea!" Jean-Louis yelled from ten feet away, the brush now so thick I couldn't see him.

"How do we get out of here?"

At long last, we burst through the tree line onto a beautiful white sand beach.

A dozen or so well-dressed Chinese couples were snapping selfies next to the water as we emerged from the brush onto the beach like a trio of wild animals poking their heads through the brush of the Serengeti.

"Uhhh," the three of us said to ourselves.

"*Nihao!*" Jean-Louis yelled at the Chinese people. They all gaped. One of them dropped a DSLR camera onto the sand. What zoo did these foreign dudes come from? *That* is a good question.

The beach had a fine curve like a black woman's ass, and looked straight east into the blue abyss of the Pacific. That California sunshine was a world away.

By now, the sun was high in the sky, ready to turn my

pasty skin a marginally more ethnic shade. To turn Ed into Eduardo. Each UV ray seemed to cleanse the spots of dirt I had accumulated on my body during my blind trekking down the wooded hillside. For an instant, I actually considered venturing down to the water to take a dip. After all, this was a beach, and swimming is something that people do at the beach.

As gut instinct was quietly pulling me toward the water, common sense slapped me in the face, as I remembered that the $H_2O$ in front of me had probably once flowed through the docks of Shanghai—the arrival and departure point of a fleet of cargo ships to a city where people piss and shit on the street. Not the kind of place that has the cleanest water flowing through it. Had I submerged myself at this beach, I probably would have emerged with a third arm. Or a tail. Maybe the water's secret ooze would have mutated me into a Ninja Turtle. Maybe.

Everybody went back to taking selfies.

"I want to sit on the damned beach," I said, exasperated, not from the day or the weekend. It was an accumulated exhaustion—the product of living in Shanghai.

"Best idea you've had all day," Jean-Louis sat down on the sand. We took our sneakers off.

Meanwhile, the Chinese couples simply stood around, somewhat confused, as if they genuinely did not understand what people actually *did* at the beach. They looked left and then looked right in an attempt to harness social clues, but everyone was just taking pictures. My suspicion of their beach ignorance was confirmed when I removed my shirt and caught more stares than an elephant riding a flaming bicycle.

There was no one else lying out on the beach. Not a single Chinese person. And there was definitely something un-Chinese about beaches. The beach is more of a hangout for greasy Italians or Brazilian beauties. The Chinese are too industrious to go dither on a pile of sand.

Miles, Jean-Louis, and I, however, were keen on relaxing on the beach for a period of time. Miles the explorer quickly grew restless and went exploring. Jean-Louis and I had our batteries depleted by the staircase climb and the sleepless night that preceded it. We passed out.

Later, my eyes crept open, startled by the sensation of alternating sun and shade. Shade? My eyes opened wider to a squadron of six twenty-something Chinese people standing around me in a semi-circle, staring. They were dressed in jeans and sweaters. I was shirtless on the sand. They didn't look away, and they weren't embarrassed.

They almost appeared to be studying Jean-Louis and me. Worse, they were blocking our afternoon sunlight.

"Jean-Louis," I whispered, "Open your eyes. I think we woke up in a science experiment."

"Huh," he mumbled, slowly regaining consciousness, not yet aware of our new friends. A girl pointed a DSLR camera at us and snapped a very loud picture. That, Jean-Louis registered.

"What the fuck?" Yep, now he got it.

"*Ni hao,*" I said, both confused and amused.

"*Ni hao!*" ("Hello!") They all smiled and nodded their heads in unison, excited that not only did they have a picture of the semi-naked white men on their beach, but they were also in a *conversation* with us. Totally new ballgame.

Jean-Louis laughed. "Whelp, that's all I really know how to say."

"*Ni men mei guo ma?*" Was the next sentence I caught from them. I could almost sense that this meant, "Are you American?"

"*Due,*" I nodded. Yes.

"*Hao de!*" One of them said. OK! This was a conversation, baby! I was doing it.

"*Zhong guo ren, ma?*" (China people?) I asked. They all laughed as if to say, "Yes brainiac, we are China people."

And then, that was sort of it. They said something else in Chinese. I just shrugged my shoulders, still sitting on the sand, implying to them that they had just explored the far reaches of my miniature Chinese vocabulary.

"*Zaijian.*" Bye! They left the soiree, with their digital snapshot as a party favor.

Miles returned not long after.

"Dude, Ed just had a conversation with some Chinese people."

"Really?" Miles was impressed.

"Yep, there were six of them. We said hello and everything."

"Woooow. Look at you guys." Miles chuckled at our linguistic ineptitude. He thinks he's so cool, being fluent in Mandarin. Whatever, I had a conversation!

"OK, guys," Miles pivoted, always spring loaded for the next adventure, "Let's go explore."

"Sure, I'm in." Jean-Louis exhaled, hesitatingly, potentially worried at the prospect of some obscure Chinese misfortune befalling him.

We moseyed toward the far end of our crescent beach, loosely in the direction of our hotel. We walked parallel to the water. This was a Buddhist island. Where were the Buddhists?

At the far end of the beach, we ran into a problem. A giant rock pile and hill blocked the most direct route back to our hotel. An old school obstacle. There, a rock-laden isthmus extended about one hundred yards into the ocean, the very tip of which rose about thirty feet above the boulder-strewn ocean below.

Hmm. Did we retreat back the way we came? How were we supposed to pass? I half expected a midget to pop out and ask us a riddle. There was no midget.

We estimated that our hotel was about one half mile on the other side of this rock outcropping, so we had to get to the other side in order to eventually make our way back on foot. The rock formations were steep enough that we could not walk right over the peninsula to the far side, but were instead forced to climb out to the very tip and go around.

"We have to do this," Miles dropped, matter-of-factly.

"I know." Jean-Louis relented.

We slogged across the sand to the start of our rock star escapade. The small pebbles between our toes quickly grew in size. We strapped on our sneakers once again and were quickly using all fours to vault up and ease down Herculean sized boulders. It took us about twenty minutes just to scramble out to the very tip of the peninsula. The sun was just now retreating back to its nightly bed below the horizon, and the salty ocean mist was rising off the water below.

About ten yards above and behind us, a small house stood atop a flat patch of grass, inaccessible from our current position at the very tip of the peninsula, amid jagged stones encircling us and gently kissing the sea below. What was that house?

God was quickly turning the dimmer down on the afternoon sky, so it was time to hustle and get our bums back to the hotel. We began phase two of our climb, on the far side of the isthmus back to the mainland. The climb was growing more technically challenging, especially given the lack of light from the island sky.

The boulders were growing larger, and the gaps between them wider. We almost considered turning back, but that was probably even more dangerous.

"*Merde! Merde merde merde* fuck fuck fuck." I heard Jean-Louis yell behind me.

"You OK?" I called back.

"Dammit. I dropped my phone into the ocean."

"Still have your wallet?"

"Yeah."

"So you're batting .500."

I turned forward again, and slid down a steeply inclined boulder, when suddenly I almost bowled over a mediating monk on a rock below. Shit! That's who lived in that isolated little house.

He was bald and wearing an orange robe, sitting cross-legged on a flat stone. His eyes were closed and his palms faced upwards as if he were waiting for the sky to dump a bunch of Skittles® into his hands.

He immediately sensed my presence and broke his mediation. He looked up at me and just stared. No expression on his face.

"Uh. Um. Uh." I wanted to tell him, "It's cool, we know Master Hui Ming," but I had no idea how to say this in Mandarin, nor would this gentleman likely know our dinner partner.

All I could muster was a little English, "Sorry, Mr. Monk. Don't mind us. We're just trying to pass through. If you could just..." He was blocking our way and not moving from his seated position.

"Would you, um, mind, if we could just squeeze, we'll be..." I turned sideways to pass by him, my ass brushing his shoulder a little bit as I scooted around toward the rock behind the monk. Miles and Jean-Louis were of no help, and followed behind me. The monk never said a word.

"Nice one, Ed." Jean-Louis goaded. "Real nice. Way to rub your butthole all over a monk."

"Well it's not like I farted on him."

"We did wreck that guy's mediation," Miles conceded.

"You know what, guys. We gave that monk some good

dinner table fodder. I bet he's psyched to tell all the other monks about this over a vegetarian meal tonight."

"I don't think they do that."

"Maybe they do. We don't know that."

"They don't."

"But they could."

"I'm pretty sure they don't..."

"But they might."

"Keep telling yourself that."

"I will."

Finally, we neared the sand once again. It was dark as we emerged from the rocky peninsula on the far side, having completed the roundabout with only a few scratches.

\* \* \*

The next day, we checked out of our hotel room and visited one final island attraction before catching the "speed ferry" (only four hours—thank goodness) back to civilization.

The attraction was, quite simply, a fifty-foot tall Buddha statue by the sea. What remote island would be complete without a fifty-foot Buddha?

After eight months here in China, I had seen many a Buddha statue before—Kneeling Buddha, Reclining Buddha, Pregnant Buddha, Great Buddha—you name it. The only Buddha's missing were Jesus Christ Buddha and Crack Cocaine Buddha.

So I wouldn't leave China being friends with any monks. Come to think of it, most of my friends were still expats, even this far into the year. Mandarin is hard, man. That afternoon on the beach was one of the better "conversations" I had managed with some Chinese people. The language barrier was real, and kind of isolating. Sometimes I really missed English.

What we had here was a failure to communicate.

I jogged through the FIS hallway to an impromptu faculty meeting one Monday morning. This was unusual.

"Good morning Mista Edooooo," Yurika yelled.

"Good morning Yurika," I cut her off.

I entered the meeting room and swung into a seat.

"We've been scammed. Linda began abruptly. I repeat: FIS has been scammed." Mr. Pancake stood in the corner. His omnipresent crescent smile had been flipped upside down. Sad Pancake.

Linda paused for effect.

"Are we supposed to *guess* the scam?" Jean-Louis asked, an indication that Linda had paused too long. She continued.

"Russell Johnson," She said as I scanned the room looking

for him, "Has been fired." *I knew it.* That guy was always shady. What was he into?

"Who Russell Johnson?" The math teacher Mr. Lu legitimately did not know.

"He taught economics," Linda explained. "Technically, he was in your math department."

"I think no. Mista Russell Johnson no ever come to math department meeting. I teach math. My students love the math."

"What happened?" Ken asked.

"Let's just say he over-promised and under-delivered. Scratch that. He issued guarantees and delivered nothing. And he lied about it."

"Explain."

"He assured us that our registration with the College Board Advanced Placement Program was complete. I contacted them, and they have never heard of FIS. I checked the grades that his students have received, and they all have a 100 percent grade in all of his classes. I then asked his students about those classes. They say that Russell would often not show up, and when he did, he usually assigned free study time. His students haven't learned anything."

"So it wasn't really much of a scam *per se*, he was more just a liar and extremely lazy," said Miles.

"If that helps you rationalize things."

"Mr. Russell Johnson is not so nice," Helga finally found something besides her ex-husband that she didn't like.

"What's worse," Linda sniffled and continued, "Is that there may have been something going on between him and Mona." Mona was the Taiwanese eleventh grader with suggestive dance moves. "But we don't know for sure."

Just the week prior, I had spied Russell in a full *embrace* with one of his female pupils. A fifty-year-old white guy embracing young Asian girls. Something was definitely amiss. I smelled a pervert.

\* \* \*

Crisis breeds opportunity. I had studied economics in undergrad, and now there was a vacancy. After the meeting, I approached Linda and Mr. Pancake in the teacher office. I knocked on the open door. Linda was typing on the office desktop computer. Mr. Pancake sat at a table in the back, counting piles of cash. *Did some students pay their tuition in cash?* I turned to Linda.

"Linda, do you mind translating for me for a moment?"

"Sure, Ed." She turned and said something to Mr. Pancake. Mr. Pancake's round face broke into a smile. He put down a handful of 100 RMB notes, snapped a rubber band around them, and jotted something into a notebook. He crossed his arms, and turned to me.

"Mr. Wu," I began. "I know that the departure of Russell Johnson opened up a vacancy for an economics teacher."

Linda translated. Mr. Pancake nodded.

"I studied a fair amount of economics in undergrad, and I believe I can teach the Advanced Placement macroeconomics course."

Linda translated again. Mr. Pancake grunted and smiled. He spoke in Mandarin. I turned to Linda.

"Mr. Wu says the job is yours, and he hopes that you can use your skills in economics to make Fudan International School even more profitable."

He extended his right hand, and I shook it. I returned his smile. The course was mine.

I walked out of the office gleeful. I had asked for a promotion and received it.

*More profitable.* I thought about his words as I strolled down the hall. The pile of money, the big smile. *He was running FIS as a business. How have I not seen this?* I felt dejected about the state of the school but happy with my own assertiveness. Like scoring a goal when your team loses. I shrank a little.

I returned to my office and emailed Russell to ask if he had left any class notes. Over time, my multiple emails were met with radio silence. We had definitely been duped by hiring this jerk.

With no starting place, I emailed my mother and asked her to FedEx my old high school AP Economics course notes. Incredibly, they had been gathering dust in my closet in New York for years. Whatever it takes.

Such are the growing pains of a young startup international ~~school~~ business.

\* \* \*

The following week, Jean-Louis, clearly frustrated that Russell Johnson had left him utterly unprepared to take over another class (this one a geography course), marched into his classroom.

"Good morning, class," he began. "Some of the teachers have been trying to find some of Mr. Russell's old homework assignments that he gave to you. Did he email anything to you after he left? All of the teachers have been trying to email him, but he never answers our emails."

Jean-Louis glanced over to Mona, the attractive Taiwanese student, who seemed perplexed.

"Mona, you seem confused."

Mona paused, and then answered. "Well, Mr. Russell emails *me* all the time."

*Uh-oh.* Probable pervert officially identified. The Chinese may be crazy sometimes, but something like this was legitimately unheard of even in this country. Of course, it takes an old white guy to shatter the innocence of our student body.

"What does he say in those emails to you, Mona?" Jean-Louis pressed for more evidence.

"He tells me how much he misses me," said Mona, with a flick of her straight hair. *Ugh!*

I'm sure the content of those emails could have killed a small cat. Maybe Russell's next appearance will be in federal pound-me-in-the-ass prison. In Thailand. The world may never know.

By the time he left us in the dust, even Mr. Pancake realized that we had essentially been swindled out of money in exchange for a plate of shame doused in soy sauce. Linda muttered to me at one point that Russell had been paid an exorbitant salary.

Russell, if you are reading this, you should not be allowed within two hundred yards of a school. And I hope when they catch you, a 300-pound inmate named Wookie decides to make you his bitch.

A few weeks later, I was playing furious catch-up to motor my small troupe of FIS seniors through the material covered in Advanced Placement Macroeconomics. I negotiated a good price for a single used econ textbook at Shanghai's English language bookstore and photocopied lessons for my two students, a pair of native English speakers named Lewis (a boy) and Guang (a girl), who were both USA-bound for college the following year. We chugged through econ lesson after econ lesson. I always stayed a couple of chapters ahead. The whole thing felt like the training montage from the movie Rocky. These were the same two kids that had made me cry earlier in the year when I overheard them in the hallway. How things had changed.

I took Miles and Ken's advice to heart: don't be lame. So, before each class, I smoked a rock of imaginary crack cocaine and repeated to myself, "ECON IS FUN!"

"Gooooood morning future central bank presidents of

the United States, or whatever Asian countries in which either of you eventually settles!"

"Good morning, Mr. Ed!" They chuckled, struggling to match my level of energy. I approached the course as if it were a forum for intellectual discourse among friends.

"Who's ready for a little *monetary policy review?*" You'd think I was peddling chocolate ice cream at summer camp. "You guys do your reading?"

"Yes, Mr. Ed," they both replied. Lewis was the straggler of the two, but in a classroom of two people there is hardly room to hide. He kept up.

I hit the accelerator. "In any economic climate, the USA federal reserve has what most widely utilized policy tool at its disposure?" I pointed to Guang.

"Open market operations," she answered correctly.

"Open market operations!" I sang it like gospel. "In a contractionary environment, what are they going to do?" I pointed to Lewis.

"Expansionary monetary policy," he answered correctly.

"Meaning?" I began to point back and forth to each of them, like a symphony conductor.

"They buy bonds."

"To increase the money supply."

"Bank loans increase as banks dispense this new excess money from the Fed."

"Interest rates decrease."

"People and businesses borrow more and save less."

"Thereby stimulating the economy back to growth."

I paused conducting. "Guys, this is like music to my ears. Amazing. You will be future bank presidents one day. Now if only you had the power to negotiate with your parents for more allowance."

"I know!" They both replied, indignantly.

"Ah yes, my children," I placed my palms together and touched my opposing fingers tips to one another in succession, like a contemplative James Bond villain. "Principal-agent negotiations are a lesson for another day. In the meantime, let's continue chatting about the wild and crazy world of macroeconomics. Who's coming with me?"

Yurika, who coined my name, "Mr. Edo," skipped excitedly to my Ancient Civilizations class, flipping an invisible jump rope under each stride.

"Good morning, Mr. Edo," said no-longer-the-linguistic-equivalent-of-a-cinder-block Kotaro. Intensive classes all in English for eight hours a day meant comprehension had finally started to penetrate my kids' pores like a nagging pimple. Clearly there were still miles to go before I could sleep, but every baby step had counted.

All my students were the beneficiaries of my shortening the distance between "work Ed" and "Duardo." My newfound casual approach had also blurred the line a bit between educator and student. We were all buddies. I was simply the highly critical and discerning one in the group, who even had a tendency to grade his friends routinely on a sliding scale from A–F.

These days, I even got the occasional high five in the hallway. In particular, I was growing more and more fond of my advanced middle school English class with each passing lesson. One day, however, a boundary was breached:

I was approached one day by Jin Mon Rho, the eighth grade Korean girl with bangs, an infectious smile full of silver braces, and a heart of gold. Jin Mon sported long, provocative eyebrows, separated only by a small demilitarized zone in the middle of her forehead. After class one Friday, she approached me and offered a token present.

"Mista Ed. Is gift for you." She gave a small bow and extended in two hands a small blue box, wrapped in a ribbon. Her body language was tender—the line between student and teacher had all but evaporated.

"Um. Uh. I, eh. Thanks?"

Not knowing the proper student-teacher protocol, I reluctantly accepted the offering. She immediately blushed and scurried out of the room.

After school, I opened the small, blue box, and pulled out a pink card, a Korean coin, and a little name tag with the name "Jin Mon Rho" written in marker. One side of the card contained a pattern of white hearts, and the other her best scripture: a letter that was appropriately titled, "Letter."

"To: Ed

"I like you<3 Gifts are a name-tag which I used at middle
school in Korea and Korea coin. These gifts are for you. Ed,
I think smiling is best among your appearance. I'm sorry
about that my gifts are small. Don't be sick, be health."

I melted. Though very grateful, a conversation between
Jin Mon Rho and me later followed which firmly outlined
the boundary between teacher and student.

"Jin Mon, I am flattered by the gift, but students shouldn't
give gifts like this to their teacher. Especially gifts with
heart emojis."

"Mr. Ed you are fatter?"

"No, *flattered*. It means I am grateful."

Though adoration still filled her eyes as I reminded her
that I was *not* Russell Johnson, my message was sufficiently comprehended. I had conquered my first serious
face-to-face with a student. I sat down at my desk after
and thought about it.

I'd spent the better part of a decade keeping the moat
surrounding my castle full of water. I guess in a way I'd
never really, truly let anyone in. Not Riley, not Molly.

Definitely not my parents. Finally, here in the Shanghai springtime, I'd had this epiphany and opened myself up to my students. I'd decided to be me. And in doing so, a girl had finally opened herself up to me. Yes, she was an eighth grade Korean with braces, but we'd connected. I'd laid down a bridge to my fortress and invited all these little Asian kids to cross over. One of them liked what she saw. How now, brown cow.

And it would have been so easy for me not to say anything, to dispatch the problem by not dispatching the problem, like poor Tanya from Toronto, recipient of my cold shoulder (or I hers?), who was likely out in the Shanghai wilderness delivering her next blow job with no closure about her brief flirtation with Mr. Ed.

But lovely Jin Mon, the friendly Korean, had at long last met adult Mr. Ed.

\* \* \*

I thumbed a piece of chalk in my right hand, its dry dust coating my fingers. Mona...Mona Mona Mona.

"Mr. Ed."

Her sleek black hair fanned like she was starring in a Pert Plus® commercial. A thin black cardigan complemented her artfully applied makeup. Her brown eyes shielded years of youthful secrets.

"Mr. Ed."

*Russell Johnson. What have you been hiding, you dirty old man?*

"Mr. Ed?"

And here I was thinking about Mona, like how when someone tells you *not* to think about something, you think about it.

"Mr. Ed? Hello? Hello?"

My eyes crossed, blurring the scene in front of me. Still daydreaming on my two feet, I began listing to my right, until my internal gyroscope sensed danger and jolted me alert once again. The world came into focus.

"Mr. Ed! Hello?" Mona stretched her arm skyward, attempting to ask a question.

"Huh? What. Oh. Yes, Mona, you have a question." I snapped back to reality.

In front of me were fifteen tenth and eleventh grade

English students. It was the usual mix of overachievers and apathetic stragglers. Everyone squinted at me, wondering whether I was indeed awake. Mona's eyes bore through me like lasers.

*"Mr. Russell emails me all the time."* In my head, I replayed her words to Jean-Louis.

"Mr. Ed? What is the homework we must do?" she asked. Sometimes, I forgot she was a high school student, just like everyone else.

"Apologies for my brief trip to outer space. Yes, my dearest children, this weekend please remember to write a first person narrative in which you pretend you are an animal. Also, don't forget to fill in your email address on this form. Have a great weekend! Adieu!"

In response to the Russell Johnson fiasco, we had decided to collect all of our students' email addresses. Later that day, Jean-Louis sat in our office, thumbing through the list of student email addresses.

"Dude, you will not believe what Mona's email address is." He had a huge smile on his face.

"Here we go," was my response.

"Putitinme17**@******.com," he shone his teeth white while anticipating my reaction.

"What?" I blurted. "Put *what* in her? Jesus."

"Put *it* in her."

"Oh, that is just sick."

"Agreed—totally sick. Disgustingly, unabashedly, incredibly, wonderfully...sick." He grinned.

"And this is the e-mail address she gave to the *school*?"

"That's the sickest part," Jean-Louis chuckled.

"Well she lassoed a middle-aged white guy with that email address."

"He probably spammed the hell out of her."

"With his 56 baud modem."

"While watching his VHS porn collection."

"And faxing her Shakespearian sonnets.

"Well, we're going to hell."

"What do the other students' email addresses look like?"

"Snugglepanda@yahoo.com, videogamesarecool@
japan.com, whenwillmyballsdrop@puberty.com. Other
nonsense."

I crooked an eye.

"OK, I made the last one up," he admitted.

"Plus five points to Mona," I conceded.

"Plus five *hundred* points to Mona."

Monitor Group
140 Broadway
New York, NY 10005

Dear Eduardo:

Congratulations! We are delighted to be able to offer you
a consulting position with Monitor in our New York office
beginning this September. Enclosed are two copies of your
offer letter. Please sign and return one copy to our Recruiting Coordinator as acceptance of this position.

Please feel free to contact us at in order to clarify any questions or concerns you may have. The deadline to accept or
reject this offer is June 1st.

We look forward to your response and the opportunity of
welcoming you on board to commence a successful career
with Monitor.

Sincerely,
Monitor Group New York

There it was in my email inbox. A signed letter with an invitation to step aboard the Path. I felt numb. At long last, things here in Shanghai were working. Should I throw this new life away? I didn't know what to think. So, I did what anyone else my age would have done. I didn't think about it.

One Saturday in the spring, Miles and I took a day trip to nearby Nanjing.

Besides the infamous mid-twentieth century Japanese massacre that brutalized Nanjing—which I won't tell you about here because I don't want to heave you into a serious depression (the book about it is called *The Rape of Nanjing*, if you're looking for a light beach read)—Nanjing was also famous for a triangular attraction named Purple Mountain. Miles and I disembarked the train and dove head first into a Nanjing taxi.

Ten minutes out of city center, the road became lined with oxygen-giving trees. Metropolitan madness dissipated into terrestrial tranquility as our four-lane road converged to two, and before you could say "People's Republic of China," we were snaking up a calm, wooded road to the mountain.

I could have been cruising through New England in October. It was serene. I could breathe. Only after living in

China could I declare that fresh air, like good water, has a distinct taste. I missed unpolluted air. The backseat windows were rolled down and the mountain air gushed into the back of our taxi.

Miles turned to me: "Ed, take a deep breath."

I inhaled slowly through my nose and held the air deep in my lungs, letting it linger an extra second. I closed my eyes and exhaled.

"God, I can breathe again."

"Every breath is adding days to my lifespan."

"My body feels like it's coming alive."

"OK, take it easy tiger," he said. "You getting aroused over there?"

"I think I am. A little bit. My nipples feel like mountaintop peaks."

Near the base of the crag, we purchased passes to visit the mausoleum of Dr. Sun Yat Sen, the storied edifice constructed at the apex of Purple Mountain. Sun Yat Sen was revered in China for his triumphs of the early twentieth century, particularly helping to overthrow the Qing dynasty. He was a revered political leader often called "The Father of Modern China." Apparently, being that awesome lands you an eternal resting place atop a huge rock, a posthumous jackpot given the Chinese affinity for shapely stones.

We slid under an archway and met a giant stone wall, etched with a stupor of Chinese characters. Of the hundreds of symbols adorning this beast, Miles could identify about ten.

"It says something about old China."

"That's helpful," I said sarcastically.

"Want to help me translate the rest?"

*Point taken.*

"This place is underwhelming so far," Miles was not impressed.

"Yeah, what gives? I thought this guy kicked ass in real life."

We looped around the wall and immediately saw an infinite set of stairs carved into the mountain at a thirty-degree angle, shooting straight as an arrow to the pinnacle of Purple Mountain. It was shamelessly imperial.

"Oh."

"Oh."

"That is a legit staircase."

We looked up. It must have been another half mile directly up this endless staircase to Dr. Sun Yat Sen's Mausoleum atop the mountain. The giant building staring down at us from the mountaintop had two giant gray pillars and a blue roof. The shingles curled up in noble fashion.

I turned to Miles: "Here goes."

After just several dozen steps, I was already huffing and puffing.

Half an hour later, we neared the top, and I could feel my stomach start to rumble. This unplanned workout was making my bowels do a somersault.

"You alright there, Mista Edo?" Miles chided.

"Feeling a bit of a rumble."

"Uh-oh. Tsunami incoming?"

"More like a mudslide."

We summited. I looked up at the imposing structure, the "sacrificial hall." The hall was guarded by massive ornamental columns, each about fifteen meters tall. The structure was ornate but austere. We joined the single-file line at the tomb's entranceway in order to get a glimpse Sun Yat Sen's burial chamber. I held my stomach, which was growing weaker by the second. His coffin was encased under protective glass in the rear atrium of this concrete grandiosity, just like Chairman Mao in Beijing. The silence was thick as we shuffled past the coffin, all the while sandwiched between Chinese tourists. We were packed in so tight, and everyone was so deferential, you could distinctly hear small denominations of the RMB jingle in people's pockets. Or maybe a gurgle from deep within the roiling GI tract of a semi-panicked American guy.

I couldn't take it any more. I had to poop. Badly.

I scurried out of the tomb.

"Good luck!" Miles called as I scampered. Incredibly, there was a standalone bathroom building at the top of the mountain. I blew past a number of lingering Chinese people and entered the bathroom. I was immediately hit with a scent that I can only describe as one part truck rest stop and one part obese armpit. I practically had to carve my way through it.

I flung open a stall door in eager anticipation of relief. There was no toilet. I looked down at the porcelain hole in the ground.

Immediacy trumped decency. I whipped my belt open and pulled down my pants. I squatted down, careful not to fall into the hole. My quads instantly started to burn, still fatigued from the climb up to the top of Purple Mountain. I steadied myself by placing my arm against the back wall of the stall so that my legs wouldn't give out.

"I could hear you groaning from like 100 feet away," Miles told me as I sauntered toward him, my evacuation complete.

"It was a hard fought battle." I probably looked pretty weary.

"Um. Who won?"

"In porcelain wars, there are no victors."

"How was the TP in there?" Miles was genuinely curious.

"Admittedly, a little rough."

"No cushion for your cushion?"

"Was more like sandpaper."

"I told you to drop one before we left this morning."

"We can't all deuce on schedule, man. It's not like brushing your teeth."

"Did you flush?"

"There was no handle."

"So you just left it there?"

"'It' is probably too tidy a term to describe what I left in there."

"Thanks. Now I've got that visual looming over me like a storm cloud. So, you zipped up and then bolted?" Miles was surprisingly inquisitive.

"The ol' zip-n-bolt," I coined it.

"You can't zip-n-bolt here. This is like one of the holiest places in China."

"Well, I zipped. And then I bolted."

"Dude."

"Dude."

* * *

Midway through our descent, I spied a nearby Chinese gentleman in his twenties snap an ultra-quick picture of me with his camera phone, clearly hoping that I wouldn't notice his furtive photography.

I instantly turned to him and raised an eyebrow of bewilderment. He looked shocked and embarrassed that I caught him, and he froze in panic.

"Paparazzi, twelve o'clock," I muttered to Miles.

I smiled at the guy. He exhaled a "phew," and then smiled back at me. In a suddenly brazen moment of restored confidence, this Chinese tourist then motioned to Miles, asking if he would mind taking a picture of him and his new friend, me. In sparkling Chinese, Miles said of course he would.

The tourist's mouth dropped. *Two white guys and one of them speaks Chinese!?* After Miles worked his photographic magic with this man's camera phone, my new buddy waved over a group of another eight Chinese tourists, who had been patiently observing the cultural exchange between the *lao wais* (white people) and the ninth member of the travel group.

"Guys! Get over here! Crazy white guy offering free pictures!" I inferred. I posed for about twenty photographs.

Turns out, this group was from a faraway province of China I had never heard of, and they were touring the East of their country for the first time in their lives. They had never seen a Westerner before. Say cheese.

I discovered later that Nina the PR Guru had thought that Miles, Jean-Louis, Ken and I had been, well, charming during our dinner adventure with the monk, Master Hui Ming. Even me. This was certainly not the review I was anticipating.

Her assistant emailed Miles to inquire whether we might be kind enough to join her that Thursday for a "business meeting" with a few of her friends at the ICS television station in Shanghai—that's "International Channel Shanghai" to all of you. Yes, Shanghai has an English language local television station, among the dozen or so free network television channels in the city of millions.

Ken and Jean-Louis both had to proctor study hall that Thursday night at school. Only Miles and I could attend the meeting.

The two of us paused and stood outside the thirty-story (everything in Shanghai is thirty stories) ICS headquarters building in downtown Shanghai. We informed the guard outside that we had a meeting.

White people? Must have important business. He waived us in without a word.

At the far end of the lobby was a swanky bar area with an array of red leather couches and black tables. It was there that we spied Nina the PR Guru. Our second meeting with her. Like a district judge presiding over the locals, Nina the PR Guru was a commanding presence looming over her posse of eight people.

The group, all Chinese, was mostly youthful, and they were substantially better dressed than the typical crew of drunk men gambling on Shanghai street corners. We approached, exchanged pleasantries in English, and sat down.

Nina the PR Guru addressed us directly:

"Hello, Miles and Ed. We are here today because we want to talk with you about International Channel Shanghai. The television shows *Shanghai Quest* and *Culture Matters* are very interesting. We want to know your opinions. Please share to us your thoughts."

*Um, what?* It appeared we had fallen ass backwards into

a planning meeting with various producers and other TV executives. How we were even remotely qualified for this was beyond me.

"I think both shows are fantastic, but could more closely align with the interests of their target audience," Miles projected with confidence. I gave him a look. In response he raised an eyebrow, a clear indication that he had never heard of either show, and was completely full of shit.

"We agree, Miles," Nina the PR Guru replied, "Thank you for your opinion." Miles was *good at China.*

Nina the PR Guru introduced me to a young female producer of the television show *Culture Matters.* Her name was Liu Wei. Miles was shuffled into a separate conversation on my other side. This woman, probably in her late twenties, started talking all about the program, which I quickly understood to be a talk show about aspects of Chinese culture that "matter," hence the obvious double entendre of its name, *Culture Matters.*

The young woman began to rattle off a few cultural topics and sought my expert reaction regarding whether they indeed "mattered."

The only thought going through my head was, "Trust me, lady, you don't want to know about my areas of cultural expertise. If you had any idea what I've done in this culture on Friday and Saturday nights, you would terminate this dialogue immediately."

"In the older shows, we have talk about restaurants of Shanghai and the power of woman. What ideas you have?"

"Ideas?" I stumbled. "Ummm. Maybe you can do a show about the bars of Shanghai."

"Hmm," was her curt reply.

"Oooor," I recovered quickly, "Maybe you can do a show that compares New York and Shanghai. I always hear people compare the two cities. I come from New York and I can assure you that they are both similar in many ways."

"Oh, that is very interesting." She genuinely seemed intrigued by my newfound creative prowess. Huge recovery. At this point, Nina the PR Guru chimed into our conversation as my counterpart informed her of my cultural wizardry.

While Nina the PR Guru and my *Culture Matters* junior exec talked television, I turned to my left and gave Miles another look.

"What the fuck is this?" I whispered to him.

"This is the life of an expat in Shanghai."

"They just presume we are experts at everything."

"Don't give them a reason to think otherwise."

In the chair adjacent to Miles sat a reserved older gentleman who had been mostly silent in this pow-wow of Chinese television executives and purportedly omniscient American undergraduates.

Nina the PR Guru addressed Miles and me. "Do you both know Mr. Jin? He is the father of Louis, who studies at FIS." Louis, son of Mr. Jin, was actually one of my best students. At the moment, he had an A- in my new AP economics class.

Mr. Jin was dressed in a tweed jacket and tie. His hair was parted too far to the side, and he used so much gel that his head appeared to be made of shiny plastic, like a Lego® figure.

Mr. Jin's speech was deliberate and nonsensical, a freight train of three-syllable words that had no place in the sentences into which they were inserted.

"Mr. Jin, you must be a proud father. Louis is an excellent student," I told him in earnest.

"The harmony of excellence has been the passion of my existence."

"Um, so you have been supportive of his studies?" I asked.

"My family is the essential natural harmony of my being."

"Right."

Mercifully, the Chinese business meeting drew to a close. Liu Wei, the producer of *Culture Matters*, stood to leave. She turned to me:

"Oh yes. There is one thing I have forget. We have episode *Culture Matters* this week. Do you want be on show?"

"You mean be *on the show* on the show?" I asked.

"Yes. You are a teacher and the episode is 'extra-curriculums' in the Shanghai schools. Do you know about this subject?"

I thought about Miles's words. "Of course I am an expert on this topic. I will be on the TV show. That sounds amazing. Thank you very much for the offer."

"Great."

*Holy shit, I'm going to appear on Chinese television.*

"Who else is going to be on the show?" I asked. My attention was now rapt.

"Well, the host of show is Mr. Sammy Yang, famous television person. Also we want for you bring your student, Royce Song, the son of Nina Song."

*Big surprise there.*

"And finally, Mr. Jin will be in the show."

*Shit.*

\* \* \*

We all parted ways. Miles and I hailed a cab back home to our domicile.

"What the hell just happened?" I asked him in the cab.

"Another day at the office," Miles said coolly.

"They asked me to appear on a Chinese talk show," I revealed.

"They asked *me* to appear on a Chinese *reality* show," he countered.

"You win."

"I always do," he jested.

We both smirked at each other.

"You've grown," was my father's impressed reply, when I gave him the no-longer-dreaded job update during one of our infrequent phone calls.

I had grown. I was a globetrotting *economics* teacher. I dined with monks and appeared on television. I pooped in shrines.

"As I told you in Xi'an, I'm proud of you." My mother added.

"Thanks Mom. Means a lot. God, it's nice to hear somebody speak English, too."

"We can switch to Spanish if it will help confuse matters."

"*Gracias, pero prefiero Inglés.*"

I yearned for home. I missed English. I had somehow managed to figure out this whole China thing—at least a little—but, man oh man, did I ever still feel like a fish out of water. China is tiring. Mandarin is difficult.

"So tell us about school."

"Where to begin? I'm now teaching our school's seniors an AP Economics course, which I took over from that psycho pervert, Russell Johnson. My students have the Advanced Placement exam in just a few weeks—early in May. So, I've been whipping them like butter."

"I thought that the Chinese don't eat dairy," my mother teased.

"OK...I've been beating them with chopsticks."

"More apt, though borderline child abuse."

"Pretty sure that beating children is the definition of child abuse," my father corrected.

"Anyway. I'm also leading a 'Grammar for Native English Speakers' class. Linda noticed that I had good grammar and basically stuffed all the native English speakers into a room to learn grammar from me. There are eighth graders and twelfth graders in the same classroom. It's like Little House on the Prairie."

"I'll admit I'm relieved," my dad said.

"And what about all those other students who can't speak English?" my mother asked.

""Like Kotaro and Yurika?"

"Yeah."

"They're getting better. You should see some of these other kids though. One little seventh grader named Valiant is like four feet tall and uses a rolling suitcase instead of a backpack." My parents laughed. "He writes all these violent stories in which everyone dies. We call him Violent Valiant."

"Best keep an eye on him."

"He's a good kid."

"What a riot. Anything else of note going on?"

"Oh yeah, I'm appearing on television tomorrow."

* * *

It was time for my Chinese television debut. I felt pretty woozy all day in the classroom. I considered canceling the talk show appearance, but as I opened up my email to compose a sorrowful apology for my impending absence, my inbox pinged with a confirmation from Liu Wei, the producer of the television program *Culture Matters*, assuring me that everything was all set for my arrival that evening and that she was "so excited" to see me again. She had been pretty gracious about the whole endeavor, and I'm sure she would have "lost face" among her peers had yours truly not shown his at that evening's taping. I was going on TV, whether I wanted to or not.

When class ended I grabbed Royce, the son of Nina the PR Guru, and we braved a taxi down to ICS television station for show time.

In the back seat of the cab, he turned to me timidly: "Mr. Ed, what do you think will happen at the talk show?"

"I don't know what to tell you, Royce. I've been told little about what to expect. Do your best, and we'll see what they throw at us." He pressed his lips together tightly. His wire-frame glasses were smudged, and his button-down shirt was untucked.

"OK," he half-whispered, meekly. He slumped in his seat. Jesus, he was *sixteen years old*. Royce, of Chinese descent but born in New York City, was fully fluent in both English and Chinese. I tried again.

"Your mom puts a lot of pressure on you, huh?"

"Yeah. She's intense. I already have a target list of US colleges that she wants me to apply to." Royce admitted.

"Wow, that would make me nervous too."

Royce perked up.

"My mom said I could write about this TV show tonight on my applications. I really hope I don't mess up. Then I'll never get into college."

Wow. For as lackadaisical as some of my students appeared, it often escaped me how intense Chinese parents could be on their kids to achieve. I sympathized with Royce. After almost a year teaching, I finally knew what to say and what not to say.

"~~You'll be fine~~. I'm nervous, too."

"You are?"

"Royce, I'm not that much older than you are. Plus, look at my face. I can barely grow a mustache. People think I'm thirteen."

"But you're my teacher."

"I was a student a year ago. I'm closer in mentality to you

than I am to your parents, even though there's this thing where we tend to equate teachers to parents."

"So you're nervous, too."

"'Course I am! Listen, I think the world's biggest secret is that no one really *knows* what they're doing. They just sorta make decisions and figure it out."

"And you think we'll figure out this talk show?"

"Well, look on the bright side. What is the subject of today's talk show?"

"Extracurricular activities at school."

"And what is the topic you know best in the world, as a *student?*"

"School."

"My man," I gave him a mini high five. "Chin up—we're gonna be alright."

We met Liu Wei in the ICS lobby and she whisked us past security, flashing her badge to the suit-clad guard as we made our way to the elevator bank.

"First, you will go to the makeup on eighth floor," she explained as she pushed "8" in the elevator. "Next, Kelly will take you to the studio on tenth floor." *Makeup? Who is Kelly?*

The elevator doors clanged open. Papers rustled, shoes scuffed, telephones rang, things beeped, and people bustled. It was an office.

Liu Wei tapped Kelly on the shoulder. He removed his headphones, swung his chair around and stood up. Kelly, it turned out, was a white guy. Such a white guy. He gave Royce and me the once-over and then extended a hand.

"How's it goin' buddies? I'm Kelly." He instantly reminded me of Spicoli from *Fast Times at Ridgemont High*. Royce and I both nodded and reciprocated the handshake.

Kelly brushed his shoulder length blonde hair behind his ears. "So, you're the two students here for the *Culture Matters* show?" he inferred as he led us to the makeup room.

"I'm a *teacher*, I corrected him." I guess I haven't aged that much.

"Oh, sorry bro."

Even though this was the International Channel of Shanghai, the entire staff was Chinese. The only foreigner of any kind was Kelly. I could not figure out what this random guy, who told me he just graduated from some West Coast hippie school, was doing in Shanghai.

In twenty words and a single handshake, I was already piecing together his life story in my head. Media major in undergrad, used to smoke a lot of pot. Parents super liberal. Not a globetrotter but aspired to trot the globe, man. Had minored in Mandarin, just to be different. Cared a lot how he looked but dressed like he wanted people to think he didn't. Moved to Shanghai alone, trying to find himself, just like me. For this one fleeting day, our Paths crossed.

"Makeup, eh bro?" Kelly asked.

We were in the makeup room. I sat in front of a mirror with bulbs encircling it like a spaceship. An attractive young makeup artist scoured and prodded my every facial contour the way a painter examines her canvas before laying down the first brush stroke.

"Yeah, man. Seems that way."

"Dude, you gotta get dolled up for them bright lights."

"Right, hombre." I went with it.

"Speakin' my language now homie."

"Bro on." I said it but wasn't sure what it meant.

Meanwhile, my giggly makeup artist began to paint. I glanced over at Royce, who was also getting "the treatment" from another makeup lady. His eyes were closed, and I think he was holding his breath.

I got a faint chill down my spine as the artist blushed my cheeks, giving them a rosy hue that popped in the mirror. The only other time I'd been powdered with makeup before was when I played Poins in my eighth grade class's production of King Henry VIII: Part II. Don't ask.

Kelly escorted us to the set. It was almost time. *Alright, Mr. DeMille, I'm ready for my close-up.*

Kelly explained to Royce and me the premise of the episode on which we were about to play talk show guest. The idea was that we were to debate the value of extracurricular activities in schools in China. The three opinions would come from a student (Royce), a parent (Mr. Jin), and a teacher (yours truly).

We greeted Mr. Jin. A few minutes later, we entered the studio floor, where I got my first glimpse of our host, Sammy Yang.

He was wearing a slick gray blazer and a blue, checkered shirt while seated contentedly behind a cheap wooden desk. Like Mr. Jin, it looked as if Sammy's hair had been parted by Moses.

There was an autographed, poster-sized portrait of Sammy Yang on the studio wall. Next to Sammy's desk was a shiny glass coffee table with nothing on it. Three boxy white plush chairs surrounded the table. The temperature in the studio was freezing. I shivered.

Kelly motioned the three of us into the white chairs next to the desk.

Immediately, Sammy dove in, without any introduction.

"I will lead the discussion and ask you questions. You will answer them. You should feel free to disagree with each other in order to cause as much conflict as possible." *Right.*

Of course, Royce and Mr. Jin were two of the most calm, composed people I have ever met. There would be no disagreements today. We were informed that there would only be *one* take of the show. No retakes. "So don't screw it up," was the message.

The lights behind the cameras dimmed, the chatter and hustle-bustle melted away, and before I knew it, a red

LED light next to the primary video camera illuminated, indicating that the show was now *recording*.

Host Sammy's face snapped into smile mode like a kid posing for a Christmas photo. He launched into the welcome-to-the-show monologue, the only sound in a now silent and dark studio behind the bright lights illuminating my manicured face.

"Culture Matters. It matters. Welcome to the show. We always think that the Chinese students are too busy. They are busy on the homework, and of course, lot of extra-curriculums arranged by the parents and so forth. Well, is extra-curriculum right, or is it a right thing to do? What about after-school activities, and after, uh, class activities? To some of the colleges in the United States, they do consider that's a very important element, for application, for student to 'applicate.' Send their applications. Let's find out through three different standpoints of view." He gestured to Royce. Royce winced.

"My name is Royce. I am a student. I like extracurricular activities."

There was an awkward pause while we all waited for the rest of Royce's sound byte that never came. Mr. Jin then broke the silence.

"The legacy of mental faculties is essential the mentalities."

*Uh.*

Then, Sammy turned to me: "Mr. Ed, what do you think? In the Chinese society right now, lot of parents just arrange lot of things for their kids. Piano classes, I mean ballet classes, I mean drawings, and/or karate, Chinese calligraphies, and so forth. On top of their homeworks and school days. Will you do the same things?"

"Well I—"

Mr. Jin cut me off. "Certainly. I think the after school program not only to give the student extra skills. And most of times, they have a special training for the mentalities. This they may cannot get from the school. I say the schools they give you the to learn most of their knowledges..."

Huh?

Mr. Jin kept going, deep in rumination over the status of the universe or something. What were we talking about again? After hearing his commentary, I needed some extra training for *my* mentalities. How can a guy say so much and also say so little? When was it time for me to say anything?

"Mr. Ed."

Host Sammy was staring at me.

"Mr. Ed?"

The red *record* light of the camera glowed like an orb in the dark studio.

My cue! I had no idea what the question was. Producers, directors, cameramen, and my fellow talk show participants were all staring at me, so I ventured:

"Hello, my name is Eduardo Mestre. I am an economics and English teacher at Fudan International School. Additionally, I am one of the sports coaches for one of our extracurricular programs, which is a club where students play soccer and football and basketball and other sports. I believe these activities are also very important for students' learning, not just in the classroom, but also out on the field. Learning happens everywhere, and that's why I believe that extracurriculars are very important for students."

Everyone in the studio visibly exhaled. My rant sorta made sense. Phew! I didn't blow my Chinese television debut. We continued across multiple topics of debate. Everyone got involved. Even Royce and Mr. Jin coalesced and had a real conversation.

Host Sammy turned to me, toward the end of the recording. "So, Mr. Ed, like the students call, why else the extra-curriculums is important?"

I drew a breath and blinked hard. When I opened my eyelids again, the cameras were gone. My students were all there, eyes scrunched and attentive. They each turned their head gently to one side, to expose one ear to more adept hearing. I turned left, the chairs occupied by Mr. Jin, Royce, and Host Sammy all faded to a blur. I turned back to the camera, which wasn't there.

"I guess what's exciting is that extracurriculars are this great opportunity to let you be you. You can pick what you want to do, what you want to be, and you do it. They're fun. If you dream of snapping photographs for the cover of Vogue magazine, join the photography club. If you routinely watch videos of Messi scoring bicycle kick goals on YouTube, then lace up your cleats and come to soccer club. So, I guess the question is not whether or not extracurricular activities are important—it's more about whether you've found something that you care enough about to pursue. Whether you've found something fun, which lets you be yourself. And if you haven't found that, you should keep searching."

What I said looked lost on Sammy Yang's face. Mr. Jin similarly looked a little vexed. They were looking for more of an answer along the lines of how important extracurricular activities are for admission to American universities, or whether being a teacher bestows societal stature. But the bigger question is whether you give a shit about anything. Participating in extracurriculars is a sign that you actually give a damn. I looked over to Royce, who smiled to himself. He got it.

Sammy Yang didn't know what to say. He looked down at his notes for a stock question. "Well, Mr. Ed, are you the passionate teacher?"

"Well, Sammy," I slouched in my chair, "I guess it's not that I'm the world's most passionate teacher. I've just discovered that even though not every student wants to sit through repetitive lessons on English grammar or economics, if you create a happy little bubble where students can relax and be themselves, where you can have a little bit of fun, those moments of magic will make you care about things about which you didn't know it was possible to care."

I peeked over, and Royce's smile grew wider. The red record light turned off. I walked out of the studio and went home. Just like that, my Chinese television career was over.

\* \* \*

The episode aired the following week to an audience of millions, which, given the size of China, was probably construed as a commercial failure. International Channel Shanghai was not done with us, however. A week or so later, a full camera crew came to FIS and followed Miles around and filmed him for an entire day for the reality show *Shanghai Quest*, which detailed the lives of expats living in Shanghai. When my students inquired about the cameras following Miles, I shrugged.

Anthony, a quick-on-his-feet tenth grader from Papua New Guinea, then asked me a wise-beyond-his-years question: "Mr. Ed, does being white in Shanghai instantly make you a celebrity?"

"Well..."

In the spring, something happened that made China the focal point of all eyes on Earth. In Sichuan province to the West, the ground began to shake violently, and the rest of the world would soon discover that 90,000 poor souls had perished in the earthquake and its aftermath. I was shocked at the astoundingly impressive response of the Chinese to rescue their endangered brethren. It was incredible. The government sent every possible resource possible to Sichuan province: men, machines, money, medicine. The public desire to contribute funds and relief supplies was so great that there were insufficient resources to actually collect all the money and supplies people were donating.

Fudan International School also did its part. We amassed supplies and pooled money. Better yet, spearheaded by PR Guru Nina Song, FIS organized a volunteer trip to go visit some of the schools in the areas where the loss of life had been great. A few weeks later, a few of us teachers would lead ten of our older students on this trip. We were going to deliver books and other supplies, as well as teach

English classes and play games with some of the students who had been most affected. It was a noble cause.

When I signed up to chaperone the trip, I got the mysterious feeling that this trip might be my last in China. But in such an unpredictable place, it can be dangerous to think so far into the future. After all, tomorrow is another day.

The following week brought the arrival of the Chinese spring holiday, meaning we had no classes on Thursday and Friday.

Adventure beckoned. Life called. The Path left a voicemail. Ever since that first faculty dinner in the Sichuan restaurant, the boys and I had long dreamed of climbing Huangshan, China's famous "Yellow Mountain." For about nine months, it was nothing more than a myth—a spectacular pinnacle that old Chinese painters fawned over. Late that spring, as Miles thumbed through a China guidebook, we learned that you could actually drive to Huangshan from Shanghai in about six hours. The myth immediately became more real. With two days off from class, we knew that this weekend was our shot.

Huangshan is the tallest mountain in all of Eastern China—1,864 meters (6,115 feet). That may not sound like a lot, but this country has a way of turning molehills into mountains. This hike would be a far cry from the island of Putuoshan or the endless staircase in Nanjing that led to the mausoleum of Dr. Sun Yat Sen.

Huangshan is no Everest, but then again I was no Edmund Hillary. In all my muscle-toning, testicle-drying gym bonanzas, I had yet to hop on the Stairmaster. Now was my chance.

Of us four amigos, not a single one was a born outdoorsman. In fact, we all hailed from cities and could not even claim suburbia as home, let alone the wicked wilderness. The only altitude I had ever achieved came via elevators and airplanes, and more recently in China, via stairs.

And there would be stairs indeed this long weekend. Many, *many, many* stairs. In fact, our guidebook informed us that one could climb the entire mountain by staying on a single staircase that ascends the entire way up. *One* staircase that ascends a vertical mile. One Path, with no deviations. That has to be some kind of record. We also read that there were a couple of moderately comfortable hotels at the summit. Amenities and creature comforts aside, this was going to be a hell of a workout.

So, our stated goal for the four days was to rent a car, navigate six hours on Chinese highways to a remote base town South and West of Shanghai in a province none of us had ever visited, climb 1,864 meters (6,115 feet) to the apex of Huangshan, spend the night atop the mountain, descend, drive all the way home, and not die. All in that order.

In the land where everything goes wrong, and a simple

errand can require two or three attempts before successful completion, this was no small ask. Ken in particular was convinced that we were all coming home in a body bag. Who grabs a pair of sneakers and a map and heads out into the abyss to climb a Chinese mountain? A few months back, I could barely buy a cell phone, and now I was going to climb a mountain?

Success hinged on at least thirty-four different uncontrollable variables—the magnitude of it all made my head spin. Tracking down a car, navigating out of Shanghai, finding lodging, locating this mountain, praying for good weather, avoiding steep cliffs, hoping we were sufficiently fit, trying not to anger any monks, and so on. It was a lot to wrestle with.

OK, step one: find a car. Once again we used the ever-powerful Nina the PR Guru as our liaison and reserved ourselves another Volkswagen Santana 3000 model Shanghai taxi from the same car rental agency that we had used once upon a time to investigate Chinese Suburbia. This was going to be a long taxi ride.

A few hours after giving our students the old heave-ho on Wednesday afternoon, Jean-Louis, Miles, and I were making preparations and fetching any gear that could be of use from our rooms up at FIS campus in order to pack up the taxi and drive it downtown to our apartment in preparation for Thursday morning's departure.

It was Ken's job to go retrieve the vehicle before we left school campus and drove downtown for the evening. Miles was tied up, so he couldn't do it.

"You don't have a Chinese driver's license," Miles reminded him. "How are you going to get the car?"

"I just have a feeling it will be fine," he replied, out of character.

Fifteen minutes before our meeting time, Ken texted us to tell us that he had a "surprise."

"Jesus. I knew that tall landmass was going to fuck this up," Jean-Louis shook his head. We hadn't even left yet. "Surprise" in China usually means there's no toilet paper, or someone just ran over your puppy. This could not be good.

In a stunning turn of events, this was a *good* surprise. Ken cruised through the gates of our school in a brand new minivan. He rolled down the window.

"Surprise!" He was beaming.

"What the?!" Miles was confused. "I thought we reserved a taxi."

Ken dove right in: "So, here's what I think happened. No

one spoke English, but I'm pretty sure it is a busy weekend for car rentals, and the agency had run out of cars."

"That can happen?"

"So, the owner of the agency, in an attempt not to lose face by screwing a bunch of whiteys out of an automobile, took it upon himself to personally lend us *his own car* for the entire duration of the holiday. And of course, no rental car agency owner rolls around in a crappy taxi. He gave me the keys to this groovy minivan you see right here, complete with plush seats, a high tech sound, and an integrated DVD system."

Jean-Louis was sold: "Ken, this is a sweet, sweet victory to begin the weekend. That said, please don't ever call a minivan 'groovy' again."

"Nice!" I belted. "We are winning!"

We *were* winning. A four-day road trip in a cramped taxi might have been rough.

The next morning, it was anchors aweigh. As we had once before in the past, we set sail westward, this time armed with Chinese roadmaps and a family cruiser, the comfort of which would have been the object of jealousy among soccer moms in any suburban landscape.

As we scooted towards some of the major highway arteries pumping traffic out of Shanghai, the ratio of tractor-trailers to passenger cars grew perilously high to the point where our van almost got swallowed whole in an ocean of metal, rubber, and exhaust. Here was the source of your GDP growth right here. The air was noxious.

"Try not to inhale," Jean-Louis said. "*Tu peux mourir.*"

"I could die? Well good thing you just spent your final breath warning us," said Miles.

"You're welcome," retorted Jean-Louis.

"Technically, that was an exhale." I butted in, and then I watched Jean-Louis inhale. "OK, now he's dead. Or at least highly diseased."

"Ken, are you holding your breath?" Miles asked.

"Nope," he squeaked, inadvertently letting out a little bit of air.

"Somebody punch him," Jean-Louis obliged.

"What the hell, Jean-Louis?"

"OK, now you're dead, too."

Though our maps were entirely in Chinese, this time we smoothly navigated west on the main highway out of Shanghai—the A3. The only major unpleasantry was the diesel diarrhea emanating from all the eighteen-wheelers on the road. For a fleeting moment, we were silent.

"What do you guys get paid?" Ken broke the silence with a sledgehammer.

"How many months you been waiting to get that off your chest?" Miles asked.

"I get paid enough to simultaneously buy myself 200 Chinese prostitutes," Jean-Louis offered.

We all tried to do the math in our heads.

"Is that like a bulk discount or sticker price?" I asked.

"Sticker."

"Hmm." Ken was drawing a mental comparison.

"Why now, tall one?" Miles reasoned.

"Well, I overheard something the other day." He paused. We waited for an awkwardly long moment. Jean-Louis finally obliged.

"Oh, really, Ken? What, pray tell, did you happen to over-hear?" He asked the required question in a high-pitched voice.

"I didn't overhear anything, as much as I was in the office at school and saw something on Linda's computer screen." He paused again.

"Oh really, Ken? What, pray tell, did you happen to see on Linda's computer screen?" Jean-Louis obliged a second time.

"The salaries of all of the Chinese teachers at FIS."

"Whooooaaaaa," the three of us replied in unison.

"Well, I just saw only two before I looked away. Wei's and Jing's." He paused a third time.

"Out with it."

"100,000 RMB each."

"Interesting," I said sheepishly.

"And that's less than you make..." Miles edged us forward.

"Yeah..."

"Jesus, Ken, what's your salary?" Jean-Louis was impatient.

"I'm not saying mine first. What if yours' are bigger?"

"I'll show you mine if you show me yours," said Jean-Louis.

"This is getting uncomfortable," admitted Miles.

Then Jean-Louis said, "OK, fine. On three."

"Fine."

"OK."

"One."

"Two."

"Wait wait wait wait!" Ken jumped in. "Dollars or RMB?"

"RMB." Please let my salary be the same as theirs, I thought to myself.

"Fine. One. Two. Three!"

"200,000 RMB!" All four of us yelled in unison.

"Oh thank God," said Ken.

"Fuck me, I should be worth more than the three of you combined," said Jean-Louis.

"Well," Miles reasoned, "the bigger issue at hand, besides our pay scale parity, is the fact that we all make *double* what our Chinese counterparts up at school make."

"Hardly seems fair..." I said the obvious.

"I think we can all agree that it's complete bullshit," Jean-Louis said what we were really thinking. "But none of us is going to do anything about it."

Twice the pay of fellow teachers with the same experience taking on the same workload teaching the same number of classes? There was only one plausible explanation: they were Chinese, and we were American. I felt undeserving.

We passed Hangzhou, a city known for the mysterious West Lake. About three or four hours into the road trip, every single car on the road disappeared. Where were we? The final stretch of our six-hour trip to the town of Tankou, at the base of Yellow Mountain, was on a newly constructed and completely empty stretch of road. Mystery abounded.

By nightfall, we reached our destination in the town of Tankou, a random little hotel (also found through Nina the PR Guru), without a hitch. We ate some unidentifiable food at a local restaurant and got to sleep. The next day was going to be a long one. We were going to climb a Chinese mountain.

Around 8:00 AM that Friday morning, the morning sun shone through our four-bed hotel room window like destiny and beckoned us to the great outdoors. It was one of those conquer-the-world mornings—the backdrop of a Frosted Flakes commercial before Tony the Tiger exclaims, "They're gggrrrrrrrreeeeeeat!"

Incredibly, as we emerged from the hotel in this Chinese mountain base camp, we met a guy on the street who ran a restaurant that served *American* breakfast. We followed him to a ramshackle establishment.

Michael Jackson's greatest music videos were playing on a television in the corner. We chowed on eggs and bacon while bopping our heads to the swanky beats of *Thriller* and *Bad*. Today was going to be a good day.

We thanked our gracious host and cook with a few extra RMB in tip and walked back to the hotel. In the lobby, we checked our maps, consolidated our gear, and set out. We left our car in the hotel parking lot, hopped in a cab, and told our cab driver that we wanted to be dropped at the base of Huangshan Mountain.

The taxi stopped by the side of the road next to a nonde-script single concrete set of stairs, which shot like a laser up the inclined hillside. There was no one else around. Just us and the Path.

Our driver turned around and smiled at us. Then he pointed up.

"This?" We asked the driver. The driver nodded.

"We just follow this set of stairs to the top of the mountain?"

"The driver says yes," Miles confirmed.

"Fuck it," Jean-Louis said, and got out of the cab. The rest of us followed.

We started climbing. Left. Right. Left. Right. Left. Right. Up. Up. Up.

After twenty minutes, we paused to catch our breath. Out of nowhere, we were overtaken by two local sherpas lug-ging a *fat Chinese guy* up the mountain. The fat guy sat in a bamboo chair contraption attached to wooden rails. The sherpas held the wooden rails on their shoulders as they forged toward us. As they approached at a much faster pace than we were moving, I caught a better glimpse of the fat guy. He was smoking a cigarette while these two guys lugged him up the ascent.

"What do you think that guy does for a living?" Ken asked.

"Bamboo magnate?"

"Importer/exporter?"

"Human trafficker."

The poor sherpas were flinging sweat like a priest flings holy water upon the blessed churchgoers. Too bad they still had an extremely long way to travel, as did we. Were they going to lug this guy one vertical mile to the summit? We pressed onward.

My muscles began to burn. We saw a bunch of monkeys. They seemed at ease climbing up and down the stairs. Step. Step. Step. Already this was the longest staircase I had ever seen or climbed in my entire life, and we had barely been climbing for one hour. We were below the tree line, obscuring any view that could pinpoint our progress.

The path steepened. A pair of monkeys joined us for a 100-meter stretch of the path. They hardly looked tired.

The surrounding dirt quickly turned to rock, and the trees

got bigger. Later, during occasional breaks in the tree cover overhead, we could catch a glimpse of the jagged, mini-mountain peaks encircling the lower levels of the range. *Whoa.*

Other than our friend in the chair, we encountered fewer than a dozen people during the first two hours of the climb. Our isolation bestowed a real sense of mysticism to the mountain and our endeavor. Rest stops grew more frequent. We were already breathing heavily.

Finally, the path leveled. We heard a murmur. As we walked toward it, the noise grew louder.

It definitely wasn't the "sound of the mountain" or the wind in the willows or the call of the wild or anything like that. The sound of the murmur was...*people*. Lots of people. I turned to Jean-Louis, Ken, and Miles, and showed them my face of bewilderment.

"I hear people."

"So many people."

"I hate people."

Eventually, the trees gave way to a sea of colored t-shirts and a million voices all talking as loudly as possible.

It was a parking lot—a massive parking lot, complete with about thirty tour buses and thirty accompanying Chinese tour groups. Every single tour group had decided to outfit its clan with red hats and monochromatic t-shirts.

There were at least a thousand people in the parking lot. CHINA!!! You have fooled us once again. Gone were our two hours of meditational silence, replaced by a swift reminder that this was a very crowded country.

Jean-Louis, sweaty and huffing from our morning climb, planted his feet down on the asphalt in the parking lot, raised his arms, and looked skyward.

"CHIIIINAAAAA!!!" He screamed to the heavens in agony.

"Fuck." I said. "God, you cannot be serious." Up above, God chuckled.

We learned that we had started our hike from the absolute bottom of the endless staircase. But there was a parking lot a third of the way up, which could cut your hike significantly. That's what about 1,000 Chinese tourists in red hats had decided to do.

Miles just shook his head and laughed. The other three of us were not as amused.

The parking lot was manic. Trinket shops. Throngs of people. The base station for a cable car to the summit. Confusing signs. No English. The one thing missing was a vendor peddling shells and oranges.

"So much for this morning's serenity," Ken said.

"Wow, this is hectic," Miles utilized one of his signature Chinese phrases.

Even Miles was vexed by the Chinese signage in the parking lot. Where did our magic staircase continue? We searched for a sign in English. Finally, we found one. It had three bits of useful instruction:

1. "Please do not enjoy the view!"

2. "Don't flirt monkeys by feeding them."

3. "Be cautious in thunderstorm."

At last, the least helpful sign in all of China. We circum-navigated the parking lot until we found a staircase that led skyward. Next to it was another sign in English:

1. "Do not fall off mountain"

2. "Do not smash head on rock."

"I think it's this way," I declared to the group. This was definitely the path. We looked behind us.

There was a kiosk to obtain tickets for the gondola ride to the very top of Huanghan Mountain. I tried to ignore the burning in my quads as we walked past the gondola entrance and continued walking.

As we marched onward, I thought about the guy being lugged up in the chair from the bottom. If he was so lazy, why didn't he just take the bus and then ride the cable car to the top? Paying two poor locals to physically drag you up the path to the summit is just masochistic. Maybe that was the point.

We continued up the staircase, which was suddenly jam-packed. Ninety percent of that foot traffic, however, was coasting down the mountain, not up.

"Looks like most Chinese mountaineers took the cable car to the top and walked down," Miles called back to us. From a purely logical standpoint, this made infinitely more sense than what we were attempting.

The only other people walking up? Porters, carrying everything from loads of clean laundry for the hotels on top, cartons of food for hungry climbers, or lazy people in chairs. Now we saw tons of guys being hauled up the mountain while sitting in a chair. They must have all been cousins of our fat, smoking friend from this morning.

All of these porters passed by me without issue. Do you know how embarrassing that is? To get lapped by someone carrying a 150-pound sack, or a 150-pound guy? I was not exactly the fittest guy up there, but these porters were making me look like a paraplegic.

"How much do you think it costs to hire two guys to carry you up?" Jean-Louis asked.

"You couldn't *pay me* to get carried up," declared Ken. "I'd be worried that they'd throw my butt off of the mountain."

"Stop worrying so much."

"Get a couple of beers in this tall guy," I said, "And he'll loosen up."

"He always does," Miles smiled.

"Task at hand, boys," Ken looked up the mountain.

"它要多少钱," Miles asked one of the guys being carried. The guy suavely dragged on a cigarette and then answered. Miles turned to us.

"It costs 200 RMB to get lugged up the mountain."

"That's like $30."

"Solid bargain."

The cliffs were getting steeper still, and though there was still plenty of tree cover, it was no longer feasible to explore off-path without falling down an endless crevasse.

Peek over the side of the staircase, and you could see straight down forever.

We could now see farther up toward the mountaintop. Some of the higher peaks rose majestically out of the depths below, and I could instantly see why this place was so famous, and the subject of such adoration in traditional Chinese art.

Each of the peaks looked as if the ground below had split open its surface for an instant, and each of these rock masses sprung forth in a desperate attempt to free itself from Earth's possessive clutches. They had jolted skyward without regard for one another, and the result was a series of disparate, jagged peaks all competing for the sky's attention. People were an afterthought in this surreal expanse.

I took more pictures on this single day than I did on any other day the entire year.

We plucked along. At one point, Jean-Louis stopped in front of me. He looked up to the radiant sun.

"Guys, we are *winning*." For a second, Jean-Louis was at peace.

A bird flew by overhead. "GAAAAAAAHHHHHHH!"

"Fuck! A bird just shat on my face!" Jean-Louis screamed. "China!" We all keeled over laughing.

Another hour or two of climbing, and we turned a corner in the path to suddenly catch a clear vista of the summit itself a couple of kilometers up ahead of us. Almost there!

We were at the bottom of one final valley—glorious green interspersed with the mountain's uniquely jagged rocks.

"Anyone know the theme song to Jurassic Park? Seems appropriate right now," I announced.

"Dun dun duuuuuun dun dun, dun dun duuuuuun dun dun," Jean-Louis was on point.

"What a freak," Miles shook his head.

"I am getting a prehistoric vibe here," declared Ken.

"Every time I look up, I'm worried I'm gonna get swooped up by a pterodactyl," I went with it. Jean-Louis instinctively grabbed his head for a second. A nearby monkey copied him.

"Weren't pterodactyls vegetarians?" asked Miles the scientist.

"Yeah, right. Giant scaly dinosaur birds swooping down to gobble up carrots and heads of lettuce," Jean-Louis pounced.

Miles paused for a second to conjure the appropriate comeback and then ventured: "Dude, carrots? Lettuce? Dinosaurs lived 65 million years ago. Human agrarian culture didn't emerge until a few thousand years ago. It's not like there were T-Rex's and then there were other dinosaurs planting vegetables. They ate grass."

"Local, organic, gluten-free, non-GMO grass," Jean-Louis parried.

"It's a wonder our ancestors survived natural selection," Ken said.

"Take it easy, mutant Charles Darwin," Jean-Louis ended it.

Up ahead, one last segment of stairs rose up through the rocks. Beyond the top step in the distance, we just saw sky. After eight hours of climbing, at last we stepped up onto that last step onto a giant landing area with pathways, and several buildings, replete with about hundreds of Chinese tourists, mostly in red baseball hats. The top of the gondola ride dropped off dozens of additional tourists every minute. There were a couple of hotels, and even a *quik-e-mart*.

"Is this it? What the fuck? It's like a fucking strip mall!" Jean-Louis cursed.

Miles casually asked something to the gondola attendant.

"This guys says that the true peak is up that way, another couple hundred meters." Miles pointed toward a quiet stone pathway, hidden among dense brush, leading up and away from the kinetic madness in the landing area.

"I suppose we go onwards? I hope the path isn't too dangerous," said Ken.

"Hold that thought." Jean-Louis ran into the quik-e-mart and emerged with a six-pack. "For the summit," he explained.

In addition to the beer, Jean-Louis bought a white baseball

cap that said "Ernesto Zedillo: Para el bienestar de tu familia." Translation: Ernesto Zedillo: For the wellbeing of your family.

*Side bar.* Who is Ernesto Zedillo? Apparently, he was president of Mexico from 1994-2000. Why a Mexican politician's campaign hat was for sale in a mountaintop convenience store in Huangshan, China, is a mystery for the modern era. Then again, in the land of chopsticks and little dicks, this was just another unanswerable question on my list of unanswerable questions. Jean-Louis placed the hat on Ken's head, flipped it on backward like a "cool guy," and no one batted an eyelash.

The sky ahead was beginning to dim. Our last pathway snaked left and right until it ran into a tilted slab of stone the size of a basketball court. We ambled up the rock on all fours until the brush around us gave way to an open-air expanse where you could see for miles. It was a revelation. We had reached the end of the Path with no further jockeying possible by which to ascend farther up toward the heavens.

We plopped down on the rock among a few dozen Chinese tourists to watch a sunset that made me forget that the rest of the world existed. I closed my eyes and breathed in deeply through my nose. I smelled...nothing. For the first time in China, I smelled nothing—just a crisp, cool gush of nothingness, nothing of which smelled like anything, which was more wonderful than everything, which was supremely...nothing.

My legs ached and my heart yearned. A few miles across from us in the distance, a series of Huangshan's joint mountain peaks rose and fell like the blade of a serrated knife, slicing the sky open, pouring radiant sunshine into the whole valley. The lush spring green of the tree line crept up toward the top of each peak, desperately trying to achieve the vertical reach of the ethereal rock.

None of the locals noticed our tardy arrival atop the slab. Everyone simply stared into the distance in silence, tracking the sun's alien glow as it arced down between the two tallest points of the range, the sky turning from a calming blue, to a fiery red, and finally to an unconscious purple as the last slice of the sun vanished perfectly into the dip between the highest crests across from our unspoiled vantage point.

Jean-Louis handed me a can of Tsingtao beer.

"Look at that," he guffawed, gesturing to the view. It was almost comical how miraculous it looked. "That is perfect. *C'est parfait.*"

"I haven't even taken a sip yet, but I know that this is going to be the best bad beer I've ever had in my life," I told him.

In quick succession, the four of us flipped a finger under the metal tab. The *ccchhhhkkkk* sound of the twelve-ounce wonder in my right hand was so pronounced, as if it were carbonated by the breath of God. The four clicks of our cans opening rippled through the small audience on the rock and two dozen heads turned around to see the commotion. To their great surprise, there were four white guys drinking beer. Their faces lit up like the fleeting sun.

"*Gan bei!*" ("Cheers!") they all said at once. They laughed. They smiled. We laughed. We smiled. We cheers'ed them back.

We posed for pictures with a posse of about thirty people from Henan province, off on their first-ever vacation. At once, one guy in the group started yelling in Mandarin, "Bring the girl! Bring the girl!"

The rest of group paused for an instant and then chanted collectively, "Yeah! Bring out the girl!"

I turned to Ken. "What the hell is happening?"

From behind the comfy confines of her mother's legs, an

adorable four or five-year-old girl emerged, as if ready
give her first recital. Instant silence.

"Hello." She said calmly, in English. Her entourage erupted
in a collective celebration of accomplishment. *English!*
*English!*

"Hello," Miles responded, in English.

"How are you?" she questioned.

"I'm fine, how are you?" replied Miles.

"Fine," she answered.

"WWHHHOOOOAAA" was the collective cheer from her
family as they all burst into applause, beaming with pride
at the performance of their youngest.

They all talked excitedly. A conversation with an American in English? Did you see that? English! Our girl spoke
English to a white person! Amazing!

Night approached quickly. We scampered down the rock
to go find lodging. Our eyes squinted to find the pathway,
the scant moonlight and the occasional pathway lamp
were our guide. Incredibly, the rest of the summit area was
vastly expansive, covering several square kilometers and

rising and falling in between about twenty peaks of varying height. It would take you half a day to circumnavigate the entire summit area, and even longer to walk along every single path and climb every stair within the summit zone.

There were five different hotels, and fresh-legged Chinese tourists were walking right off of the gondola to the top and meandering off to their various accommodations as we lumbered our final steps of the day, feeling weary and beaten, decades older than we did early that morning.

We ate some ramen from the quik-e-mart, booked four beds in the cheapest dormitory-style hotel we could find, and shut our eyes.

My face hit the pillow and I entered another dimension.

I was awoken abruptly in the darkness by loud voices and the smell of smoke. *Fire! Fire!*

My heart skipped a beat. I jolted upright and hit my head on the bunk bed on top of mine. A quick survey of the scene around me yielded no fire, but rather two Chinese dudes talking really loudly and smoking cigarettes. Cigarettes...in a cramped, shared hotel room with multiple strangers sleeping and only one small window to direct fresh air to everyone's lungs. Ken, Jean-Louis, and Miles had also woken up thanks to these two highly considerate gentlemen.

"*Zhèlǐ bu kĕ yi,*" ("Here not able") I declared to them, in my finest moment of Mandarin to date. They responded something I didn't understand, extinguished their cigarettes, and exited the room with their bags, loudly sounding off their discontent with my "request," as if it were a personal effrontery and an infringement upon their right to smoke in a shared, nearly windowless closet. Sorry, guys. Sorry for being so selfish.

"Countries are like people. They all have assholes," Jean-Louis mumbled as he fell back asleep.

After we spent the next day exploring some of the surrounding peaks at the summit of Huangshan, we ducked into a restaurant near our hotel to refuel. "Holy shit, this menu is amazing!" I exclaimed as I read over the restaurant's expansive offerings. And it was amazing, not so much for the food itself but for the incredible name-translations of the dishes:

"Explosion Crisp Cucumber Garlic"

"Tofu Peppery Burn"

"Sweet-and-Sour Cakes Ribs"

"The Red Side Doufuru"

"Calming and Ingredients"

"Huangshan Pair of Stone"

"Nutrition Old Chicken"

"Chicken Farmers"

"Emblem Flavor Brine Fight"

"Baijun Alter Artillery Vegetables"

"Peanut-Drunk Fruit"

"Emblem-Halogen Xiangan"

"Hongxiangsu Date of Juice"

"Xiangguchaorou Tablets"

"Oyster Sauce Dishes Expense Heart"

"Five-City"

"Emblem of Fans"

"Head Hotpot"

"Shujun Out of Free"

"Fans"

"The Legs"

"Duck Blood"

"Jifu Pills"

"Depth Burden Dumplings"

I looked up to see our waiter standing over me impatiently. Everyone else had ordered. "Uhhhhhhhhhh," I scrambled and pointed, "Calming and Ingredients? And the, uh, Emblem of Fans?"

Thankfully they were both tasty—one was a soup and the other was a plate of vegetables. Both could have benefited from a sturdier translation, but the seasoning was on point.

\* \* \*

Waking up on Sunday morning felt like a cold shower. To successfully complete our weekend, we would need to descend the mountain and drive for hours back to Shanghai (again, all without dying), all to ensure that our eager pupils would have something to learn on Monday morning.

To add one additional hurdle, there was a miniature white squall atop the mountain that morning. The view was gone. God bottled up his sunshine once again. It was raining. Conveniently, our hotel sold ponchos (Made in China!).

The first hour down was a little hairy, but there were no casualties. About a quarter way to the bottom, we stumbled upon a curious rock formation that was brutally out of place among all the jagged peaks of Huangshan. About five meters tall and just off the path was the aptly named "Mobilephone Stone." I saw the sign depicting the name of the rock before I actually saw the rock itself. I was about to roll my eyes before I looked up at what appeared to be a giant cell phone made entirely of granite. The body of the rock was strikingly similar to an average flip phone, but the real highlight was that peculiar weathering and winds actually gave the thing a rock antenna. The Mobilephone Stone, situated among wondrous ancient cliffs and peaks, was the perfect metaphor for old vs. new China.

A little farther down, we found an abandoned portable carrier chair, the same exact style as that which we observed the first day in Huangshan when two porters were lugging the overweight guy in a chair up the mountain. Jean-Louis took a seat in the thing while Ken and I attempted to hoist him up a few stairs. We could barely get Jean-Louis-plus-chair off the ground before we dropped him, nearly resulting in an inadvertent tumble down the rest of the mountain.

"My bad, Jean-Louis," I apologized, "I guess I wasn't cut out to be a Sherpa."

"No shit, Sherlock," Jean-Louis said as he stood up and rubbed his ass. "Stick to the classroom."

Only four hours after we set off down the mountain, we hit

the bottom. We made it. We were triumphant conquerors of Huangshan. The fun wasn't over, however.

By some miracle, we found a taxi at the bottom of the mountain to drive us back to the hotel parking lot in Tankou where we had deposited our automobile just three days prior. Just like that. Huangshan was only a spectacular memory.

We ate one last meal at a local restaurant before driving back to Shanghai. We picked the most inoffensive looking local spot and took a seat. We were, however, the only patrons in the restaurant—bad sign.

The family that ran the joint was mesmerized that they had four genuine foreigners eating at their spot. They wore magnetic smiles and rained questions in Mandarin upon poor Miles. After a couple of painful minutes, the family of four disappeared back to the kitchen to prepare our food.

"Apparently they recommend some kind of chicken soup and are going to make it specially for us," Miles filled us in.

"Chicken soup sounds fantastic." Thank you indeed. A tasty chicken soup was really going to hit the spot.

For the next several minutes, we were recapping the triumphs and glories of our weekend conquest.

"Guys, we are winning!" Ken pumped his fist, continuing our weekend catchphrase. We had done great. We had navigated to and summited a legendary Eastern China mountain.

Our conversation was interrupted when, out of nowhere, we heard a piercingly loud "GAAAWWWWK" ring clear as day from the kitchen.

Jean-Louis ducked reflexively, thinking another bird was about to poop on him.

I knew better. It was, without a shred of doubt, the sound of our chicken being murdered and turned into soup.

As we all slowly turned our heads toward the kitchen, Jean-Louis whispered: "Still winning."

For those of you who have never had the distinct pleasure of hearing a chicken get slaughtered, I can assure you that the sound of its neck being snapped is one that will haunt my dreams forever.

But I was still hungry. About twenty minutes later, the entire family of four—parents and two young sons— together brought out a massive vat of soup, their proud creation. The mother gently placed a gigantic cauldron in the center of the table. Her husband and progeny gathered behind her, eagerly awaiting our reaction.

In the vat of soup was an *entire chicken*. The feathers were plucked, but otherwise the entire thing was intact. Head, feet, and all innards were still present and accounted for. I looked down at the table. There were only chopsticks and spoons for the broth. No knives, buzz saws, or other sharp objects. The four of us stared at the chicken.

"Well guys, when in China..." In a veteran move, I armed my right hand with a pair of chopsticks, stood over the vat of chicken, grabbed the bird by the neck with my sticks, and sunk my teeth into its hindquarters. It was delicious.

The family cheered.

The four of us took turns passing the bowl/entire chicken around until all that remained were chicken parts nobody was looking to chew or swallow. If we could conquer a mountain, we could conquer a chicken.

And so it was back to the road with a bird swirling around in my stomach that had been alive an hour ago. It's a man-eat-bird world out there.

About halfway back to Shanghai, our minivan now on a highway zooming along at breakneck speed, we were still talking about how awesome we were for "winning" all weekend long.

"Who won this weekend?" posited Ken from the passenger's seat of the minivan.

"WE won," Jean-Louis and I simultaneously echoed from the backseat.

"And we are *still* winning," chimed in Miles.

"YEAH we are," I was invigorated by what a successful trip it had been.

"Woooooo," Ken gave his fist pump a soundtrack.

"Yeeeaaaaaah," all four of us were hooting and hollering. "We are winning at China!"

Suddenly, out of nowhere, the car rumbled with a massive double sound. *THUD. THUD.* The car jerked violently before straightening out again.

"What the hell was that?"

"What the?! Is the car alright?" I hushed in a panic.

"What the..."

I turned around and saw out of the back window that we had run over a wild dog with our minivan! *Fuck!* I saw multiple chunks of the dog's carcass strewn about the highway. We definitely killed it, all pieces of it. I turned back around in my seat, my eyes wide. All of us sat in silence for a second until Jean-Louis whispered from the backseat:

"We are no longer winning."

"We are no longer winning," the three of us agreed.

The animal kingdom took a small hit that day, but the human population did not, as we later arrived safely back in Shanghai without further incident.

The mountain was conquered. The teachers were tired. Somewhere, the dog and the chicken were approaching the Pearly Gates.

I stared out of my classroom window, envisioning the
ghost of Huangshan rising up on the horizon. All I could
see were the concrete peaks of the Shanghai skyline. The
mountain was gone. I sighed.

This particular week was atypical for one gigantic reason:
Helga, math teacher extraordinaire from Turkey, had
arranged the one-week visit of a dozen high school students from a school in her hometown in Turkey. Hide
your children: the Turks were invading!

Each of the Turkish students introduced themselves at
an all-school meeting and said a few sentences in English
in front of the one hundred attendees. I'm sure we can
all remember studying a foreign language in high school
and dreading the thought of speaking up in front of the
entire class. These poor kids had the doomsday triple play:
addressing one hundred strangers in a foreign country in
a foreign language. Poor Eurasians.

Each of them, though—with names such as Gizem and

Nicolai—spoke enough English to hang proudly on their refrigerator door. Still, they were a long ways away from fluent. I was not surprised to learn that the three best English speakers of this group of turkeys would be attending my *Native English Speaker's Grammar* class for the following five days. What creativity could I invoke?

"Good morning, students," I commenced the first lesson. "I hope you have all had a wonderful weekend." Addressing my three new students, I said, "Looks like we've got three new passengers on board Air Fudan International School. I'm your pilot, Mr. Ed. Today we'll be cruising at 30,000 feet. Or as they probably tell you in Turkey, 10,000 meters. In the event of an emergency, there are life preservers under your seat. Please put on your own oxygen mask before assisting other passengers." All my students laughed. The three Turks looked like their plane was going down.

"Today, we are going to have some fun. We will be doing some creative writing, but the exciting part is that you are all going to be crafting stories *together*. I want each of you to get out a piece of paper and a pencil." This was some rustling, shuffling, and muffling as my command was executed. My Turkish pupils also followed suit after first stealing glances at the other kids in the room to make sure they were correctly following my instructions. *This is the easy part, guys.*

"Now, I want each of you to write the title and first sentence of a story and then pass your paper to your neighbor on your left. When you receive a piece of paper from your neighbor, you will then write the second sentence of *that* story. In the end, we should have eleven different stories, each with eleven sentences. Every one of you will have written one sentence in each of the stories."

How did I come up with this concept? Come up with distinct lesson plans for several hundred classes and you'll get pretty inventive, too.

And so, eleven pens met eleven papers, and eleven pairs of lips attempted to mask silent giggling as each student strung together a capital letter and a period and then passed off their budding masterpieces to their seatmates. The process later became more intriguing as students had to first digest all the sentences already on the page before adding theirs to the bottom. Even the Turks were loving it. At the end of the class, I read all of the stories aloud, first scanning them myself to ensure all were appropriate. Ten of them certainly were, consisting of the usual illogical but mildly humorous adventures of animals and princesses and robbers and airplanes and Nintendo.

The final story, on the other hand, was the sort of material you saw on your television on shows like *Cops* or *America's Most Wanted*:

"The burning sky churned and toiled upon itself. Scared, she ran across the busy roads of America, her home and her fear. Suddenly, she heard the terrifying sounds of helicopters above her. The FBI had arrived, now she was shaking fast because of her fear. She was hiding 20 kilograms of marijuana in her closet and she would be busted. Then, she decided to burn all of it in her fireplace. But, her cousin Danny was a drug addict and stole all of the drugs and had a party. The party was so good. However, the cops came and arrested everyone for illegal drug possession; remember, drugs are bad. After that everyone has gone to prison and lived happily ever after. But there was a problem."

Oh boy. Story content aside, I was feeling pretty impressed with my kids. Despite their affinity for ganja, their work was impressive. Stories like these were the exception, not the norm.

Minus this single story, my class activity had been a giant success, so I decided to try it with my middle school grammar students, whose English capabilities were not as polished. What resulted rivaled the high school kids' story more than I expected:

"The girl, who is the prettiest in the world, came to Shanghai to an international school. Girls hate her and boys looked up her and like her a lot. One day, the boy who is the most handsome in the world appeared. Boys hated him and girls liked him a lot. Finally, the handsome boy and the pretty girl were dead because all students in the high school killed them."

Sigh. They were only middle-schoolers, but already some of the jealousies and insecurities of adolescence were surfacing. American, Chinese, Korean, Japanese, Taiwanese...some things just don't change.

The last sentence of the story was written by violent Valiant, the clever but tiny seventh grader with the wheeled, rollaway backpack who would always write action stories more suitable for a John Woo film than for a composition in English class. It was apparent that in this story there would be no "happily ever after." The stories may have been silly, but there was something magical about holding up a piece of paper that all of your students have written together. I wanted to hang each story on my refrigerator.

\* \* \*

By Friday, the Turkish students and our hodgepodge FIS troupe were all so close that it seemed there was hope for all global cultures to get along. It almost gave credence to the average Miss America contestant's advocacy for world peace. I had not given Helga sufficient credit. Later in the week, I told her how impressed I was that she had organized a delegation from her country to come visit us. She smiled back. For once, she didn't have to say anything.

"Welcome you, the Fudan International School," he began in broken English, "We are so very grateful you come help. Every day I have sadness."

The school principal at the refugee camp had deep, sullen eyes that had seen too much death. We were in Sichuan province with a small volunteer group of FIS students and small faculty entourage. There was dirt under our feet and a fleet of makeshift caravans around us.

A bell rang through a loudspeaker. Out of the caravans strode thousands of students with heads slung low. They were the survivors. Many of their classmates were with God now, victims of a massive earthquake several weeks prior. No one seemed to notice us.

Another bell rang. It was time for us to teach. We divvied up our student group and approached our rooms, ready to try to teach these earthquake survivors a bit of English.

I walked into the classroom and met five rows of desks

with fifty gaping first graders, all ages six or seven. Their eyes stuck to me like magnets, their ears perked in anticipation for the moment when I would open my mouth to speak foreign words. A handful of older FIS students, some Koreans and some Hong Kongese, stood behind me. Here I was, the lone white guy in a classroom of young Chinese earthquake survivors, as they waited for me to part my lips.

"Hello students," I declared affirmatively.

One hundred eyes looked at me emptily. One kid even scratched his head. I thought of Kotaro. This time around, I was not discouraged. A year in China will teach you some things about resilience.

I cupped my hand to my ear and tried again, even louder this time.

"I saaaid...helloooo stuuuuudents!" The words projected deeply from my belly.

One hundred eyes lit up slowly. "Heeellooo, teacher," replied all the students in surprising harmony, hesitant but coordinated. We all smiled at each other.

"Hooow are you?" I continued.

"I'm fine, thank you, how are youuu?" was their perfectly choreographed reply. They chuckled.

That's all it took. The chasm between us was melted with a few choice words. It felt a connection. My heart went out to them.

My FIS student assistants distributed books, pencils, pens, and other sundries. We played Simon Says. I mattered.

I exited the classroom and gave my FIS student volunteers a high five. Royce Song gave me a gentle nod. Out in the noon daylight in the school's courtyard, students began to point. And gape. And nudge their friends. It's quite likely that, in this small city in central China, we were the most foreign looking group that these young students had ever seen.

The passive, uninterested glances from most Shanghai residents had sometimes made me forget the fact that I was a foreigner in a peculiar land. Shanghai residents were used to seeing foreigners.

Out here, however, that was not the case. We were no longer in Shanghai. This was a remote city in a remote province in the remote west of the remote third world. Foreign folk simply did not travel through here. Our quiet arrival was a distant memory.

I turned to Ken and Miles, "Oh boy."

"Oh boy," Miles repeated.

"Does this make you guys nervous?" Ken asked.

"Feels like they're ready to jump us or something," I concurred.

"That kid there is just staring at me. Literally staring." Ken's eyes nervously locked in on one local student as he walked.

"Well stop staring back, dumbass," said Miles.

"I can't stop now. Neither of us has blinked."

"Dude, they are *all* staring at us."

"I can't blink." Then, Ken, tripped on a rock, fell to his knees, and flung his box of toys and books all over the schoolyard. That made him blink.

An awe-faced young girl with a bowl cut approached me with puppy dog eyes.

"Aww, you are very sweet," I told her. "Do you speak any English? *Wǒ jiào Ed.*"

She paused for a moment but didn't say a word.

Then, she thrust a panda bear notebook and a purple pen skyward.

"Dude, she wants your autograph," Miles muttered. *Autograph?*

"I'm not sure that I would sign..." Ken hesitated.

"Aw, c'mon. No harm no foul?" I jested. The little girl's eyes grew wider.

"You are very well behaved!" I told her.

I grabbed her notebook and purple pen, and scribbled a short message:

Study hard in school!

Mr. Ed :)

She stared at my signature and then hugged her panda bear notebook.

"You signed it?" Miles asked, incredulously.

"Yep."

"Watch, now they're *all* gonna want an autograph," Ken forewarned.

"Oh please, it was for one girl. Live a little. Look how happy she is."

"Yeah, we'll see about th—"

Suddenly, a handful of grinning students surrounded me, waving notebooks. So, I signed a few more autographs, my inspirational message now shorter for each kid.

"Stop signing them!" Ken warned. "You're pouring fuel on the fire."

"I can't tell them 'No.' I'm not a monster!" I chuckled, even though it was immediately clear that Ken was right.

Kids now came sprinting in groups of fifty, and I instantly found myself mobbed by a small ocean of screaming Chinese schoolchildren. I peddled backward from the center of the school playground until my back was against a metal trailer; another hundred autograph seekers who barely reached the height of my crotch were now bombarding me with pens and notebooks. I was trapped! I signed and signed as fast as I could.

A stone's throw away, I could see Ken and Miles were also surrounded.

One little girl snuck her way to the front of the group around me but possessed no notebook. I shrugged to her, and she pointed at her arm. So, I autographed her arm. I was now signing body parts! Sign. Sign. Sign. Breathe. Sign. Sign. Sign. It was a stampede, and only my pen could keep me from getting crushed.

"Ed! What have you done?!" Ken was alarmed.

"Quick, run for the administration building!"

We shook off the throng of autograph collectors, grabbed our things, motioned to our FIS student volunteers, and ducked into the administration building.

"Hi Dad."

"Hi Ed."

"How are you? How's Mom?"

"Good! Busy. Right now I'm staring out the window onto our apartment terrace. Guess what I see?"

"The buildings across the street?"

"The terracotta warrior that you guys bought in Xi'an."

"Outstanding."

"Your mother had to drive her minivan to a port in New Jersey to pick it up because it got flagged by Homeland Security."

"Can't entirely say I'm surprised."

"We miss you."

An emotion. My dad actually had them. I couldn't believe it.

"I miss you guys too." I really did. Just when I had begun to hit my stride in China, I found myself yearning more and more to return the States. I pondered my job offer letter.

"How are things at school?"

"Honestly, pretty solid."

"Yeah?" He beckoned to hear more.

"Yeah. My twelfth grade economics students just took the AP Exam. Think I'm finally finding my groove."

"Great to hear. What else?"

"Well, this is still China. My Mandarin still sucks, last week we ran over a dog with a minivan, I just volunteered at an earthquake relief site, and I don't think I've eaten a salad in months."

"So what's next?"

"After China?"

"*After* China?" He inferred a lot from the word *after*.

"I'm not sure, but I do know that there will be an *after* China."

"So you're coming home? Taking the job?"

I mulled over his question.

"I think I've found what I was looking for."

"So do we have a graduation of sorts? Or a closing ceremony?"

Everyone looked at Linda for an answer.

"We have nothing planned," Linda conceded.

"I want to plan something," I blurted, before I had a moment to process exactly what this meant.

"You want to plan a school graduation for us?"

"Um. Yes. Yes I do." I'd transformed from Mr. Um to Mr. Yes.

"It should involve the entire school and faculty," Linda pondered out loud.

"I agree. It should be an all-school ceremony."

"OK! You're the man, Mr. Ed. Let us know if you need any help." Everyone stood up to leave the meeting.

Wait, what? That's it? Just...go plan a graduation?

Well shit, let's organize a graduation. Though few kids were technically "graduating" from our high school, all students and a number of parents would later attend this version of a closing ceremony. There were to be diplomas, awards, closing remarks. Dear Lord.

After the faculty meeting, I sauntered back to my desk. Had I just bitten off more than I could chew? Maybe.

I took out a piece of paper and a pencil. I wrote the date in the upper left hand corner. I wrote my name in the upper right hand corner. In the middle at the top of the page I wrote "Graduation."

On the line below, I wrote the word "Fuck" four times. I scratched my head like Kotaro. Then I shook my head and crossed out the first four words and wrote out a list.

Graduation

~~fuck fuck fuck fuck~~

1. Come up with award categories and select winners

2. Buy / make / invent awards to hand out

3. Find and book a venue

4. Schedule and invite parents

5. Set up the venue with a stage, chairs, podium, etc.

6. Devise a program for that day

7. Find a keynote speaker

8. Write a program

9. Don't shit pants

10. CHINA!!!

It was a long list. This was going to be a lot of work. For once in my life, I wasn't daunted. Later that day, I got to work on item number one. I opened up a blank word document on my computer and started literally inventing awards to give to our students:

"Most improved English writing"

"Excellence in Mathematics"

"Earnest and Persistent Effort in the Study of English as a Second Language"

"Excellence in Chinese" (I wasn't about to win that one—Miles had it on lock—though had there been an "Excellence in China" award, I might have been in contention for at least second place. *Ni hao!*)

To all my student winners—who no doubt listed these awards on their CVs when applying to college—I apologize for the fact that I completely invented them. I Googled some of them, and others I just pulled out of thin air like a magic spell from Harry Potter.

I promise, my children, these awards are still as special as all of you.

It was a slow process, because I kept switching screens on my laptop and staring at the offer letter from Monitor Group.

Over the next several days, I prepped.

I brought Mr. Lu, the Chinese math teacher, across the street to help translate as I negotiated with a Fudan Fuzhong school administrator to use their gymnasium as a graduation venue.

"FIS wants this space! We can use it! Graduation ceremony. OK!"

The Fudan Fuzhong school administrator nodded at me and smiled. The subtlest hint of respect from a school whose students had beaten me in a track race, and often made me feel inadequate. He gave us the space for the ceremony.

Next, I asked Mr. Pancake (through his translator) to be our keynote speaker. Mr. Pancake may have been our cash-counting, profiteering head administrator, but he was the only natural choice.

His translator replied, "Mr. Wu honored speak at the FIS graduation."

I solicited feedback from other FIS faculty members about which students should win awards. The biggest question I had was what to actually hand students when they won an award. I asked Jennifer, the FIS office admin and local Shanghai resident.

"There is Trophy street near Bund."

"Trophy *street?*"

"Yes. Trophy street."

The next day, I negotiated with a small old lady for a bag of trophies. The stars were aligning. If they could turn satisfaction into a drug I would smoke it. Is that the dorkiest thing I have ever said? Maybe. The best part about it all? I think I finally felt like me.

That Monday late in June commenced the final week of my first year as a teacher at the Fudan International School in Shanghai, China. School is funny that way. It's singularly the only work we do in this world that is so closely tied to the passage of time, with these annual doorways in and out, all packaged so neatly. It's a tidy structure in a world of entropy. But peel back a layer and the thing stinks underneath till you cook it just right. My year of teaching was just about to come out of the oven.

Jean-Louis, particularly, saw the end in sight as he had to leave China early that Wednesday in an attempt to make it home for a friend's wedding that next weekend. Just like that, the Western world was once again beckoning us back as best it could.

Exams Monday and Tuesday were the final brush strokes on the academic painting I had begun back in September. After my last class with my lowest level English learners, all my students filed out of the classroom, except for one.

"Mr. Ed, thank you very much for teaching me to speak in English. I am many more happy today. One year ago, I was sad. Today, I am happy," Kotaro stood tall and looked me in the eye. He didn't scratch his head, and his voice didn't quiver.

"Kotaro, I cannot describe how proud I am to call myself your teacher."

"Thank you Mr. Ed. Today I feel, *eto, eto*, different."

"You have a bright future ahead. Keep your chin up." I recycled some advice from my parents' anniversary cocktail party a year earlier.

Classes were officially over. That Wednesday evening, we held a prom for our students. Have you ever wondered what an end-of-year high school dance is like in China? No? Then I shall tell you. That afternoon, the hallways were abuzz with talk of *the dance*. There were only four or five student couples in student body, so this was going to be the largest single-mingle since the advent of Match. com.

Around 4:00 PM that afternoon, it was time to say goodbye to Jean-Louis. He had been accepted to McGill Law School, openly embracing the fate from which he once ran, if only briefly. For now, he was heading back to North America a touch early for a family wedding. Miles, Ken, Jean-Louis, and I were gathered in the teacher's dormitory.

"Mr. Ed."

"Jean-Louis."

"*Monsieur* Ed."

"*Mon frère*," I dropped some French back at him.

"It's time."

"After all that, you're off to law school. Life moves full circle."

"I know. I sorta knew it all along."

"The sun is setting, my friend," I orated, "It has been a fantastic year."

"It has," he sounded wistful.

"Do you need money for the cab ride?" Ken asked.

"Got enough to spare for a foot massage at the airport," Jean-Louis whipped out his wallet to prove he still he had it.

"One last shot of whiskey?" Miles offered.

Sure, why not. Right there in the teacher's dormitory, Miles poured four glasses of whiskey. We threw them back, just like our wild days from the fall.

We laughed and we reminisced. It still didn't feel real. An hour later, we helped Jean-Louis into a taxi.

"*Au revoir!* See you fucks in the next life!" He yelled out the window with a big smile.

Just like that, he was gone. Our fearsome foursome was reduced to a terrible trio.

"He will be missed," we all agreed. We stood in silence for a minute.

"He would want us to finish that bottle of whiskey, right?" I tested the waters.

Ken agreed: "Oh, absolutely."

So, at 5:00 PM on a Wednesday, the three of us got drunk in the teacher's dormitory at Fudan International School, one hour before we were supposed to chaperone our school prom.

\* \* \*

An hour later, heads buzzing, we crossed our neighborhood roadway, Guoquan Lu, and found the Fudan Fuzhong gymnasium, where FIS prom was being held.

What the hell does "prom" look like in China? My head was swimming in whiskey as we busted through the gym double doors, expecting the beady eyes of our innocent students to accompany their very conservative dance moves. Remember the Christmas party?

Something had changed. The lights were dimmed so much that it took my eyes a moment to adjust. It was my ears, however, that were most surprised.

The DJ had tossed aside the golden oldies and was instead blaring some of the dirtiest rap music I have ever heard.

*I'm all about that fucking*

*tell me you game for mouth sucking*

*follow it up, white pow and a beer...my luck man*

*I'm comin hot as hell, big ol' dick*

*for yo' sweet lips*

"Jesus, who is this DJ that we hired?" I slurred to Ken.

"Oh my God, it's Valiant, the miniature seventh grader." Miles scouted little Violent Valiant on top of the stage with headphones on. His head was barely tall enough to see above the table, but sure enough, he donned a pair of monster headphones and was taking this Fudan International School prom to places that our Christmas party could have only dreamed.

I scanned the rest of the room. Our students were all dancing...dirty. These innocent little tykes from my classroom were all grinding on each other. I guess they did learn a thing or two this year. Mona, the Taiwanese temptress, appeared as if she had definitely been clubbing before. She was swaying suggestively, and it was clear that this wasn't her first rodeo. Tonight, I let it go.

I had barely taken in the scene when I was approached my Yurika—stocky seventh grade girl and coiner of the nickname that hung with me for the entire year, "Mr. Edo." It was impossible to take the conversation seriously while another seventh grader was spinning dirty beats.

"Mista Edo! You dance? We dance?"

"Umm, hello Yurika."

"This music is so good!"

*Bust my nut, deep gut, down that throat,*

*Hope my swimmers can float*

"Yurika, do you understand these words?"

"I like it. But I not understand."

*She could suck more heads than a Hoover*

*A downright, down tight, groover*

*Phew.* Yurika did not understand the lyrics.

"In that case, Yurika, this is *outstanding* music. And highly exemplary of some annals of American culture."

She furrowed her brow. "OK. Thank you, Mr. Edo!"

*Fiending to screw and a mouth dripping yum*

*She tilt her head back and swallow my cum*

I was sweating, but I tried to calm myself with the assurance that some innocence among my seventh graders still prevailed. After all, they had no idea what these words meant. The faces of the older kids told me that they, too, struggled to decipher the wise words of wisdom from America's leading hip-hop artists.

A few songs later, my whiskey buzz was still pulsing. Ken's eyes showed that familiar destructive glint.

"We've got to get out on that dance floor," Ken literally shoved me out onto the dance floor.

"Yes!" Miles and I agreed. So, three *lao wais* entered the dance floor, and there was a widespread, joyous scream among the female student body, audible over Flo Rida, T-Pain, and Li'l Wayne.

I hustled over to the center of the dance floor and dropped my head. Left foot, right foot in tune with the bass. Repeat. My neck loosened, and my head began to wander together with the music over the loudspeaker. My hips couldn't help but obey, and my arms were futile to resist. Somehow, the whiskey tied it all together. Once again, for old time's sake, I danced wildly on a dance floor in China.

This time, the group of spectators was not a throng of indifferent Chinese and expat revelers but the adoring eyes of my students, unaware that I was buzzing and even less aware that the particular rap music enlivening their school prom was grimier than most internet porn.

Eventually, the pace changed. *Take My Breath Away,* the '80s classic, reverberated through the gym as every last student was slow dancing. It was magical. I wanted a hug.

Instead, I got a punch in the arm from a clumsy Ken.

Miles jogged up to the two of us, a little wide-eyed.

"I'm gonna go meet my Chinese girlfriend."

"That's still a thing?"

"She's conveniently peripheral."

"Good luck. Wear a Jizz Bone," I told him. He jogged off through the double doors and disappeared.

I turned to Ken. "That encounter is going to go well," I said sarcastically.

"What do you think they talk about?"

"Politics?"

Prom was winding down.

"Hell of a night, eh?" Ken said.

"Wednesday night fever."

I proofread my email response to Monitor Group. Some words stuck out. Excited. Opportunity. New York. Business team. Accept. I clicked send.

I accepted the job. Officially. I was leaving China. Back full circle to where young Edward grew up and a more mature Ed would return. I think I finally understood that "Me" is comprised of all the little pieces that make us human. The past is a long time, and sometimes we all try to be something that we haven't been before. One day along the road in life, you look back and realize all the fun and all bullshit you've been through is what makes you whole. I was Edward, I was Mestre. I was the attention-seeking third child, the desperate high schooler still trying to fit in. I was Ed, the laid-back college boozer. I was Mr. Ed, a guy on his own Path who'd found the right balance of all these pieces. I'd worked hard. I'd gotten help. Not just my parents. Everyone had helped me onto the Path. Off the Path. Creating a new Path. Chin up. Life. So spin me around. Hear me roar. Throw me in the air. Shuffle the deck. Lord, got to keep on moving. Onto the next version of myself.

We cleaned up. We packed. We settled debts and said goodbyes. Miles, Ken, and I moved out of our downtown apartment just as the construction site across the street indeed reached the thirtieth floor, now completely obstructing our view. For the first time in my life, a portion of an apartment deposit was returned to me. (Third time is a charm!) By now, my appetite for gratuitous destruction and general negligence for my own abode had finally abated. Thankfully, here in China, I had managed to channel most of my destructive forces *outside* the four walls of my living space.

Graduation took place on Friday morning. The entire faculty from my school knew that this was my show. It was the culmination of a year of teaching and the biggest and strangest experience of my life. Today, I was about to emcee an entire school graduation. What could possibly go wrong?

Just thirty-six hours after prom, and we were back in the same gymnasium. There was an anticipatory hum of conversation. Our entire student body, now eighty students, was seated in parallel rows of chairs. Proud parents craned their necks from their seats behind. There were flowers. There was a stage. A banner that read, "Fudan

International School" hung proudly overhead. My palms were sweaty.

"You ready, man?" Miles turned to me, genuinely concerned.

"You can do this." Ken put a friendly arm on my shoulder, rooting for me in earnest. I exhaled, stood up from my chair in the audience, and approached the stage. The murmurs of the crowd quieted down to a tense electricity. I approached the microphone. All eyes were on me.

Down in the front row, Linda's motherly face emanated encouragement. She bowed her head gently, trying to coax out my first words. Ken and Miles nodded from the back corner. They could hardly contain their goofy smiles. Math teacher Mr. Lu was rapt with attention. FIS head administrator Mr. Pancake scanned the room, his brow furrowed, his face stuck in a permanent smirk.

My eyes wandered down into the student body. Kotaro, Valiant, Yurika, Mona, Jin Mon, all my students. They all grinned as my eyes met theirs.

I stepped forward and grabbed the microphone with my right hand. This was it, the moment to demonstrate that I had made it. I was a big boy with a big job, all grown up and presentable. My heart rate cooled a bit as I took in a breath and began my rehearsed opening words.

"Wel—"

I got out half a syllable before someone screamed.

"Mr. Ed! Mr. Ed! Mr. Ed!"

*What was going on? What was wrong?*

It was Helga. She stood up from the audience in a panic. Everyone craned their neck to understand the commotion. She belted in a high voice as she made her way to the stage, sidestepping rows of faculty and parents seated in the back of the auditorium. "I almost forget. I have math awards to give out to my students!"

"Uh, Hel—it seems, er," I stammered into the microphone. "It appears that Helga has some awards to give out."

I relented. Put on the spot, I had no choice but to yield the floor to the chatty Turkish math teacher one last time. HELGA!!! She approached the stage, but rather than take the microphone, she handed me a thick stack of papers. They appeared to be math certificates.

"Oh, thank you, Mr. Ed. You please read the maths certificates now."

"Uh, ok." Our entire conversation was broadcast to the audience via the microphone I was holding. Before I could mutter another word, Helga dashed off the stage and hopped back into her seat. I was left holding a pile of "maths" certificates, which I now had to dole out before I could even begin the graduation proceedings. I looked down at the top certificate and began to read the award and the name into the microphone.

"The award for bronze level series two algebra achievement with distinction goes to...Dong Hun Kim!" The audience started to clap vigorously. *Helga, you have stolen my thunder!* Dong Hun Kim came to the stage to receive his award.

"The award for bronze level series two algebra achievement with *high* distinction goes to...Mizuki Tanaka!" More thunderous clapping. *This is going to take a while.*

There were gold levels and silver levels and A levels and B levels and, forty-five minutes later, I was sure I had handed a math certificate to two-thirds of our student body. I felt like a guy wearing a hot dog suit handing out street fliers. The applause had grown increasingly weary, and the main event hadn't even taken place yet. HELGA!!!

By the final certificate, I could make out the sound of individual people in the audience clapping. I spied one student sleeping in the audience.

Certificates gone, I composed myself, took a deep breath, and spoke to the congregation.

"At last, we have completed handing out the math certificates." Sarcastic applause. "Welcome," I continued with no interruption, "to the Fudan International School Graduation and Awards Ceremony."

Thunderous clapping returned.

"Thank you for your patience, students, teachers, family, and friends. Ten months ago, you all stepped through the doors of this young school, unaware of your surroundings and unsure what to expect." I paused for effect, to the nodding of everyone in the audience. "Look around now. Look at what we have, and look at what we have built together. You, our students, have earned this. As you head into the summer holiday, hold your chin up high, because today is a proud day for our humble little school."

The room fell silent with reflection. Even the students with poorer English grasped the tone of my words.

"We are now ready to begin handing out the FIS school awards." Raucous applause. For me. For us. For FIS.

"The award for improvement in the study of English as a second language goes to...Kotaro Sato!" Kotaro's face exploded in surprise. His seatmates nudged him, and he flew up to the stage, his feet barely touching the ground.

I shook his hand firmly. "Congratulations," I whispered. I handed him a copy of the Oxford English Dictionary, as well as a Chinese scroll with the name of his award written on it. He departed the stage and the parade continued.

"Excellence in the study of economics goes to...Guang Sung!"

"Achievement in creative writing at the middle school level...Valiant Cho!"

And finally, character awards.

"The first annual FIS compassion award goes to a student who always has the needs of others at heart. Please put your hands together for...Jin Mon Rho!" She put her hands to her heart and took to the stage.

Merely a few weeks back, each of the trophies, books, and scrolls that I handed out were a mere figment of my imagination. Today, each of them was a tangible memento of accomplishment and growth. I beamed.

After the last of the awards was handed out, Mr. Pancake thumped up towards the stage to address the congregation in Chinese. I handed the microphone to our keynote speaker. Ten months in China, and I still have no idea what he said. My ~200-word vocabulary would always suffice to order beef noodles, drink copious liters of beer, and negotiate with ~~prostitutes~~ street vendors, but that was about it.

Mr. Pancake motioned with his hands for the entire FIS faculty to come on stage. There would be no Chinese to English translation of his speech this time around, only Chinese. *Uh-oh.*

He began:

"Hello students, hello teachers, hello.............. school ............... students....................... thank you." At this point Mr. Pancake paused and everyone clapped. I also clapped. He continued. This is what I understood:

"................................... school ......................................
...................................................year..............................
.......................................teachers...................................
dumplings...........................................thank you."

All the students and parents rose out of their chairs and began to applaud. Their body language told me the applause was meant for *us*, and I stood solemnly with the other teachers and absorbed the praise. I turned to my left, and I saw Ken also clapping, because his cultural ignorance told him we were simply clapping. Just because.

I elbowed him. "The students are thanking *us*, dude."

"Oh, shit." He immediately pulled his hands behind his back, defensively. Miles just rolled his eyes. I hoped that wherever Jean-Louis was, he could feel the rumbling gratitude.

There is something invigorating and emotionally buoyant about receiving applause. Forget all those self-help books—I am going to start selling CDs of people clapping.

Mr. Pancake concluded the graduation and awards ceremony, and everyone filed out of the gymnasium. I was the last one through the double doors out of the gym. I turned back. The friendly "Fudan International School" banner still hung proudly atop the stage, and the many rows of empty chairs were haphazardly scattered all over the gym. Overhead sunlight, filtered through a hazy filter of clouds, tiptoed through the windows on the wall opposite the door. I turned around and walked out.

We retreated from the gym where graduation was held, over to the FIS school library. To my utmost surprise, upon entering the library, now teeming with books, all of the students were seated calmly, and I could smell that something planned or rehearsed was about occur. *This is what an intervention must feel like.* Indeed, my instincts were correct.

Sonia, the Slovakian ESL teacher, spoke up: "At this time, we ask that all the teachers who are departing FIS please stand in front of all the students, because the students have something to give you." I looked quizzically at my similarly confused colleagues who were also leaving the school: Ken, Miles, and Rachel—the biology teacher who helped Linda with school administration.

We lined up in a row facing our student body, and four students rose simultaneously and approached the four departing teachers. In unison, using both hands, they each extended a book to each one of us and took a bow. I was speechless, full of thanks but simultaneously empty for words.

Eventually, I eked out a stunned, "Thank you." As the pupil population looked on in anticipation, I flipped open the cover of the book to find a collage of images of our school. Each page contained a picture of one of my students, along with a personalized message to me about how I influenced them during the year. *Wow.* I started to tear up. I was never the guy for whom friends went all out and over the top. No one ever threw me a surprise party. My yearbooks from high school and middle school contained sparse signatures with lukewarm well wishes. But now this.

FIS Yearbooks were distributed. I generously signed as many as I possibly could. It's the least I could do to return the time and effort all the students in the school generously put towards the creation of our parting gifts. For most of our students, this was the first time they participated in a Western-style, end-of-year school celebration. This was the last of a year-long series of firsts, for them and for me.

There were tearful goodbyes, camera flashes, and hugs all around. It was in that instant that I witnessed the success that our little school had somehow become. We had really done it.

Mr. Pancake approached me, with no translator. He extended a strong right hand. I shook it in earnest.

"*Xie xie ni*," ("Thank you") he told me. His silly smile was replaced by a muted thankfulness. I answered him in English.

"Thank you, Mr. Wu, for the opportunity," I began, emboldened by the knowledge that he wouldn't understand what I was about to tell him. "Thank you for letting me teach the economics class, and for hiring me in the first place. Please don't forget what we have built here. This is so much more than a profit-generating economic enterprise. It's a level playing field. A launch-off point for both students and young teachers alike. Be careful with what we have. Pay everyone the same. Treat everyone equal. Believe in this place. Good luck, and I wish you the best."

I clasped his right hand with both of mine. He nodded affirmatively. In a way, I think he understood. He walked out of the room, and that was the last time I ever saw him.

Meanwhile, all my students came to pose with me for a barrage of selfies. Grammar for Native Speakers, AP Economics, Middle School English, and Ancient Civilizations: the four last marks I left on Fudan International School in the spring of that year. I flashed peace sign after peace sign. Today, there were no grades or exams. These kids had helped me as much as I had helped them. In that way, today we were equals.

Linda approached.

"How did you know?" I asked her.

"How did I know what?" She beamed devilishly.

"That recruiting a bunch of twenty-two-year-old American teachers to an international school in Shanghai wouldn't be the managerial backfire of the century."

"Well, Mr. Ed, when you've been around as long as I have, you learn a few things."

"We had a twenty-minute phone conversation before you offered me this job."

"That's not to say that I didn't have a large number of other twenty-minute phone conversations with other people who did *not* get the job."

"That sentence contained like a quadruple negative. I think you're telling me there were actually other candidates for the job."

"Always the grammarian." She looked proud.

"You saw something in me."

"You underestimate yourself. I heard it in your voice then, and I see it in your face now."

"I don't know what to say."

"You're off to do great things, Ed. Keep your chin up."

Finally, she whispered some good news in my ear and walked away. I sought out Lewis and Guang, the seniors who had taken the College Board Advanced Placement Economics exam.

"You guys got perfect scores on the AP Exam," I told them.

\* \* \*

An hour later, I sat alone on my bed in the teachers' dormitory. I opened the book my students had given me and began to read. Here's a highlight reel:

Dear: Mr. ED

Hi! I am Eve.

I am so sad to hear that you will leave the school. You were my homeroom teacher and my English teacher. I was able to learn English in regular class this semester because you taught me well in last semester. Thank you! Don't forget FIS! Bye!

From: Eve

Dear. Mr. Ed :)

Hi, Mr. Ed. :)

Do you really go back to your home town next semester?? Please don't leave us...I'm so sad...Mr. Ed, you're a nice teacher. I will miss you so much...I hope we will meet again later. I wish everything will be okay with you...Good luck :)

Gwen

To Mr. Ed

Thank you great teacher!! You look good in red! :) We will miss you.

Mona

To. Mr.Ed.

Hello~Mr. Ed! I'm Valiant! I heard that you'll leave and you'll not teach us next year. Also, you said you will work for a company...You were the best teacher in the world! Good-bye! I hope to see you again.

Valiant

Dear → Mr. Ed

You're my history teacher also you're my homeroom teacher. I can learn about history of Roman and middle age.

I do not forget you so you do not forget us. I want to see you again.

From→ Yurika

Mr. Ed :)

Hi! Mr. Ed

I'm Jin Mon Rho. First, I'm so sad that you leave FIS! Also, I really thank you for everything to you. My grammar skills are better than before. I'm very happy :). I hope to see you again and you can come to Shanghai again. Sometimes my scores were bad...I'm sorry about that. But, don't forget about me :) and goodbye.

Jin Mon

Mr. Ed is gentle, handsome, and interesting teacher. I like Mr. Ed's lesson. Thank you !!! Great teacher!!! Good bye!!! Great teacher!!!

Kotaro

Kotaro...I had no words, but he finally did. To this day, it was one of the greatest gifts I've ever received in my entire life.

The next morning, I sat with Miles and Ken in the common room of the teacher dormitory. No one said anything. My bags were packed, and in twenty short minutes I was headed to Shanghai Pudong International Airport with a one-way ticket to JFK Airport in New York.

"Quite a year," I muttered to break the introspective silence.

"Fuck," Miles sighed. For once, he sounded tired.

"Where to even begin? You guys are great." Ken was dumbfounded that it was over, shaking his head back and forth in disbelief. That's the thing about China: you won't believe it until you live it. In a word...wow.

"I can't believe you guys are leaving," Miles grinned as he addressed both Ken and me. Ken was headed back to the States a week later. He wanted to work in marketing in New York. He was gearing up for another job hunt slog, but now he had a year of teaching experience in his side holster. We vowed to stay in touch.

Miles was leaving Fudan International School but remaining in Shanghai to "seek out other employment." His wanderings in China would continue, this time without a defined direction.

"You gonna stay with what's-her-name?" I asked him.

"My Chinese girlfriend?"

"Yeah."

"I'll keep her in my back pocket."

"Your ace of spades."

"Eh, my nine of clubs."

How do I say this? Miles was just *better* at China. It wasn't just his Mandarin; it was his level of calm and even temper in a place that made everyone crazy. China made me crazy. Literally. Crazy. Between its debaucheries and delights, you can quickly lose your mind. There were days when I wanted to scream. There were days when I did scream. There were days when people screamed at me. Miles somehow didn't have those.

What about the other Muppets? Helga, Linda, Mr. Lu, Jennifer, Mr. Pancake, even our Puerto Rican Dean of

Students. They all stayed at FIS. The torch now glowed bright in their hands.

It was Ken's turn: "Miles, we all know you're made for this place. You should never leave."

"So true." I nodded. I looked at Ken. "But we did great. I don't think that there's anything about this year that I would do differently."

"Besides nearly drowning in that baby pool," Ken added.

"And sucking at your job for the first couple of months," noted Miles.

"And bribing those security guards when you wrecked the bush in the courtyard of our apartment complex."

"And almost killing that motorcyclist when you tried to cross the road."

They went back and forth.

"OK, OK, OK, there are *some things* I would do differently. But it was great. I don't know what else to say."

"China—there are no words," Miles added a touch of philosophy.

"So that's it, I guess."

"That's it."

I gave my buddies an obligatory man hug, grabbed my two duffle bags, and headed out to the street to grab a cab.

In my finest Mandarin, I told the cabbie where I was going.

"*Wo qu ji chang Pudong.*" He understood me clearly. We haggled back and forth on the price. He relented. I tossed my duffels into the trunk, slid into the backseat, and we sped off one last time into the concrete abyss.

# EPILOGUE

My father's old suit fit me snugly amid the cool September air. The pleats on my pants and the tie around my neck made me feel important. *That guy has some place to be,* I imagined passersby thinking. Check that—everyone was wearing a suit. No one was looking at me. I stood on the sidewalk of lower Manhattan and stared up at the fifty-story glass tower overhead. My new home. It wasn't a banking job, but it was close.

How did this happen?

Well, in a way, doing the "China thing" for a year helped me figure out what I actually wanted in life. Or at least what the next version of me wanted. What I wanted wasn't drastically different from everyone else: I wanted a job that challenged me, made me think, and set me up for success. I wanted to be around people whom I could talk to. In English. I wanted to be near my family. Most of all, I wanted to feel as if I'd earned it.

Pieces of me make up a crazy, daring world adventurer. I still have the occasional penchant for spontaneity, but on so many levels I'm just like everyone else. This next version of me felt like Me. I knew it. At least for now. Until the next thing, you know?

My dad was right. Sometimes, to figure out what you want to do in life you just have to pick something. To decide. But it literally took me moving to China to discover that. In a way, I still don't know who I am. I just know that all of these pieces of me that I keep collecting add to the puzzle. If I just keep picking things, one day I'll wake up, look in the mirror, and realize I'm happy.

So I began a career in business, just like so many of my graduating peers from Duke University. Some of my undergraduate classmates later admitted to me that they always wondered, "What if?" before starting their jobs. Well, I lived "What if?" What if I just moved to China? I *did* move to China. I moved to fucking China. I fucking moved to fucking to China. China, man.

Sometimes you have to pick the "What if?" option. Just yell, "Fuck it" really loud. Reinvent. Do something for yourself. Do it because you want it, not because other people think you should.

From the depths of Shanghai nightlife, to the chalkboard in my classroom, to the pinnacle of Huangshan, to the cramped bunk aboard the Putuoshan Ferry, to the Great Wall and the Xi'an terracotta warriors, and back to New York City once again. It was a soul-searching adventure that brought me full circle, right back to where I had started.

At orientation that morning, in the Monitor Group's forty-ninth floor corporate conference room, I looked around the table at my fifteen new peers in their smart clothing, starting their smart new jobs at this smart company. There were no Turkish divorcees nor garrulous Chinese math teachers. Everyone sat still. The floor-to-ceiling glass window behind me framed the beautiful Manhattan skyline. We introduced ourselves to the group one by one. At last, it was my turn.

I stood up and put my hands in my pocket. My eyes swept the conference room left to right.

"Good morning, everyone. My name is—."

# ACKNOWLEDGEMENTS

To the nation of China, I apologize. To my students, I was horrendously unqualified to teach you. Thank you for treating me with the type of respect that helped to turn me into an adult. You all deserve the world.

To my wife Sophie. I couldn't have done it (or anything) without you. Thanks for showing me the light, and encouraging me to open up, to be weird, and to never give up.

To my son Rafa, all the naughty things in this book were done by an imposter who has the same name as your dad.

To my parents, for everything. My siblings, for shaping me. My in-laws, for being the best in-laws ever. The team at Scribe, for helping me get this football across the goal line. To all the friends and family who read versions of this along the way, your feedback truly made this book. Thank you. To all the amigos, teammates, roommates, co-workers, and acquaintances whom I've met on this long crazy winding road of life, you've made me...me.

The hardest part of writing a book about yourself is admitting to the world that you're not perfect. This project took me a long time. A really long time. To be honest it was mostly a fear of putting myself out there. What would people think? Am I proud of who I was? Of who I am now? In the end we're all pretty complex creatures. My year in China was a formative one, and I hope after reading this book you can see why. Gan bei.

# ABOUT THE AUTHOR

 EDUARDO MESTRE grew up in Manhattan but now lives in Park Slope, Brooklyn, with his wife, Sophie, and young son, Rafael. Like everyone else, his twenties were a confusing blur. He is no professional writer, but after publishing this passion project, he officially earns fifty participation points toward a writer merit badge. Years after Shanghai, he now helps run a startup in the vegetable space. He is officially all grown up. PS: Years later, he goes by "Ed."

92078497R00281

Made in the USA
Middletown, DE
05 October 2018